ADOMNÁN, ADHAᴍʜNAN, EUNAN

To the memory of
FRANK D'ARCY
who also knew Adomnán

Adomnán, Adhamhnán, Eunan

Life and afterlife of a Donegal saint

BRIAN LACEY

FOUR COURTS PRESS

Typeset in 11pt on 13pt GaramondPro by
Carrigboy Typesetting Services for
FOUR COURTS PRESS LTD
7 Malpas Street, Dublin 8, Ireland
www.fourcourtspress.ie
and in North America for
FOUR COURTS PRESS
c/o IPG, 814 N Franklin St, Chicago, IL 60610.

A catalogue record for this title is available from the British Library.

ISBN 978–1–84682–963–5

Like the 'infringers' of the medieval *Cáin Adamnáin* (to be discussed below),
the author is donating all royalties received from the sale of this book to
the Raphoe Cathedral Restoration Project.

SPECIAL ACKNOWLEDGMENT

The publication of this book has been made possible by the generous
financial support of Donegal County Council.

Comhairle Contae
Dhún na nGall
Donegal County Council

Printed in England
by TJ Books Limited, Padstow, Cornwall.

Contents

Abbreviations

AFM *Annals of the kingdom of Ireland by the Four Masters*, ed. J. O'Donovan, 7 vols (2nd edition, Dublin, 1851–6; repr. Dublin, 1990).

AI *Annals of Inisfallen*, ed. S. Mac Airt (Dublin, 1951).

AU *Annals of Ulster i*, eds S. Mac Airt and G. Mac Niocaill (Dublin, 1983).

CS *Chronicum Scotorum*, ed. W. Hennessy (London, 1866).

JRSAI *Journal of the Royal Society of Antiquaries of Ireland*.

Lacey, *CC* Brian Lacey, *Cenél Conaill and the Donegal kingdoms, AD 500–800* (Dublin, 2006).

Lacey, *Lug* Brian Lacey, *Lug's forgotten Donegal kingdom: the archaeology, history and folklore of the Síl Lugdach of Cloghaneely* (Dublin, 2012).

Tig *Annals of Tigernach*, ed. W. Stokes, *Revue Celtique*, 16–18 (1895–7).

Genealogical tables

Prologue

REFERENCES TO ADOMNÁN IN THE ANNALS

1. **AU/CS** 624 Nativitas Adomnani abbatis Iae.
2. **AI** 625 Natiuitas Adamnáin.
3. **AU/CS** 679 (Quies Faeilbi abbatis Iae).
4. **AFM** 684 Adamhnán do dhul go Saxaibh do chuindgidh na braite do beartsat Saxain tuaisceart leo a Muigh breagh an bhliadhain rémraite. Fuair a haisec uatha iar ndeanamh feart & miorbhal fiadh na slogaibh, & do bheartsat onóir & airmhidin móir do iaramh imailli re hoghaiseacc gach neith ro cuinnigh cucca.
5. **AU/CS** 687 Adamnanus captivos reduxit ad Hiberniam .lx.
6. **Tig** 686 Adomnanus captious reducsit ad Hiberniam .lx.
7. **Tig** 688 Adamnanus reduxit captious in Iberniam.
8. **AU/CS** 692 Adamnanus .xiiii. anno post pausam Faailbhei ad Hiberniam pergit.
9. **AI** 696 Adamnán do chor chána for Érind.
10. **AU/CS** 697 Adomnanus ad Hiberniam pergit & dedit Legem Inocentium populis.
11. **AFM** 703 Adhamhnan mac Ronáin, abb Iae Coluim Cille, decc an 23 do September, iar mbeith se bliadhna ficheat i nabdaine, & iar seacht mbiadhna seachtmoghat a aoise. Ba maith tra an ti naomh Adhamhnan, do réir fiadhnaisi naoimh Béda, óir ba derach, ba haithrighech, ba hurnuighthech, ba hinnneithmhech, ba haointeach, & ba measardha, daigh ní loingeadh do shír acht dia domhnaigh & dia dardaoin nama. Do roine mogh de féin do na subháilcibhsi, & beos ba heagnaidh, eolach illeire tuicsiona an naoimhscrioptura diadha.
12. **AU/CS** 704 Adomnanus .lxx.uii. anno aetatis sue, Abbas Iae, pausat.
13. **AI** 704 Adamnan, abb Iae & sapiens, quievit in Christo.

These thirteen entries (AU and CS are doubled-up as they more-or-less repeat each other) are the sole references to Adomnán/Adamnán in the Irish annals,[1] which all derive ultimately for the period up to about 740 from a chronicle

---

1 Translations to English will be found in the appropriate place in the main text below.

assembled originally on Iona. Evidently there are repeated variations in the entries copied here and they can, therefore, be reduced effectively to six or maybe seven separate items in total. Numbers 1, 2 and 11 are clearly retrospective, as will be seen below. No. 3 refers to the death of his predecessor but can be accepted as signalling Adomnán's succession to the abbacy of Iona. Numbers 4, 5, and 6 are duplicates of each other and No. 7 is almost certainly a duplicate of No. 6. Thus, it seems that really only four, or maybe five, separate bits of contemporary information about Adomnán were preserved in the annals. However, a great deal more about Adomnán's life, work and reputation can be gleaned from other sources.

Let us begin!

Introduction

> In ruithen & an lasair & an lia lógmhar ocus ind lóchrand laindreach ... ID
> EST SANCTUS ADAMNANUS .i. an t-uasalshacart náemh, int-í Adamnán.

> The ray of light, the flame, the precious stone, and brilliant lamp ... THAT
> IS SAINT ADAMNÁN, that is the noble and holy priest, Adamnán.

> *Betha Adamnáin* (mid-tenth century)

T*osach eolais imchomarc*, 'Inquiry is the beginning of knowledge',[1] is a saying attributed to Adomnán's friend (and perhaps 'pupil') Aldfrith king of Northumbria, known also by the Irish name Flann Fína (see chapter 3 below). We can see, for instance in the book he wrote about his predecessor and hero, the *Vita Columbae*, that Adomnán himself was a consummate practitioner of that philosophy. In the *Vita*, and indeed in his other great work on the sites and monuments of the Holy Land, *De Locis Sanctis*, Adomnán was assiduous in telling us not only what he knows about his subject but *how* he knew such things. That matter is still topical for us today – maybe even more so! In our world, *how* we know something is becoming perhaps of even greater importance than what we know, claim, or think we know.

There are at least four ways of referring to the subject of this book and it is not always easy to decide which to use in any particular context: Adomnán, Adamnán, Adhamhnáin, Eunan. Apart from exceptional cases the name Adomnán will be reserved below for the real historical individual whose life spanned the last three-quarters of the seventh century, while Adamnán will refer to the variously fictionalized culted 'saint' of later times. The other two names are the forms in use in modern Irish and English.[2]

By whatever name he is referred to it is not all that easy to get to know him. As we saw above very little contemporary information survives for him. We have, of course, his own writings but very few personal details can be gleaned from those. Much of the later comment about him, especially from the early medieval period, is either highly distorted or outrightly fictional and, in some cases, deliberately misleading and dishonest. He is certainly not unique in that sense; many medieval characters, perhaps especially ecclesiastical characters, 'suffered' similar fates. Many individuals celebrated as 'saints' have been condemned

---

1   C. Ireland, *Old Irish wisdom*, pp 76–7.
2   See also chapter 12 below for other variations of his name.

to be remembered only by a series of pious platitudes and legends. But all of them – if they actually existed – were once real people, with all that phrase implies. Adomnán was definitely such a real individual; at one time a genuine living Donegal person. He also seems to have been what we might call a very good person, but not a plaster saint! Indeed, despite the title 'saint' having been conferred on him posthumously, maybe he wasn't a saint in any sense? I have neither the qualifications nor the requisite faith to make such a judgment; but I can respect the informed judgment of others and a tradition that has lasted for over thirteen hundred years.

In the *Vita Columbae* Adomnán set out to make a portrait of a man he honoured as (and, indeed, effectively 'made' into) a saint. I will be content here if I can make a reasonable portrait of a good (and undoubtedly a 'saintly') man. If I met him, I think I would share few of the same beliefs as Adomnán, most particularly his religious views, but I can most certainly acknowledge his integrity and achievements.

Writing about Adomnán in 1995, the late Richard Sharpe said: 'It would be too much to say that we can approach his personality'.[3] But we can know some things about the real Adomnán. We have a few hard facts; we can work out a few other things; and we can speculate within the boundaries of the known facts. We can also critically analyse the later fictional and propagandistic material about him to see what people in later times made of his story with a view to exploiting it for their own purposes. Such an analysis allows us to exclude those things from a consideration of his real historical life.

We only have about six or seven actual annalistic entries for Adomnán, including references to his birth and death. Not very much to reconstruct an extraordinarily eventful and productive life that lasted almost to his eightieth year! In addition, we do have the references to him by other ancient writers, most notably the great Northumbrian author, the Venerable Bede. We also have some clues as to the reputation he left behind him. There are good modern annotated editions of his various writings and much has been written about specific aspects of his life and work, especially by scholars in recent times. This is I think, however, the first attempt at a full-length monograph about him that tries to describe his story in as complete a form as we can know it; perhaps the first since the somewhat disappointing *Betha Adamnáin* was composed over a thousand years ago (see below, chapter 9).

To some extent Adomnán has always played second fiddle to his predecessor and relative Columba or Colum Cille. This was as much his own 'fault' as that of others because of the marvellous public relations exercise on behalf of the earlier man that he engineered in the *Vita Columbae*. Some people might think that it

3   R. Sharpe, *Adomnán of Iona*, p. 43.

is close to being a mortal sin to say it, but there is a lot of evidence to suggest that Adomnán may have been at least as important – and maybe a bit more so – than Columba.

This study challenges some of the traditional views about the birth and early life of Adomnán and, particularly, about his connection (or, actually, lack of it) with the foundation of the church and bishopric of Raphoe. It will be necessary, therefore, to spell out in detail the evidence of the ancient sources and to provide a strong critique of those sources in the light of modern research, especially regarding the dates of the texts offered as proof of various issues and events. Much of this book consists of assessing the opinion of other historians, along with examining the ancient sources. Because of the nature of scholarship and the paucity of the contemporary sources, the same 'well' having to be drawn from repeatedly, it is a fact that several people will have arrived at broadly the same ideas about some of the issues dealt with here. I hope all the people whose work I have read and studied feel that I have acknowledged them properly and adequately here. As on previous occasions, I have to emphasize my indebtedness to William Reeves, who published his works on this topic over 150 years ago.

This book has been written in Donegal, in fact being here was the main impetus for commencing it, during the Covid 19 lockdown and cocoon (*dianghlas, clutharú agus neadú, mar a deireann siad anseo*) in the middle six months of 2020. As with Adomnán himself and the plague of the 680s (see below, chapter 3) the current health crisis did not obstruct the work too much; if anything, it provided the sanctuary and opportunity to carry it out. It was, however, with the greatest regret that in the early days of the lockdown I became aware of the death of a personal friend and one of the most important scholars who had worked on Adomnán and his writings, Richard Sharpe. *Ar dheis lámh Dé go raibh a anam uasal.*

The part of west Donegal where I live (and am 'locked down') is remote from the main libraries that hold the material relevant to this study, and not yet lucky enough to have consistent access to the internet. I couldn't have finished this study, therefore, without the assistance and friendship of a number of people who commented on my draft and sent me copies of relevant publications. I am especially grateful to Colin Ireland, Tomás Ó Canann and Patrick Paul O'Neill. I am in debt in a very particular way (and not for the first time) to Nollaig Ó Muraíle for his compliments, encouragement, corrections, additions and advice. The collegiality of all these people, especially Nollaig, makes work of this nature such an enormous pleasure. As always, I am indebted to the staff of Four Courts Press – especially, in this instance, Martin Fanning – for their good-humoured help and professionalism. Despite all their efforts and help, however, it won't come as too much of a surprise if some errors and important omissions remain throughout this work. I hope Adomnán, at least, will forgive me!

In the text that follows I have made extensive use of D.P. Mc Carthy's synchronisms of the Irish annals (fourth edition), published on the internet on 11 April 2005. One knotty problem that is dealt with below is the chronology of Adomnán's visits to Northumbria (chapters 3 and 6). While I am fully aware of the differing views on this matter and the work of a number of scholars who have examined it, I have opted here to follow especially the chronology of David Woods as outlined in his publications cited in the bibliography. I am, of course, conscious, in this, as in all other matters addressed in this book, that ongoing and future research will inevitably change our understanding of these issues. As the great Belgian historian of the Middle Ages and philosopher of history, Henri Pirenne (1862–1935), wisely said:

> Bien différente de celle de l'artiste, l'œuvre du savant est fatalement provisoire. Il le sait et s'en réjouit, puisque la rapide vieillesse de ses livres est la preuve même du progrès de la science.[4]

> Very different to that of the artist, the scholar's achievement is unavoidably provisional. He knows and rejoices in that, since the fact that his books go out of date so quickly is proof itself of the progress of science.

As if in proof of that, just as I finished the first draft of this study I became aware of the impending publication of James Houlihan's book on the *Lex Innocentium*. I read the book as soon as it became available, to my personal great advantage and (I hope) to the improvement of this work. To recycle a phrase used by Mark Stansbury about Adomnán's own *Vita Columbae*,[5] some of the very important points made by James Houlihan had to be 'stitched on' to this study at a late stage. Even later, when this book having completed its anonymous academic review stage was already undergoing final editing at the publishers, I was alerted by Michael Ryan about an important new article interpreting Charles Thomas's significant excavations on Iona.[6] Michael generously sent me a copy of the article. This too required some 'stitching' – even 'darning' of my text – although, happily, only one actual error (the date of the monastic enclosure on Iona) had come to light as a result. I trust that the short time I had available to digest these two extremely valuable recent publications is not too evident in my use of and citations from them. It might have been wiser to take another of the bits of advice attributed to Adomnán's friend, Flann Fína (king Aldfrith of Northumbria):

> *Dligid étnge aimsir*, 'an inarticulate person deserves time'.[7]

4   Quoted in G. Gérardy, *Henri Pirenne*, p. 4.
5   M. Stansbury, 'The Schaffhausen manuscript', p. 73.
6   E. Campell & A. Maldonado, 'A new Jerusalem'.
7   C. Ireland, *Old Irish wisdom*, pp 74–5.

PART ONE

Adomnán's historical life

CHAPTER ONE

Adomnán's Donegal

Adomnán, whose life extended throughout the last three-quarters of the seventh century, was a Donegal man, although the county of that name would not come into existence until almost a thousand years after his birth.[1] For all that we know most of his life before about the last third of it may have been spent mainly in Donegal as we have little or no contemporary evidence about his career before he became abbot of Iona in 679. There was no single name in medieval times to describe what we now know as County Donegal. Within a few decades of the county's creation, however, a number of small additional adjustments were made to its extent. The most notable of those changes for our purposes here was the significant transfer of the ancient ecclesiastical settlement of Derry and its immediate hinterland out of the county into the new British 'plantation' unit of Londonderry. Prior to that Derry was not only part of but a highly significant part of Donegal.

But long before that, reaching back into prehistoric times, Donegal as we know it had a recognizable geographical integrity.[2] This resulted principally from the structure of its landscape and the barriers formed around it by the mountains and rivers and by its juxtaposition with the Atlantic Ocean. As far back as we have written records, those physical geographical characteristics were reflected, although of course not slavishly followed, in the political divisions of its territories, as will be outlined below.

For many centuries the traditional understanding of the geography and history of early medieval Donegal was passed down to us through the prism of the late medieval propagandistic accounts prepared on behalf of the ruling Uí Domnaill family. But their version of events and contexts presents us with a highly distorted view. The available contemporary records, when studied objectively and in detail, convey a very different picture to those politically motivated, falsified Uí Domnaill historical and geographical narratives.[3]

1 County Donegal, 'one of the last counties in Ireland to be established', came into existence on 1 September 1585. It derives its name from a much older settlement on the banks of the Eske, just where that river enters the sea. The name, meaning 'fort of the foreigners', is unlikely to 'predate the ninth century ... the *gaill* referred to were in all probability Vikings', D. Mac Giolla Easpaig, 'Place-names and early settlement in Couny Donegal', pp 149, 161–2.

2 In the absence of a contemporary single name in medieval times, the term Donegal will be used throughout this book to refer in a general way to the territory now known as County Donegal. In addition, as explained above, Derry will be treated as having been part of that territory up to the time of the seventeenth-century Plantations.

3 See, for instance, Lacey, *CC*, pp 33–47; and Lacey, *Lug*, pp 117–27.

Writing, and with it 'history' – the account of the past as revealed in contemporary written documents – arrived in Ireland as a part of the cultural package associated with the introduction of Christianity. But it isn't until about the middle of the sixth century that we begin to get sufficient written material from which we can now reconstruct, reasonably accurately, significant events and polities. As far as we know Christianity had arrived in Donegal – in the eastern parts at least – over one hundred years and possibly about one hundred and fifty years before Adomnán was born. However, much of the older pre-Christian society and culture, including aspects of its pagan religious practices, remained intact and would continue to do so for a long time afterwards. But the impact of Christianity on Donegal had been significant from a relatively early date, apparently. Adomnán was born into a world where the leading figures in his local society were most definitely Christian or, at minimum, facilitated the practice of that religion. He was born about the end of the first quarter of the seventh century (for dates, see below). This was a time of great change in what we now think of as Donegal; especially for the aristocratic family or dynasty to which he himself belonged, Cenél Conaill, the 'kindred of Conall'. We cannot be certain if the Conall from whom those people were named, and from whom we get the name Tír Chonaill, was a real historical figure. We have no contemporary historical evidence to confirm (or deny) his existence. If he lived at all and was not some sort of mythical or originally deistic figure, as seems possible,[4] then he did so before the onset of 'history'.

Conall, whether fictional or real, is said to date to before the period when contemporary written records were made (or from which, at least, they survive) that would allow us to reconstruct the details of his actual life.[5] In the legends in which he figures and which were only written down in much later times, legends that might preserve some aspects of what actually happened but which cannot now be taken at face value, Conall is claimed to have been one of the sons of the equally legendary Niall Noígiallach, 'Niall of the Nine Hostages'. In those legends, the details of which claim to be set in the period before the onset of 'history' proper, it is argued that Conall and three of his brothers (who, with one exception, are said to have been born in Donegal) came north from their father's headquarters at Tara (Co. Meath), drove out the existing rulers of Donegal, that is, various branches of the Ulaid, the people who gave their name to Ulster, and took possession of that territory. On the summit of the archaeologically, mythologically and historically important Croghan Hill close to Lifford – the Tara of Donegal – Conall was said to have been given the privilege by his

4 See, for instance, T. Ó Canann, 'Ua Canannáin genealogies', pp 176–8.
5 A pre-Christian 'Conall' character (or character with a cognate name) is claimed as a founding figure of several early medieval population groups in the northern half of Ireland.

brothers of dividing up among them the thus 'liberated' lands and setting out its various political subsections. Those legends are not 'history'; as we have them now they are a late medieval Uí Domnaill propaganda narrative.[6] However, they do suggest to us how the people at the time they were written down might have imagined the process by which the political geography of the lands in which they lived had come about.

In attempting to reconstruct the evolution of the actual political geography of early historic Donegal we are fortunate in two respects. St Columba left Donegal about 562 and shortly afterwards founded the tremendously influential monastery on the Hebridean island of Iona.[7] One of the very first things he and his monks did when they settled was to commence (or perhaps, continue) the keeping of a written record of significant events. Those records expanded over time. Strictly-speaking, the 'Iona Chronicle' (as those records came to be known) no longer survives, but substantial portions of it were frequently copied and partially-fossilized versions of sections of it are preserved in what are known now as the Irish annals of later medieval times.[8] We cannot say if the monastery on Iona was or was not the only institution to make such records from the sixth century onward but most definitely theirs is the only such chronicle to survive from before about AD 740 preserving for us unique historical information about Ireland and Scotland. As many of the monks on Iona had an Ulster and, indeed, a Donegal background, what must have been their natural interest in events in their homeland is well represented in the information that has been preserved. From our perspective now the notes they made about those events represent the very beginning of the contemporary written record of Donegal, Ulster, Irish and, indeed, Scottish 'history'.

6   Lacey, *CC*, pp 33–47; T. Ó Canann, 'Máel Coba Ua Gallchubhair and his early family background', p. 57.

7   Although very few Irish people have been officially canonized as saints, traditionally many leading figures of the early church were popularly acclaimed as such. That terminology will be followed uncritically here. The founder of Iona was probably originally called some version of the Latin name Columba, borrowed into Irish as Columb. In Irish (and English) he is generally known now by some form of the name Colum Cille. Despite legends claiming that he was called that from his childhood following the abandoning of an earlier name Crimthann, it is most likely that he was only called Colum Cille posthumously as part of the hagiographical development of his cult. The names Columba and Colum Cille are used interchangeably below depending on context

8   The most authoritative account of the evolution of the Irish annals is to be found in D. Mc Carthy, *The Irish annals*. There is a lot of chronological confusion and repetition in the annals, especially for the very earliest periods. Below, as far as possible, use will be made of Dr Mc Carthy's revised synchronisms as available online. Dr Mc Carthy's dates are often at variance with those in the modern printed editions of the annals and also with dates that have become well-known in popular culture, such as, for instance, dates for the birth and death of Columba and his departure for Iona.

The second piece of 'good fortune' for us in this respect is that around the same time, or close to it, that Adomnán was writing his major study about his predecessor and relative, the *Vita Columbae* (see below), a cleric from the west of Ireland, Tírechán, was writing an account of what he believed to have been a journey made by St Patrick through the northern parts of Ireland in the fifth century. That account, which doesn't have a contemporary title of its own, is now usually called the *Collectanea*. According to Tírechán, as Patrick progressed around the country, he founded churches in the various kingdoms that he visited. Tírechan's Patrick travelled what is essentially still the main routeway up the east side, the agriculturally fertile and economically richer side, of Donegal, founding a number of churches as he went. Probably unintentionally, Tírechán's late seventh-century narrative provides us now with various clues about the secular geopolitics of Donegal in Adomnán's day.

Tírechán's account portrays Patrick as a travelling missionary in Donegal, baptizing the leading natives and founding churches as he proceeded. Most of those churches are given names that include the element *Domnach* or *Domnach Mór*, a term borrowed into Irish originally from the Latin root word *Dominus*, 'the Lord'. In that sense a church, a *Domnach*, was 'the Lord's house'. Whatever about who actually founded them, it is evident that *Domnach* place-names reflect some of the earliest cohort of Christian churches in Ireland in general, and Donegal in particular.

Our interest in the *Collectanea* in this context is less in what it purports to tell us about St Patrick, than in what it actually does tell us about the geography of Donegal as it was perceived by Tírechán in the late seventh century. He describes the country Patrick allegedly passed through as a series of *campi* (Latin equivalent of the Irish word *maige*), which is often translated as 'plains'. However, as Thomas Charles-Edwards pointed out,[9] *campus* (singular) might be better translated as an area of 'well-cultivated land' in contrast to the wild uncultivated mountains, bogs and woodlands that were and are still a common aspect of the Donegal landscape. In fact, the various *campi* in Donegal mentioned by Tírechán (translated below in the singular as *Mag*) seem to have been actually separate polities or small kingdoms, what were known in Irish as *tuatha*. We take up Tírechán's account of Patrick's travels as the latter crosses the River Drowse, the modern southern border of the county.[10]

> [Patrick] blessed ... the river Drowes, which now contains many large fish, or the kind (of fish that was there) has been increased in size.

9   T. Charles-Edwards, *Early Christian Ireland*, p. 13.
10   Original text in Latin and translation by Ludwig Bieler, *The Patrician texts*, pp 160–1. The persons and places in Donegal mentioned by Tírechán are examined and contextualized with full references in Lacey, *CC*, passim.

The river Drowes had no fish before, but since then it yields a catch to fishermen ...

He also entered Mag Sereth across the river between Es Ruaid [Assaroe] and the sea, and founded a church in Ráith Argi [not yet satisfactorily identified but probably close to Es Ruaid], and camped in Mag Sereth. And he found a good man of the race of Lathru, and he baptized him and his young son with him, who was called Hinu or Ineus; his father had bundled him in linen (and carried him) round his neck, because he was born on the way, coming with his father from the mountain: and Patrick baptized the son and wrote for him an alphabet and blessed him with the blessing for a bishop; later (Hinu) gave hospitality to Assicus [an assistant and follower of Patrick] and his monks in Ard Roissen, that is in Ráith Cungi [Racoo] in Mag Sereth, in the time of the kings Fergus and Fothad. And he [Patrick] founded a church in Mag Latrain and the great church of Sírdruimm [tentatively identified as the Dorsum Tómme – Druim Tuama or Drumhome – referred to by Adomnán in the *Vita Columbae*, see below], which is held by the community of Daminis [the monastery on Devenish Island in Lower Lough Erne] in Doburbar [perhaps either Lough Erne or the estuary of the River Eske]. And he proceeded over the Gap of the Sons of Conall [Bernas Mór, Barnesmore] to Mag [n]Itho and founded a great Church there [*aeclesiam magnam*].[11] And he went to Mag Tochui[r] [the northern end of Inishowen] and built a church there [Domnach Mór Maige Tochuir, Carn Domhnaich or Carndonagh] ... and from Mag Tochuir he came to (the plain of) Dul [Tempull Mag Dula, i.e. Templemoyle near Eglinton, Co. Derry][12] Ocheni [the River Faughan in Co. Derry] and built seven churches there.

Although not mentioned by Tírechán, as well as Carndonagh there was another allegedly early *Domnach* church in Inishowen said in later sources such as the Tripartite Life of Patrick to have been founded by the latter saint.[13] That

11 Domnach Mór Maige nItha, now Donaghmore Church of Ireland. It is located at the foot of Croghan Hill. In the sixth, seventh and eighth centuries that hill was the 'Tara' of Donegal and the *caput* of Cenél Conaill (Lacey, *CC*, passim). Most definitely the young Columba's royal relatives would have been based there and in the surrounding countryside, and it is likely that the yet to become cleric himself was familiar with the area if he did not actually live there. There must be a strong likelihood that it was at the church of Domnach Mór Maige nItha that the young Colum received some of his first exposures to the Christian church and its teachings. Adomnán too must have been very familiar with that area, although Donegal geopolitics had altered somewhat by his time (see below).
12 B. Lacy, 'The Uí Meic Cairthinn of Lough Foyle', p. 10; B. Lacey, 'County Derry in the early historic period', p. 125.
13 W. Stokes, *The Tripartite Life*, p. 157,

was *Domnach Bile*, now Cooley just on the south-west edge of the town of Moville. That ancient church was located in one of the subdivisions of Inishowen, Bredach,[14] at an extremely important strategic location overlooking the narrows where Lough Foyle closes over before being joined with the open Atlantic Ocean. Those narrows also provided a significant (if dangerous) crossing point by boat from the Inishowen peninsula to what is now Magilligan in Co. Derry and onwards to the rest of mid-Ulster.

But despite the alleged associations of the churches at Carndonagh and Cooley with St Patrick, the monastery founded by St Mura at Fahan (*Othan*) is believed to have been the chief ecclesiastical centre for the rulers of Inishowen, Cenél nEogain. Fahan was the church closest to Elaghmore, *Ailech Mór*, the original Cenél nEogain *caput*, about ten kilometers to the south-east.[15] The church at Derry was actually slightly closer to Ailech, but it was on the other, southern, side of a wetland boundary valley (the Pennyburn Depression) and belonged to the Columban and Cenél Conaill sphere of influence. That situation continued up to about 800. Following the Cenél nEogain defeat of Cenél Conaill at the Armageddon battle of Clóitech in 789, the former took control of the whole of Donegal north of Bernas Mór, including the ecclesiastical settlement at Derry and the site of the monument later known as the Grianán of Aileach. But in the time of Columba and Adomnán both of those sites were in Cenél Conaill territory.[16]

A number of genealogical traditions about Mura of Fahan are preserved, including one that he belonged to the Dál Fiatach who are mostly associated with what is now Co. Down.[17] Together these sources would appear to indicate that Mura's floruit was in the early decades of the seventh century, although we have no precise dates for him. As we will see below, although they belonged to different generations, and also to different, neighbouring but opposing kingdoms, Mura's later years probably overlapped with the young manhood of Adomnán. It is certainly not impossible that they could have met. The *Fragmentary Annals of Ireland* has an elaborate story in which Áed Uaridnach of the Cenél nEogain, apparently in 602 and definitely before he is said (probably falsely) to have become king of Tara, is brought into association with Mura.[18] Áed is not stated to have been the donor/lay-founder of the Fahan monastery, which is said to have existed already, but, in the story, not long after he became

14 Lacey, *CC*, p. 115.
15 B. Lacey, 'The Grianán of Aileach'. Lacey, *CC*, pp 105–11. It should be noted that the better-known Grianán of Aileach is not the same site as *Ailech Mór*.
16 B. Lacey, *Medieval and monastic Derry*, pp 1–13.
17 Lacey, *CC*, pp 91 and 163; P. Ó Riain, *Corpus genealogiarum*, p. 72: 557. Other Dál Fiatach connections with Inishowen are tentatively hinted at in the early sources (see Lacey, *CC*, pp 162–3).
18 J. Radner, *Fragmentary Annals*, pp 4–9.

high-king, he is credited with having granted 'fertile lands to Muru of Othan'. Áed's death is recorded in 610.[19]

We have no date for Mura's death, although his feastday and probable anniversary was celebrated on 12 March. On general genealogical grounds, William Reeves calculated that he may have died about 645,[20] a date that seems broadly acceptable. Adomnán would have been in his late teens or early twenties at that time (see below). No early written Life of Mura survives but in the middle of the seventeenth century John Colgan, himself from Inishowen, assembled some not very useful notes about him in the *Acta sanctorum Hiberniae*.[21] At 657 the annals record the death of Cellach son of Sárán, abbot of Othan Mór (Fahan).[22] Reeves suggested that Cellach was probably the immediate successor of Mura.[23] Cellach almost certainly belonged to the Cenél nÉogain. His own pedigree is not preserved but an individual belonging to the Cenél nÉogain with the unusual name Sárán does occur at roughly the appropriate time, that is, the end of the sixth century.[24] In fact, Cellach appears, also, to have been the brother of Damongóc Ailithir son of Sárán[25] (Table 1) who, as we will see, was associated with an ecclesiastical establishment on Tory Island. The latter church seems, initially at any rate, to have been a 'sister' or even a 'daughter' church to Fahan.

Table 1: Early Cenél nÉogain, including St Mura of Fahan and the Tory clerics

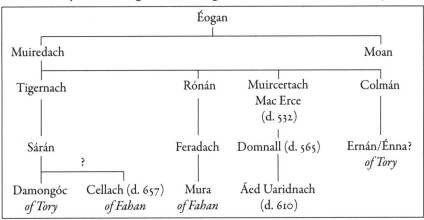

19 AU2 612.1. For his alleged but unlikely kingship of Tara see Lacey, *CC*, p. 214.

20 W. Reeves, 'St Mura', p. 271.

21 The notes were translated into English from Colgan's Latin by John O'Donovan. See M. Herity, *Ordnance Survey letters, Donegal*, pp 14–16.

22 A Tig; AU2 658.1 has 'Cellach son of Sárán or Rónán'.

23 W. Reeves, 'St Mura', p. 271; W.J. Doherty, *The abbey of Fahan*, p. 25.

24 M.A. O'Brien, *Corpus genealogiarum Hiberniae*, p. 180: 146d45. When we have no dates for an individual, a calculation of roughly 30 years per generation is presumed and added or subtracted as appropriate from a known (annalistic) date of a related person.

25 P. Ó Riain, *Corpus genealogiarum*, p. 8: 40.

The visible archaeological remains at Fahan have been described and discussed on several occasions.[26] Specifically, the date and associations of the main cross-slab there has been the subject of a great deal of discussion and speculation. Macalister's reading of the doxology, 'Glory and honour to the Father, the Son and the Holy Spirit', written in Greek (and Greek characters) along the north edge of the slab, is no longer easily legible.[27] It has been accepted, however, that this inscription provides a *terminus post quem* for the monument, as the latter formula was adopted by the Council of Toledo only in 633. Various dates from the seventh to the tenth century have been proposed for the cross-slab but on present evidence it would appear that it postdates the life of Adomnán, although its somewhat Pictish appearance indicates that a connection with Scotland at a slightly later date is very likely.[28]

Returning to the quotation above from Tírechán's *Collectanea*, two things might be pointed out at this stage as significant. Although Tírechán's Patrick travels all the way through east Donegal and on northward to Inishowen he, as it were, 'skirts around' Columban and Cenél Conaill Derry, and no mention is made of it in the text. While there is no suggestion anywhere that a church existed in Derry in Patrick's time, Tírechán was writing at least a century after the foundation of that church, at the time (or certainly close to it) when Adomnán was abbot of Iona and comarba (head of) the federation of Columban churches in Ireland and Britain. A church in Derry not only existed by that time but was closely associated with the *Familia Columbae*.[29] But no attempt is made in the *Collectanea* to suggest any kind of relationship or *entente* between Columba and Patrick, or their respective churches. On the other hand, Adomnán is quite respectful of the latter, referring near the beginning of the *Vita Columbae*, in the second preface, to *sancti Patricii episcopi*, 'the holy bishop Patrick'. Actually, earlier in the *Collectanea*, Tírechán had explicitly referred to some tension between the churches of the two saints. Writing about the cleric Assicus, one of Patrick's followers, Tírechán describes some time that the former had spent in Donegal.

> The said Assicus took refuge in the region north of Slíab Líacc [*Montem Lapidus*, Slieve League] and stayed for seven years on an island, [*in insula.* Bieler translates this as 'in a hermitage'] called Rochuil [possibly Rathlin

---

26 See B. Lacy, *Archaeological survey*, pp 268–9.

27 R.A.S. Macalister, 'The inscription on the slab at Fahan Mura, Co. Donegal', pp 89–98; R.A.S. Macalister, *Corpus inscriptionum insularum celticarum*, pp 118–20, No. 91. For other more-or-less contemporary Greek 'associations' with Donegal it might be worth pointing out that in the *Vita Columbae* Adomnán, as it were, plays with the Greek equivalent of the name for Columba, and that the Schaffhausen manuscript of that text has the 'Our Father' written in Greek on its last page (see chapter 5 below).

28 B. Lacy, 'Fahan, Tory, Cenél nEogain and the Picts'; Lacey, *CC*, pp 286–8.

29 B. Lacy, *Medieval and monastic Derry*, pp 25–39.

O'Birne, where there is an early church site][30] west of Slíab Líacc; and his monks searched for him and found him in the mountain valleys with his metalwork, and his monks took him forcibly with them, and he died in their company in the solitude of the mountains, and they buried him in Ráith Cungi [Racoo] in (Mag) Sereth, and the king gave him and his monks after his death grazing for a hundred cows with their calves and for twenty oxen, as an offering for ever, for he [Assicus] said he would not return to Mag Aí [the part of Co. Roscommon where his church of Elphin was located] because they had lied about him, and his bones are in Mag Sereth in Ráith Cungi. He was a monk of Patrick's, but the community of Colum Cille and the community of Ard Srátha [Ardstraw Co. Tyrone] claimed him.[31]

The conflicting claims between the communities of Patrick and Colum Cille as to which of them owned the bones (relics) of Assicus probably can be explained by Mag Sereth's (in which Ráith Cungi was situated) changing hands between the Cenél Cairpre and the Cenél Conaill, almost certainly during the reign of the latter's king Domnall mac Áedo (and during the young adulthood of Adomnán) in the middle of the seventh century (see below). The reference to the community of Ard Srátha also claiming the bones is more difficult to explain but presumably it also is a reflection of conflicts in the secular and ecclesiastical politics of the time.[32]

The second point about Tírechán's account of Patrick's journey through east Donegal that is worth highlighting is that no mention is made of the significant early ecclesiastical figure Brugach mac Dega.[33] In fact, Brugach mac Dega may have the distinction of being the very first Christian from Donegal for whom we have any real evidence. Brugach is associated with the church of Ráith Maige Aenaig (or Enaig) in east Donegal, territory through which Tírechán's travelling Patrick had to pass.[34] Brugach figures in stories about Colum Cille and (more

---

30   P. Walsh, 'The monastic settlement on Rathlin O'Byrne'.
31   L. Bieler, *Patrician texts*, p. 141.
32   B. Lacey, *CC*, p. 69.
33   There are two slightly different pedigrees for Brugach (see B. Lacey, 'The church of Ráith Maige Oenaig', pp 216–17). Despite the fact that he is always referred to as Brugach mac Dega (the latter word now pronounced 'jay' but in Old Irish with a hard 'g'), in fact his father in both pedigrees is named as Énna. Daig (the nominative that gives the genitive Dega) is shown in both pedigrees as six generations before Brugach. But, given his very early Christian associations, the question arises was Brugach known at some stage as something along the lines of a *mac Dé*, 'a son of God'? I am grateful to Nollaig Ó Muraíle for discussion and advice on this point, and for preventing me from pushing the suggestion too far!
34   As is normal, Brugach's name is spelt variously in different sources but they are sufficiently close to indicate that the same person is being referred to. The same is true about the name of his church although in that case the differing spellings may have a bearing on the identification

anachronistically) also in stories about Adomnán (see below). In some sources he is said to have been baptized or ordained by Patrick, for instance in the early ninth-century Tripartite Life of Patrick as part of a discussion about the ecclesiastical antecedents of a bishop Coirbre of Coleraine in Co. Derry:

> Bishop Brugach, who is in Ráith Maige Aenaich in Crích [the territory of] Conall, is he who conferred orders on bishop Coirbre. Patrick, then, had conferred orders on Bishop Brugach, so that in that matter Coirbre is a descendant of Patrick.[35]

In the Martyrology of Donegal and the Martyrology of Gorman Brugach is listed as a saint with a feastday on 1 (and 3) November. In the Middle Irish Life of Colum Cille composed in Derry in the mid-twelfth century he is shown meeting Colum Cille as a boy.

> [The child Colum Cille] and his fosterer went at Christmas time to Brugach mac Dega, the bishop of Ráith Maige Aenaig in Tír Énnai. His fosterer, the cleric, was given the charge of performing priestly duties in that place on the festival day. He, [the fosterer] however, was seized with self-consciousness and was unable to chant his allotted psalm, which was *Misericordias*. Thereupon the son of grace, Colum Cille, recited the psalm on behalf of his fosterer, though previously he had read only his alphabet, and the names of God and of Colum Cille were magnified by that great miracle.[36]

In hagiographical terms the story seems to imply that by the middle of the twelfth century some sort of debt was owed by Ráith Maige Aenaig (or by its ecclesiastical successor, Raphoe, see below) generally to Colum Cille and his followers, and most probably specifically to the Columban church at Derry.

Ráith Maige Aenaig (with various spellings) can probably be identified as the place known today as Rateen, seven kilometers due north of Lifford, near the west bank of the Foyle.[37] Previously, the consensus had been that it could be identified with Raymoghy, near the east shore of Lough Swilly, approximately ten kilometers north-west of Raphoe and twenty kilometers south-west of

---

of its location. In both these cases and in others, names have been silently standardized here to avoid confusion. See B. Lacey, 'The church of Ráith Maige Oenaig', pp 214–18; Lacey, *CC*, pp 249–50.

35 W. Stokes, *The Tripartite Life*, pp 166–7. The beautiful Church of Ireland church in Coleraine, dating from the seventeenth century onwards, is dedicated to St Patrick.

36 The Life is edited and translated in M. Herbert, *Iona, Kells and Derry*, pp 211–88. For this quotation see p. 235.

37 See B. Lacey, 'The church of Ráith Maige Oenaig'.

Derry. However as will be argued below (chapter 8), Ráith Maige Aenaig disappears from the contemporary annalistic records following references to it in the mid-to-late eighth century. From the beginning of the ninth century, it seems that it was succeeded institutionally by a newly founded church at Raphoe eight kilometres to the south-west and, probably significantly, in a similar sort of physical geographical location.

Whatever about the location of Ráith Maige Aenaigh it is probably relevant, as we will see, that Brugach should be referred to in the martyrologies, in the Tripartite Life of Patrick and in the Irish Life of Colum Cille, as a bishop. However, contrary to all other evidence he also appears, as will be discussed below (chapter 8), in the Raphoe recension of the *Cáin Adamnáin* of about the year 1000,[38] almost certainly incorrectly as a king who is hostile to Adomnán. It should be pointed out also at this stage that the chronology of his appearance in the Middle Irish Life of Colum Cille and in the Tripartite Life of Patrick fits much better with the known historical facts than with his peculiar and unchronological appearance in the *Cáin Adamnáin*.

There are some hints that Christianity may not have been evenly present in all parts of Donegal in the sixth and seventh centuries. One such non-Christian district may have been the original territory of the Síl Lugdach in the Cloghaneely area on the Atlantic north-west coast. The people of that little kingdom seem to have been slow to give up their devotion to their eponymous pagan 'god' Lug, although they seem to have been definitely Christian by the end of the eighth century.[39] There is no doubt, however, about the early adoption of Christianity in the territory of the Síl Lugdach's immediate neighbours to the east, Cenél Duach. Almost certainly it was Cenél Duach that provided four of the abbots of Iona between the death of Columba and the appointment of Adomnán in 679.[40]

There is also evidence for the early arrival of Christianity on Tory Island, fifteen kilometers out from the Síl Lugdach coast. Although there are elaborate legends about Colum Cille's presence on Tory before he went to Iona, there is no historical evidence to substantiate those claims. Those legends seem to date to several centuries later when the cult of St Colum Cille was widespread and dominant in Donegal, for instance after 800 when, as we will see, the promotion of that cult was adopted by the Síl Lugdach rulers of that time. In fact, as we have seen above, the church on Tory in the seventh century seems to have been connected with the Cenél nÉogain church at Fahan, rather than with any foundation connected to Colum Cille or his people, Cenél Conaill.

---

38   For convenience, the term *Cáin Adomnáin* (with an 'o' in Adomnán) refers to the original Law of 697. The term *Cáin Adamnáin* (with a middle 'a' in Adamnán) refers to a Raphoe text of *c.*1000. See below for full discussion of both texts.
39   Lacey, *Lug*, passim; B. Lacey, 'The ringed cross at Ray, Co. Donegal', passim.
40   Lacey, *CC*, pp 98–100; and see below.

The earliest account of the Columban foundation on Tory occurs in the Middle Irish life of the saint composed in Derry in the second half of the twelfth century, that is, six hundred years after the alleged event.[41] This merely states that: 'He [Colum Cille] founded Tory and left a venerable man of his *familia* there, namely Ernaíne'. Ernaíne, Ernán or Mo Ernóc of Tory is noted in several other sources. Interestingly, his pedigree as outlined in the corpus of saints' genealogies claims that he belonged not to Colum Cille's kindred, Cenél Conaill, but to their opponents, Cenél nÉogain (Table 1). This is also the case with the only other two named persons who are likewise said to have been associated with the church on Tory: Damongóc Ailithir ('pilgrim') and Énna Toraid, although the latter is probably just an alias form of the name Ernán.[42] Damongóc's pedigree, as mentioned above, suggests that he was a brother of Cellach the abbot of Fahan who died in 657. In fact, no one connected with the earliest traditions of Tory (excepting the later retrospective legends concerning Colum Cille) belonged to the Cenél Conaill. Despite its later associations this is what might be expected. The people who lived on the adjacent part of the Donegal mainland, the Síl Lugdach, almost certainly did not form part of Cenél Conaill either despite later claims that they did.[43]

Although we have no accurate dates for them, based on their positions in the genealogies and their relationships with the individuals for whom we do have dates, both Ernán and Damongóc would seem to have been living around the time that the annals recorded that 'the church of Tory was constructed' in 621, although Ernán belonged to an earlier generation. For 615 the annals recorded the 'slaughter' or the 'devastation' of Tory. Perhaps the 621 construction of a church there was in succession to the destruction of an earlier one in 615.[44] Those dates are shortly before that of the birth of Adomnán (see below). A note about Tory in the annals for 733 describes it as having been 'profaned' (*dehonorauit*), suggesting that reverence for it as an ecclesiastical site had continued throughout the lifetime of Adomnán.

The arrival of Christianity in Donegal is not recorded specifically in contemporary historical documents. But circumstantial evidence in Tírechán's *Collectanea*, especially the list of *Domnach* place-names, and the legends and traditions about Brugach mac Dega of Ráith Maige Aenaig make it abundantly clear that the new religion had been well established there by the time that

41 M. Herbert, *Iona, Kells and Derry*, pp 192–3, 260.
42 P. Ó Riain, *Corpus genealogiarum*: Ernán, p. 5: 16, p. 71: 538, p. 84: 662.40; Damongóc Ailithir, p. 8: 40; Énna Toraid, p. 71: 538 and note.
43 D. Mac Giolla Easpaig, 'Places and early settlement in County Donegal', p. 155; Lacey, *Lug*, passim.
44 *Occisio*, 'slaughter' (AU 616.1); *vastatio*, 'devastation' (Tig = 615). *Hoc tempore constructa est ecclesia Toraige* (Tig = 621.).

Columba was born about 520. Again, we cannot be definite, but it is certainly possible that it was St Patrick or one of his associates that was responsible for its introduction and for the establishment of a source of basic Christian education in Donegal. That source, whatever its nature, would give us ultimately two of the most famous clerics of the sixth and seventh centuries in these islands: Colum Cille and Adomnán.

Turning to secular political geography, until recently it was understood widely that in the sixth and seventh centuries Cenél Conaill already dominated most of Donegal with the exception of the Inishowen Peninsula. However, there is growing evidence now that this was not the case.[45] Instead, it seems that from the mid-sixth century when we begin to have records for it, Cenél Conaill was a small but rich and powerful dynastic kingdom in the historic area of Mag nItha; that is, the lower valley of the River Finn and the surrounding areas north of the Barnesmore Gap. This is an area that contains exceptionally good agricultural land. In addition, the area has many other geographical advantages such as access to a navigable river system. Those assets provided the economic basis for the political (and military) success of Cenél Conaill up to the end of the eighth century. There is a concentration of archaeological sites and the locations of mythological, legendary and historical events centred on Croghan Hill there, and in the vicinity of an adjacent dramatic bend in the River Finn, which probably indicates the nodal centre during that period for Cenél Conaill, their *caput*.[46] From that original area they began to spread out in several directions, into territories previously held by a number of quite separate independent population groups and petty kingdoms. It appears that we can document that expansion, step by step.[47]

One of Cenél Conaill's first conquests appears to have been the small Cenél nÉnnai kingdom immediately to the north of them.[48] Allegedly Cenél nÉnnai took their name from Énna, a brother of the legendary Conall son of Niall and one of the team who helped conquer Donegal from the Ulaid. These were the people to whom Ronnat, Adomnán's mother, is said to have belonged.[49] Ronnat is also referenced in the *c*.1000 *Cáin Adamnáin* (see below, chapter 8). The boundary given there between the Cenél Conaill and Cenél nÉnnai territories was the bridge of the Swilly. The problem about this for identification purposes is that there are at least three separate Swilly's and Swilly bridges in Donegal: one near Dunfanaghy;[50] the River Swilly (with a number of associated place-names

45 Lacey, *CC*, passim; Lacey, *Lug*, passim.
46 Lacey, *CC*, pp 45–6, 52–4, 131–41; B. Lacey, 'The "Bend of the Finn"', passim.
47 Lacey, *CC*, passim, especially fig. 120, p. 239; and figs 8, 9 and 10 and accompanying text in Lacey, *Lug*.
48 Lacey, *CC*, pp 120–31.
49 P. Ó Riain *Corpus genealogiarum*, p. 172: 722.21.
50 Ordnance Survey of Ireland (OSI) 6" Sheet 26.

and bridges) which flows into Lough Swilly near Letterkenny;[51] and a Swilly townland to the north of Lifford through which flows the Swillyburn and across which there is a modern Swilly Bridge.[52] Although we would tend automatically to think of Lough Swilly and its associated river as the principal place of that name, it seems more probable that the Swillyburn is the place referred to in the *Cáin Adamnáin*, and that the area north of the Swillyburn and continuing on to Derry was the original territory of the Cenél nÉnnai.[53] Perhaps significantly, as we will see, Raphoe is located north of the Swillyburn in what is posited here as Cenél nÉnnai territory.

Although now a relatively-speaking insignificant stream except at its exit, the Swillyburn, which runs into the Foyle about six kilometers north of Lifford, has been a major boundary since late medieval times, at least.[54] It is a boundary between townlands; it is the boundary between the parishes of Taughboyne and Clonleigh; it defines a significant section of the boundary between the diocese of Derry and the diocese of Raphoe the origins of which date back to the twelfth century. In the early seventeenth century, the Swillyburn was also used at the time of the Plantations in Ulster as the boundary between the English 'precinct' of Lifford and the Scottish 'precinct' of Portlough. At its western end the Swillyburn passes between Raphoe and Tops. Tops Hill, where the probably Bronze Age or Neolithic Beltany Stone Circle and related features are located,[55] is usually identified as the place mentioned in that area in ancient sources as Carn Glas. Carn Glas was evidently an important boundary marker, which, in the twelfth century, was used as one of the main points to demarcate the diocese of the Cenél nEógain (that is, the diocese of Derry, approximately) from the diocese of the Cenél Conaill (that is, the diocese of Raphoe, approximately).[56] If that identification is correct, then it is very likely that Tops Hill had served also as a boundary marker in earlier times as well.

There were, of course, several groups of people in Ireland during the early medieval period who were known as the Cenél nÉnnai, including one in Fermanagh near the south-eastern border of Donegal.[57] As regards the Cenél

---

51 OSI 6" Sheet 60.
52 OSI 6" Sheet 63. Close to the latter is the village of Ballindrait, *Baile an Droichid*, which was known formerly as *Droichead Adhamhnáin*, 'Adomnán's bridge'. This is an obvious place to suggest for the bridge/border location mentioned in the *Cáin Adamnáin*. However, Ballindrait is located on the River Deele (*Daol*) not the Swillyburn (see below, chapter 11).
53 Lacey, *CC*, pp 122–3.
54 Lacey, *CC*, fig. 69, p. 123.
55 B. Lacy, *Archaeological survey*, pp 72–3. The circle is undoubtedly an ancient ritual location. The name 'Tops' might appear to be an English word but in Irish it can mean 'a light or torch', '*top teineadh*, a blaze of lights', Dinneen, *Foclóir*, p. 1232. I am grateful to Mary Harte for this explanation.
56 E. Hogan, *Onomasticon*, p. 162.
57 M. Ó Duigeannáin, 'Notes', pp 138–9.

nÉnnai of north-eastern Donegal, F.J. Byrne wrote that there is 'no evidence of a dynastic family descended from Énna [son of Niall Noígiallach]' in that area 'before the eleventh century'.[58] However, there is circumstantial evidence, in the traditions surrounding the early sixth-century clerical figure, Brugach mac Dega of Ráith Maige Aenaigh (see above), which points to the presence of a people of that name in that area at that time, but who had no connection with the Uí Néill. Despite the patronymic by which he was known, Brugach's actual father was said to have been Énna and it was possibly the latter who was the eponym of a non-Uí Néill but early Cenél nÉnnai population group in that part of Donegal.[59] The territory of those people probably extended from the Swillyburn to Derry. Derry is located at the east end of a ridge of hills the highest of which (now called Hollywell Hill) was known to the English surveyors around 1600 as Knockenny, presumably an anglicization of Cnoc Énnai.[60] In a poem in the Book of Fenagh, Conall Gulban, the eponymous ancestor of Cenél Conaill, tells Énna:

> Go thou to Derry of the troops; ...
> Énna settled in faithful Derry,
> The fort of Calgach son of Aithemhan.[61]

At no point from the late sixth century onward did Derry belong to, or have any associations with, the Cenél nÉnnai. If there was no truth in those lines in the poem, it is hard to see why anyone would have wanted to invent such claims. Thus, Derry was probably a Cenél nÉnnai secular site before it became a Cenél Conaill church founded, according to legend, by the Cenel Conaill cleric Columba but almost certainly actually founded by another individual called Fiachra mac Ciaráin, a second cousin once removed of the founder of Iona.[62]

The ridge of hills running from Derry on the east through Cnoc Énnai in the middle terminates on its western side at Greenan Mountain. The well-known Grianán of Aileach cashel on the summit of that small mountain almost certainly dates to no earlier than around AD 800, but it is situated inside a presumably earlier prehistoric earthen enclosure – a hillfort(?).[63] Whatever the original date of that enclosure, it was almost certainly used by Cenél Conaill as a boundary marker and observation position from the late sixth century onward when they conquered the area and took control of the former Cenél nÉnnai lands. Cenél

58 F.J. Byrne, *Irish kings* (2001 edition), p. xvi.
59 B. Lacey, 'The church of Ráith Maige Oenaig', pp 216–17.
60 J. Bryson, *The streets of Derry*, p. 197.
61 W. Hennessy & D. Kelly, *The Book of Fenagh*, p. 403.
62 B. Lacey, *Medieval and monastic Derry*, pp 31–6.
63 B. Lacy, *Archaeological survey*, pp 111–12.

Conaill then established the border between themselves and the Cenél nÉogain of Inishowen to their north along the wetland (but now reclaimed valley) below Greenan Mountain, the Pennyburn Depression mentioned above. Cenél Conaill's arrival in the area was possibly signalled by the record of the battle of Druim Meic Ercae in 578, in which their king, Áed mac Ainmerech (Table 2), defeated the Cenél nÉogain.

Table 2: Early Cenél Conaill I, including Colum Cille

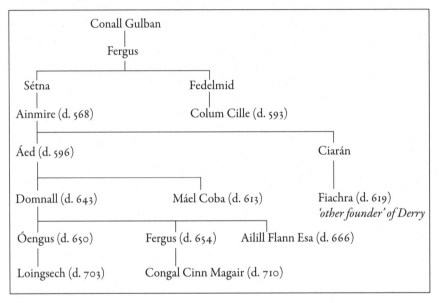

Druim Meic Ercae is often identified as a site in Co. Tyrone,[64] although it is illogical that these two Donegal kingdoms would have been fighting each other at such a location at that time. A much stronger possibility is that Druim Meic Ercae was somewhere along the southern boundary of Cenél nÉogain territory to the north of Derry and Greenan Mountain, just north of the Pennyburn Depression. There are many 'drum' names in that area but none now appear to reflect the form Druim Meic Ercae. However, if such was the location, then the name Druim Meic Ercae probably indicates a connection with the somewhat earlier, sixth-century shadowy Cenél nÉogain king, Muircertach Mac Ercae.[65]

Probably in a related move shortly after that battle in 578 and in order to 'fix' their side of the new boundary, the Cenél Conaill church at Derry was founded by their king Áed mac Ainmerech and his nephew, the ecclesiastic Fiachra mac

64 G. Mac Niocaill, *Ireland before the Vikings*, p. 80; A. Mac Shamhráin '*Nebulae discutiuntur*', p. 82, n. 17.
65 Lacey, *CC*, pp 199–200.

Ciaráin, the so-called *alius fundatoris* of Daire Calgaigh (Derry).[66] Despite the well-known legends, there is no evidence that Columba was involved in that foundation, at least not in any primary capacity. The handing over to the church of what had probably been up till then an important Cenél nÉnnai settlement – and maybe ritual-site – would have been another example of the tactic frequently used by victorious early Irish kingdoms in granting away one of its defeated enemy's significant secular sites to the church, in order to 'neutralize' it politically.

As outlined above, Cenél Conaill seem to have originated in the area north of the Barnesmore Gap, the lower valley of the River Finn and the territory known as Mag nItha. The area south of the gap extending to what is now Donegal town and beyond became known as Tír Áeda. There are two explanations as to how it got that name. One derives from the mythical character also referred to in the name of the anciently famous (but now destroyed) waterfall on the Erne, Es Áeda Ruaid.[67] However, that waterfall lay well south of and outside the territory of Tír Áeda when we first encounter it. The association with the mythical Áed seems unlikely, at least as the primary explanation of the name. The other explanation is also legendary but is at least grounded in real history. This suggests that it was conquered before the end of the sixth century by the powerful Cenél Conaill king, Áed mac Ainmerech, from whom, accordingly, the territory was named.[68] That claim does make historical sense and further, as we will see below, Áed seems to have conquered as far south as the church at Drumhome.

Thus, starting from the Cenél Conaill base at Croghan Hill in the lower Finn valley, Áed conquered the whole of the east side of Donegal, all the way from Derry in the north to Drumhome in the south. This was the territory through which passed (as it still does) the principal route from Connacht into western Ulster, the route followed by Tírechán's Patrick in the *Collectanea* (see above). Áed then established (or in Drumhome's case possibly re-established, see below) important boundary churches at each end of his enlarged kingdom. Those churches, Derry and Drumhome, are the only ecclesiastical sites in 'Donegal'[69] referred to by name in Adomnán's *Vita Columbae*. At least one of the reasons for this may have been because they marked the northern and southern boundaries, respectively, of the Cenél Conaill kingdom into which Adomnán himself was born. Although in a quite different context, that late sixth- and seventh-century political reality may also be the explanation of what was, almost certainly, a nostalgic and propagandistic but redundant title used in the annals in 921. When Cináed son of Domnall, allegedly a direct descendant of Áed mac Ainmerech,[70]

66 B. Lacey, *Medieval and monastic Derry*, pp 27–34.
67 D. Mac Giolla Easpaig, 'Places and early settlement', p. 158; Lacey, *CC*, pp 72–3.
68 T. Ó Canann, 'Trí Saorthuatha', p. 24 and p. 40, n. 30 and references cited therein.
69 Which, as described above, in this context includes Derry.
70 M. O'Brien, *Corpus genealogiarum*, p. 164: 144f18.

died in that year, he was described as the 'superior [*princeps*] of Derry and Drumhome, and chief counsellor [*cenn adchomairc*] of Cenél Conaill ...'.⁷¹ But by that date and for the previous 130 years, Cenél Conaill had lost control of everything north of the Barnesmore Gap following their disastrous defeat at the battle of Clóitech.⁷² Cináed's 'Derry' title was probably nothing more than a *soi-disant* aspiration and claim, that would not have been recognized (or even make contemporary sense) in the *realpolitik* of the tenth century.

The land around Drumhome had been conquered by Áed mac Ainmerech before his death in 596, but it was probably still relatively dangerous, contested border territory at the time of Adomnán's birth in the 620s. That is one of the reasons why it seems unlikely that he was born near there as is often claimed (see below, chapter 2). The church at Drumhome was situated on the northern side of what was at the time most probably another significant wetland valley. The land there has been improved since medieval times and, as there have also been some related modifications along the coast, the local topography has changed considerably. Nowadays, the former wetland is represented mainly by the course of the much-drained and restricted Ballintra River, as well as by a series of small, connected lakes.

In the sixth and seventh centuries the church of Ráith Cungi (Racoo) was situated on the opposite, southern side of that wetland valley. The valley, which was probably also the boundary between the two territories mentioned in this area by Tírechán in the quotation used above, Mag Latrain to the north and Mag Sereth to the south,⁷³ almost certainly became the boundary between Cenél Conaill and their neighbours to the south, Cenél Cairpre, during the reign of Áed mac Ainmerech. According to the Tripartite Life of Patrick, Cenél Cairpre disputed the control of south Donegal as far north as Racoo until the time of their king Muirgius son of Máel Dúin who died in 698.⁷⁴ However, Cenél Conaill did actually cross the valley and conquer Cenél Cairpre territory as far south as the Erne somewhat earlier, during the reign of Áed mac Ainmerech's son Domnall and his sons, as will be demonstrated below. The Tripartite Life extols Muirgius as 'a wonderful king of the tribe of Cairpre' but perhaps what was actually being praised was that he was the first of his people to accept that by then their kingdom had lost the territory between Racoo and the River Erne, which river now formed their new border with the Cenél Conaill to the north.

We seem to be able to plot the advance of Cenél Conaill as they pushed southward against Cenél Cairpre. Most of this advance took place during Adomnán's lifetime and was reflected, to some extent at least, in the *Vita*

71 AU 921.6.
72 Lacey, *CC*, pp 307–10.
73 L. Bieler, *The Patrician texts*, pp 160–1.
74 W. Stokes, *The Tripartite Life*, p. 149. AU 697.6.

Columbae. The powerful Cenél Conaill king Domnall mac Áedo died in 643; the Annals of Tigernach claims that this occurred at Ard Fothaid. Ard Fothaid is usually identified with the massive hillfort-type earthwork at Glasbolie.[75] That fort was located on the south side of the wetland valley referred to above, that is, on what had been until recently the northern border of Cenél Cairpre territory. Writing about fifty years later Adomnán (who would have been in his late teens in 643) has Columba voice a particularly 'cosy' prophecy about the death of the otherwise very combative Domnall:

> He will never be handed over to his enemies; but will die at home in his bed, in a peaceful old age, in the friendly presence of his household.[76]

Adomnán adds that all this happened as predicted. In somewhat overdoing the prophecy, it is possible that Adomnán was claiming a special title for Domnall's house at Ard Fothaid, something that would make sense if he had only recently moved there having actually conquered it and the surrounding territory from Cenél Cairpre. Whether that is the explanation or not, without doubt Domnall and his sons did continue to move south towards the Erne, conquering the land as they went. We can see that from the record of the battle of Dún Cremthainn in 650[77] in which two branches of Cenél Conaill fought each other and Óengus son of Domnall fell (Table 2). Dún Cremthainn, now Dungravenan, is a promontory fort on the north bank of the Erne, on the western edge of the town of Ballyshannon.[78] That this battle occurred there between two factions of Cenél Conaill makes it absolutely clear that, by then, the Cenél Conaill had reached the Erne and had established it as their southern border. When the death of another son of Domnall is recorded sixteen years later, he is described as Ailill Flann Esa.[79] (Table 2) His name surely proves his connection with the most famous *es* (waterfall) in the area: the Es Áeda Ruaid, the great but now destroyed waterfall on the Erne just below Ballyshannon.[80]

All this seems to prove conclusively that by 650, first under Áed mac Ainmerech, and then under his son Domnall, and then under Domnall's sons Óengus and Ailill and their immediate relatives, the Cenél Conaill kingdom had

---

75 B. Lacy, *Archaeological survey,* pp 114–15.

76 R. Sharpe, *Adomnán of Iona,* p. 120. The Andersons give a slightly different, even 'cosier', translation: 'He will never be delivered into the hands of his enemies; but will die on his bed by a peaceful death, in old age, and within his own house [*intra domum suam*], surrounded by a crowd of his intimate friends.' Anderson & Anderson, *Adomnan's Life of Columba,* p. 231.

77 AU 650.2.

78 B. Lacy, *Archaeological survey,* pp 227–9.

79 AU 665.1.

80 The waterfall was one of the great wonders of ancient and medieval Ireland but was destroyed in the 1950s to facilitate a hydro-electricity scheme.

been expanded all along the east side of Donegal from Derry in the north to the Erne in the south. By the time its king Muirgius died in 698, Cenél Cairpre had probably accepted that their northern border, and the southern border of Cenél Conaill, was without any doubt the River Erne. That is probably the reason why he was praised in the Tripartite Life.

Immediately to the west of the Cenél Conaill territory of Tír Áeda, that is west of the River Eske, was a forest perhaps remembered today in the name of the parish of Killymard.[81] Beyond that again and further west of the River Eany, reaching out to the westernmost Atlantic peninsulas, was the territory of Cenél mBogaine. The later genealogies claimed that these too were a subsection of Cenél Conaill.[82] But they had their own king, Sechnasach mac Garbáin, as early as 607 according to the Annals of Tigernach. It is much more likely, therefore, that they were a separate and quite independent people. Such an interpretation has implications for the often-stated view that almost all of the early abbots of Iona belonged to the kindred of Columba. A seventeenth-century source claims that the fourth abbot, Fergna, belonged to the Cenél mBogaine.[83] But earlier sources refer to him as Fergna Brit, suggesting a British origin for him. As we will see below there is other evidence that throws doubt on the repeated claim that most of the early abbots of Iona were related by blood to Columba.

We can see in the annals evidence for Cenél Conaill attempting to expand into Cenél mBogaine territory. That is probably the explanation for the killing of their king by Domnall mac Áedo in 607.[84] An entry for 613 is probably also really about Cenél Conaill expansion into Cenél mBogaine territory.

The slaying of Máel Coba son of Áed in the battle of Sliab Tuath, *Bélgadhain, alius in the battle of Sliab Truim*. Suibne Menn was victor.[85]

---

81 The meaning of this place-name is disputed. Nollaig Ó Muraíle (pers. comm.) and others have suggested *Cill Ua mBaird*, 'the church of the Ua mBaird', based on a number of late medieval sources. But the first part might alternatively (or also) reflect *coille* meaning 'wood'. Significant forestry survived in this area until the seventeenth century at least (Day & McWilliams, *Ordnance Survey memoirs*, p. 95; E. McCracken, 'The woodlands of Donegal', p. 62). Notably, there are no ringforts or related sites of the early medieval period in this closely defined area, suggesting an absence of settlement there at that time – possibly because the area was still densely wooded.

82 M. O'Brien, *Corpus genealogiarum*, p. 165: 144f53.

83 See W. Reeves, *The Life of St Columba*, p. 372. But M. Herbert (*Iona, Kells and Derry*, pp 39–40) suggests that the Cenél mBogaine connection was a fictional attempt to provide Fergna with a Donegal pedigree.

84 Tig.

85 AU 614.1. Tig adds that 'Suibne Menn killed him [Máel Coba]'. Italics indicate a secondary hand.

Máel Coba of the Cenél Conaill (Table 2) was a son of Áed mac Ainmerech and was said to have been king of Tara at the time of the battle. Suibne Menn is said to have been king of Cenél nEogain.[86] Sliab Tuath is usually identified with Bessy Bell mountain near Newtownstewart in Co. Tyrone.[87] But John O'Donovan was almost certainly correct when he suggested that the real location of the battle was near Sliab Tuath in Donegal, a prominent mountain actually in Cenél mBogaine territory, nowadays known in English as Slievetooey.[88]

North of what was the main Cenél mBogaine territory and the Gweebarra estuary is the largely agriculturally barren area that now forms the rocky Gaeltacht parish of the Rosses. This area appears to have been largely uninhabited until post-medieval times as it is almost devoid of visible archaeological sites of all earlier periods. An important exception is the early church site at Templecrone, Tempull Cróna, together with the nearby small coastal island of Oileán Cróna. Templecrone is located in the significantly named Termon townland which, itself, was probably an island in early medieval times. Seven kilometers north of Templecrone is the site of Dún Gleo[89] on another small but strategic coastal island. Tempull Cróna and Dún Gleo seem to have marked the actual effective northern boundary of Cenél mBogaine territory although both were very remote from the main settlements of those people further to the south. The saint of Tempull Cróna, Crón daughter of Díarmait, is said to have belonged to the Cenél mBogaine but we have no precise dates for her.[90] On the basis of her pedigree (she is said to have belonged to the fifth generation after the eponymous Énna Bogaine) it is likely that she lived in the first half of the seventh century. According to the late fictionalized genealogical framework, the Cenél mBogaine were descended from Énna Bogaine (sometimes just Bogaine) who is said to have been a son of Conall Gulban but, in other sources such as the *Echtra Conaill Gulban*, Bogaine appears as a son of Niall Noígiallach.[91] Notwithstanding that confusion, all the medieval sources agree that Cenél mBogaine was part of Cenél Conaill but, as we have seen, it is much more likely that it originated as a separate and quite independent kingdom. Again, as we have seen, the annals almost certainly allow us to see Cenél Conaill attempting to conquer and expand into Cenél mBogaine territory. That seems to be the explanation for the

86 For Suibne see Lacey, *CC*, pp 219–22.

87 E.g., G. Mac Niocaill, *Ireland before the Vikings*, p. 90; Mac Shamhrain 'The making of Tír nEogain', p. 61.

88 AFM sub anno 291, vol. i, p. 122, note h.

89 Dún Gleo is actually about 8kms north-west of the town of Dungloe which, nevertheless, takes its name from the ancient Dún. I am grateful to Patrick Boner for assistance with the geography of that area and for drawing my attention to the article 'Dungloe what's in a name' by Sean Boner on the Upper Rosses History Discussion Forum Facebook page.

90 P. Ó Riain, *Corpus genealogiarum*, pp 8: 38, 76: 622, 82: 662.24.

91 M. O'Brien, *Corpus genealogiarum*, pp 163 and 165: 144d20 and 144f52.

killing in 607 mentioned above of Sechnasach mac Garbáin, their king. In the genealogies, a Garbán, almost definitely the father of that Sechnasach, is said to have been a grandfather of St Crón of Templecrone (Table 3).

Table 3: Early Cenél mBogaine including St Crón

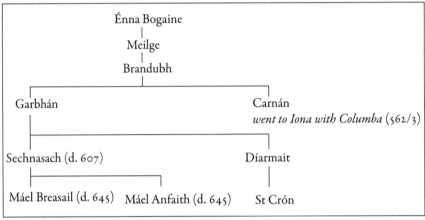

Énna Bogaine
Meilge
Brandubh

Garbhán — Carnán *went to Iona with Columba* (562/3)

Sechnasach (d. 607) — Díarmait

Máel Breasail (d. 645) Máel Anfaith (d. 645) St Crón

If those relationships were correct, then that would place the floruit of Crón in the middle decades of the seventh century. Her lay contemporaries for whom we do have dates died, apparently, in the mid-640s.[92] As we know that clerics often lived longer than their secular relatives – many of whom would have led more violence-filled lives – Crón's death may not have occurred until as late as the 660s or even the 670s. In other words, a considerable part of her adult life must have overlapped with that of Adomnán. We can only speculate as to whether or not they ever met but, as we will see below, Adomnán was especially noted for his concern for women. In any case, Crón was a very important Donegal woman who was an overlapping contemporary of Adomnán. Although we know very little about her, she must have been a remarkable person. The fact that this early cleric was a woman is especially interesting. Apart from her significance in the Christian life of the community at the time, she is the first woman who, independently in her own right, is recorded in Donegal history. She is the only named early female clerical figure directly connected with Donegal for whom we have any information. Her feastday is 7 July.

In the following century another female 'saint', Samthann (died *c*.738), is connected by dedication with the church of Ernaidhe (Urney) on the right bank of the River Finn (in Mag nÍtha, but now in Co. Tyrone). Samthann's main church was at Clonbroney (near Granard, Co. Longford) in the midlands but her genealogy links her with the Dál Fiatach of Ulster. At least part of her adult

92 Lacey, *CC*, pp 81–2.

life must have overlapped also with that of Adomnán. Her tenuous links with the north-west of Ireland seem to have come about from an alleged connection with two Cenél nÉogain kings of Tara, Áed Allán (d. 743) and Niall Frossach (d. 778).[93] Cenél nÉogain certainly did have some connections with the Dál Fiatach[94] and during the reigns of the two latter kings Cenél nÉogain made considerable inroads into the territory in which Urney is situated.

North and north-east of Templecrone and Cenél mBogaine territory – on the mainland opposite Tory Island – were the lands of the Síl Lugdach who have been mentioned above. The late genealogies claim that they too were part of Cenél Conaill; however recent research has shown that they actually constituted a quite separate, independent people and petty kingdom.[95] From the eighth century onwards the Síl Lugdach, most probably with the assistance and permission of their overlords, Cenél nÉogain, began to grow into a very powerful kingdom that spread out from their original remote western location to take over some of the richer lands of east Donegal. In the process they took on aspects of the identity of the former Cenél Conaill rulers of those lands becoming as it were 'more Cenél Conaill than the Cenél Conaill themselves'. As part of that transformation they also assumed the role of principal devotees of the cults of both St Colum Cille and St Adamnán (*sic*). From the late eighth century their newly acquired lands contained many of the locations and monuments associated with the memory of the early parts of the lives of both of those individuals.[96] These included: (i) the sites connected with the birth and childhood of Columba; (ii) the ecclesiastical settlement at Kilmacrenan, which was the principal centre for the preservation and propagation of the lore of Colum Cille in early medieval Donegal; and (iii) a church at Raphoe, newly founded about 800, linked, retrospectively, with Adomnán (see below).

In 880 or thereabouts, one of the Síl Lugdach, Flann son of Máel Dúin (Table 4), is said to have become abbot of Iona and, hence, leader of the Columban federation of churches in Ireland and Scotland.[97] They would go on to play a major role in the preservation of, and almost certainly also in the propagandistic distortion of, various aspects of the Columban heritage, including some of the traditions about Adomnán. Their decendants of later medieval times, the Uí Domnaill (and the Uí Dochartaigh), also vigorously cultivated and exploited that Columban patrimony.

93 Lacey, *CC*, pp 293–5 and 303–4.
94 See, for instance, Lacey, *CC*, pp 38, 45, 162–4.
95 Lacey, *Lug*, passim.
96 Lacey, *Lug*, especially pp 54–69.
97 M. Herbert, *Iona, Kells and Derry*, pp 74–5. But for a critical view see also T. Ó Canann, 'Clann Fhiangusa and the pedigree of Flann mac Maíle Dúin', pp 20–2 and below, chapter 11.

Table 4: Síl Lugdach genealogies

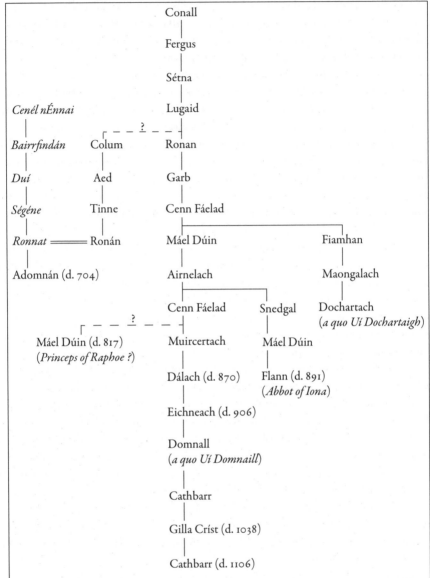

The Síl Lugdach version of their 'embroidered' genealogies, including the false pedigree of Adomnán showing his descent from Lugaid son of Sétna (and the Cenél nÉnnai pedigree of his mother). Also, the pedigree of Máel Dúin son of Cenn Fáelad the probable *'princeps* of Raphoe', as suggested below (chapter 8). The latest name here, Cathbarr mac Gilla Críst, was the Síl Lugdach/Uí Domnaill aristocrat who commissioned the *cumhdach* or shrine-box for the *Cathach*.

In the sixth and seventh centuries, immediately to the east of the Síl Lugdach territories was the petty kingdom ruled by Cenél Duach. The later genealogies claim that they too were part of Cenél Conaill[98] but, again, it is much more likely that they also were, in fact, an independent kingdom. Apparently, they had their own king from a very early period and one of those, Báetán son of Ninnid, is in some sources (but almost certainly falsely) claimed to have been king of Tara.[99] Báetán's grandfather, the father of Ninnid, was said to have been Duí, the eponym of Cenél Duach. The eighth abbot of Iona, the predecessor of Adomnán, was Failbe who was a descendant of a Duí son of Ninnid (Table 5),[100] allegedly belonging to what might be called Cenél Conaill proper. Three other early abbots of Iona (Laisrén, Ségéne and Cumméne) are said to have been descendants of Feradach son of Ninnid (Table 5).[101]

Table 5: Possible Cenél Duach (or associated) abbots of Iona

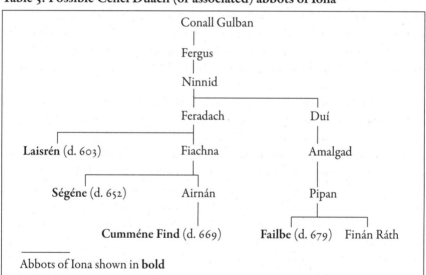

Conall Gulban
|
Fergus
|
Ninnid

Feradach — Duí

Laisrén (d. 603) — Fiachna — Amalgad

Ségéne (d. 652) — Airnán — Pipan

Cumméne Find (d. 669) — Failbe (d. 679) Finán Ráth

Abbots of Iona shown in **bold**

However, the possibility of two Donegal Ninnids of the same generation, one of whom had a father Duí and the other of whom had a son Duí, while not impossible, is, to say the least, suspicious. That suspicion is strengthened by the tradition that Failbe the abbot of Iona had a brother Finán who was said to have

98 M. O'Brien, *Corpus genealogiarum*, p. 164: 144f30–39.
99 F.J. Byrne, *Irish kings*, p. 275; E. Bhreathnach, *The kingship and landscape of Tara*, pp 187 and 216. Lacey, *CC*, pp 97–8 and 198–9.
100 P. Ó Riain, *Corpus genealogiarum*, p. 54: 339.
101 Ibid., p 54: 336, 337 and 338.

been the founder of the church of Ray (Ráith) in Cenél Duach territory.[102] In fact Ray, situated on the right bank of the similarly named boundary river, was almost certainly a Cenél Duach border church, suggesting that Failbe may also have belonged to Cenél Duach rather than to the regular Cenél Conaill. If that was so, then it is another problem for the repeatedly stated claim that most of the early abbots of Iona belonged to the kindred of Columba, Cenél Conaill.

East and north of Cenél Duach was the Fanad area. This was the home in the sixth century of the Corpraige to whom, according to what is probably the most reliable tradition, Eithne, Columba's mother, is said to have belonged.[103] There is very little evidence for those people and it is clear that Cenél Conaill conquered that area within Adomnán's lifetime. One of Domnall mac Áedo's sons, who died in 654, was called Fergus of Fanad (Table 2), while the latter's son, Congal Cinn Magair (Table 2),[104] took his name from a district on the west shore of the adjacent Mulroy Bay.[105] Congal Cinn Magair would later be involved with Adomnán as one of the so-called 'guarantors' of the *Cáin Adomnáin* (see below, chapter 4). Thus, during the seventh century and during the lifetime of Adomnán, just as in Tír Áeda and Cenél mBogaine we can see Cenél Conaill influence also spreading incrementally into the Fanad and Mulroy areas of north-west of Donegal.[106]

To the east of Fanad across Lough Swilly lay Inis Éogain, the territory of Cenél nEogain. The latter were the principal rivals and, at times during Adomnán's lifetime, the outright enemies of Cenél Conaill. From the late sixth century at least the northern boundaries of the latter kingdom came right up to the wetland valley, the Pennyburn Depression, which also defined the southern edge of Inis Éogain. The southern side of that frontier was emphasized and reinforced 'spiritually' by the former Cenél nÉnnai settlement (and possible pre-Christian ritual site) at Derry which in the late sixth century was 'converted' to a Cenél Conaill border, Columban monastery.

South of the Pennyburn Depression and Derry was Adomnán's country, the homeland of both of his parents. The area between Derry and the Swillyburn was, as outlined above, probably the original territory of Cenél nÉnnai, his mother's people, although it was conquered by Cenél Conaill about the last quarter of the sixth century. There seems to be no reason why the tradition that Adomnán's

102 Ibid.: pp 76: 623 and 82: 662.25. For the suggested late eighth- early ninth-century date for the stone cross at Ray and its possible connections with Iona see B. Lacey, 'The ringed cross at Ray'.

103 P. Ó Riain, *Corpus genealogiarum*, p. 61: 397; p. 78: 651 and p. 173: 722.23.

104 Fergus's death is recorded at AU 653.4; however, he is not given the 'Fanad' epithet until the reference to him in the entry for the death of his son Congal in 710 (AU 709.3).

105 John O'Donovan, in M. Herity, *Ordnance Survey letters, Donegal*, pp 46–7.

106 Lacey, *CC*, p. 239, fig. 120.

mother belonged to the Donegal Cenél nÉnnai should not be accepted (see below, chapter 2). There is a suggestion in some of the legendary material about Cenél Conaill characters (e.g. Conall Gulban and Columba) that children were born in the homeplace of their mothers, not in their fathers' homes.[107] If this was so, then Adomnán may well have been born and raised in this area. Indeed, Raphoe itself, with which he is later connected by legend, was almost certainly originally part of Cenél nÉnnai territory before being conquered and absorbed by Cenél Conaill about half a century before his birth.

107 E.g., Lacey, *CC*, pp 35–7.

CHAPTER TWO

Adomnán's birth and early life

In his surviving writings Adomnán himself tells us almost nothing about his origins: who his parents were, where he was born and where he grew up. Neither do we know where he commenced what was evidently, based on the output of his later career, a very thorough and wide Latinate, Christian education. In fact, he gives us only one hint about his place of birth when in the *Vita Columbae* he refers to *nostram Scotiam*, 'our Ireland'.[1] There is a tenth-century Life, the *Betha Adamnáin*, which will be discussed below (chapter 9), but it contains no biographical details about his early years and is, in effect, a *roman-à-clef* about events and individuals in the tenth century rather than Adomnán's life in the seventh. But below we will try to tease out some additional information that might narrow the search for the place of his birth.

He did confirm for us, however, what his unusual and rare name was: Adomnán. Whether or not he had that from birth or adopted it later in his life as his specifically clerical name we cannot say.[2] Although he did not himself provide us with the original version in Irish, four times in the *Vita Columbae* he latinized his name in the phrase *mihi Adomnano*, 'to me Adomnán', the second syllable clearly spelt 'om'.[3] The name Adomnán is made up of three elements: (i) the emphatic 'Ad'; (ii) the root 'omn', derived from a word meaning 'fear', 'awe', 'terror' or some such concept; and (iii) the suffix 'án', a hypocoristic or endearing term. It is important to stress the spelling Ad-omn-án as it is often cited later, inaccurately, with the second syllable spelt as 'amn', that is, Adamnán. In fact, the latter comes to be the accepted spelling from around the beginning of the ninth century at least and from that form was derived the modern formulation Adhamhnán, anglicized as Eunan.[4] Spelt with either a middle 'o' or 'a', it is a comparatively rare name. But at least three other relevant Adomnáns or Adamnáns (their names spelt variously in different sources) are known from roughly the same period:

---

1 Anderson & Anderson, *Adomnan's Life of Columba*, pp 540–1.
2 But see G. Márkus, '*Adiutor Laborantium*', p. 151, n. 28.
3 Anderson & Anderson, *Adomnan's Life of Columba*, pp 200–1, 318–19, 508–9 and 533–4; and for a discussion of his name pp 92–3. See also the Schaffhausen manuscript, *Generalia* I: 9a, 50a, 120b and 132a.
4 However, the spelling Adamnán with an 'a' is already used in the law tract *Crith Gablach*, dated by its editor to 'the opening years of the 8th century', i.e., close to the time of the death of Adomnán of Iona (D. Binchy, *Crith Gablach*, pp xiv and 21).

(i) Adomnán was a bishop of the church of Ráith Maige Aenaig in east Donegal who died in 731. He will be discussed further below (chapters 8 and 9).

(ii) The Venerable Bede tells us about an ascetic Irish monk who, in the 680s, belonged to the monastery of Coldingham in what is now Berwickshire, near the border between Scotland and north-eastern England. Although Bede gives us his name in Latin, it appears that it would have originated in Irish as Adamnán.

(iii) In the genealogy of the Conmaicni of Cuil Tola, cited in the Book of Fenagh,[5] one individual is assigned the name Adamnán. Although we have no precise dates for him, a rough calculation based on a generation length of *c.*30 years would seem to place him as being alive in the early eighth century and to have overlapped with the lifespan of Adomnán of Iona. His name may even have contributed to the legend of *Scrín Adhamhnáin* in Co. Sligo (see chapter 11 below).

It has been suggested in both medieval and modern times that Adomnán or Adamnán was an Irish form of the biblical name Adam, meaning something like 'little' or 'dearest' Adam. The twelfth-century additional notes to the Martyrology of Óengus make this explicit in the entry for the 23 September feastday: '*Adomnani abbatis Iae*[6] – *Adamnan .i. diminutiuum a nomine quod est Adam*', 'Adomnán abbot of Iona – Adamnán, i.e., a diminutive of the name Adam'.[7] *Sanas Cormaic* or Cormac's Glossary, attributed to Cormac mac Cuilenán who died in 908, also has: *Adamnán .i. homunculus .i. disbegad anma Ádam*, 'Adamnán, i.e., a little man, i.e., a diminutive of the name Adam.'[8] But, as pointed out above, it seems clear now that Adomnán was in fact derived from a root word in Irish, *omun*, meaning something like 'fear', 'panic' or 'terror'. In that sense the full name Adomnán would have meant originally something like: 'man of great dread',[9] or even 'great, little [or "dear"] man of fear', perhaps referencing the 'fear of' God. In a fascinating essay on this subject Gilbert Márkus drew attention to the use of a cognate word in a reference to a plague in 826.[10]

5 See also O'Brien, *Corpus genealogiarum Hiberniae*, p. 319: 161b15 where the individual is referred to as Adomnán (*sic*).

6 This first part with the 'o' spelling is identical to the reference to him in the retrospective entry on Adomnán's birth in the Annals of Ulster (623.2).

7 W. Stokes, *The Martyrology of Oengus*, pp 210–11.

8 K. Meyer, *Sanas Cormaic*, p. 1.

9 Anderson & Anderson, *Adomnan's Life of Columba*, pp 92–3.

10 G. Márkus, '*Adiutor Laborantium*', p. 150.

Adomnae mor for Herinn n-uile, .i. robudh plaige o m. Iellaen di Mume.

Great terror in all Ireland, i.e., from the warning of plague given by Iellán's son of Mume.[11]

Márkus goes on to distinguish the subtlety between the etymology of a name and the evolving meaning that was derived from or attached to it. He argues that Adomnán's name can be understood also to mean 'little Adam' and equates it with the rare Latin word *homunculus*, 'little' or even (in modern Scottish and Ulster parlance) 'wee' man, which appears to have been a favourite of Adomnán.[12] Márkus further suggests that the use of the word *homunculus* in the Latin poem *Adiutor Laborantium* (see below, chapter 10) is in effect Adomnán's signature as its author. It seems very probable that Adomnán was fully aware of that word as a sort of pun on his own name!

Adomnán's birth is noted in AU, Tig and CS for the equivalent of the year 625.[13] The AU reference for that year has *Nativitas Adomnani abbatis Iae*, 'the birth of Adomnán, abbot of Iona'. Evidently this is a retrospective note entered, at the earliest, subsequent to his appointment as abbot on Iona in 679, and possibly subsequent to his death. His death entry in AU (and in Tig) for 704 says that it was: *.lxx.uii. anno etatis sue*, 'the 77th year of his age' (CS says 78th). Pádraig Ó Riain has disputed the reliability of this 77 figure, arguing that it was cited in imitation of Adomnán's own similar calculation of the age at which Columba had died. The latter, according to Ó Riain, was an artificial age generated by Adomnán from the ancient and medieval esoteric 'science' of numerology, reflecting multiples of the number 7, which 'stood for completeness and perfection'.[14] Ó Riain says that the figure 77 was calculated by Adomnán for Columba by allowing the latter 43 years in Ireland before he left for Iona and 34 years in Scotland before he died there, that is, 4+3 = 7, as does 3+4; 43+34 = 77. The argument derived from this is that some anonymous annalist decided to use the same false, but numerologically perfect, age for Adomnán. The problem with this is that whoever that annalist was they are likely to have recorded it at or close to the time that Adomnán died. Both the latter's death and the noting of it took place on Iona where many of the monks would have been familiar with

11   AU 826.6. For discussion of Iellán etc., see Kenney, *Sources*, p. 477. Mention of this reference seems timely, as this book is being written in the midst of the Covid 19 lockdown.
12   G. Márkus, '*Adiutor Laborantium*', p. 147. Márkus points out that of the 12 known occurrences of the word *homunculus* in literature between AD501 and 735, 8 of them come from works by Adomnán. The word 'wee' as used in English is derived, of course, ultimately from the Gaelic word *beag/bhig*, 'small', or 'little'.
13   AU 623.3; CS 624. Tig mistakenly says *báss* ('death of') when what was intended was *nativitas* ('birth of').
14   P. Ó Riain, *A dictionary of Irish saints*, pp 53–4, with further references cited therein.

at least what was claimed to be their abbot's age when he died. Richard Sharpe calculated that if the annalist who recorded those details was correct and if, as is also almost certain, Adomnán's feastday, 23 September, reflects the anniversary of his death, then that meant that he had to have been born sometime between 24 September 627 and 23 September 628.[15] As opposed to that, Jean-Michel Picard noted that the annals were agreed that in the year following Adomnán's birth there was a solar eclipse and, as the only appropriate eclipse occurred on 10 June 625, Adomnán's birth had to be in 624.[16] Thus we have various possible dates for the year of Adomnán's birth (as we do also for Columba): 624, 625, 627 and 628. Modern scholars are as uncertain about the issue as were the medieval chroniclers. As things stand, there can be no certainty about any of those dates, but the strong likelihood is that Adomnán was born sometime in the middle of the third decade of the seventh century.

Since William Reeves suggested it in the 1850s, several modern authors have concluded that Adomnán's origins may have been in Tír Áeda[17] in the southeast of Co. Donegal, a name now anglicized as the barony of Tirhugh, the area between Donegal town and Ballyshannon and the Erne Estuary. That suggestion was based on Adomnán's mention in the *Vita Columbae* of the church of *Dorsum Tómme* or *Druim Tuama* (Drumhome) in the middle of that area, and of his hearing a story about the night of Columba's death from an old monk who was buried there.[18] Reeves claimed that the story 'almost implied that Adomnán was, in his boyhood, living in that neighbourhood.' However, Adomnán himself says that he heard the story when he was a *iuvenis*. That word is normally translated as 'a young man'. It is certainly possible that he did have some connection as 'a young man' with *Druim Tuama*, maybe as an aspirant or junior cleric there. However, as Mark Stansbury pointed out, the word *iuvenis* can also refer to a person up to their middle age: 'Adomnán is consistent in calling Columba a *iuvenis* before he left Ireland at the age of 42.'[19] It may be that in using the same

15 R. Sharpe, *Adomnán of Iona*, p. 44.

16 J.M. Picard, 'Adomnán and the writing of the "Life of Columba"', p. 4 and p. 14, n. 13. However, D. Mc Carthy's synchronisms of the Irish annals gives the year of Adomnán's birth as 625.

17 W. Reeves, *The Life of St Columba*, p. xli; R. Sharpe, *Adomnán of Iona*, p. 44; T. Ó Canann, 'Máel Coba Ua Galchobair', p. 41.

18 Anderson & Anderson, *Adomnan's Life of Columba*, pp 532–7; R. Sharpe, *Adomnán of Iona*, pp 230–1. The monk's name in contemporary Irish was given as Ernene mocu Fhir-roide. But Gilbert Márkus noted that Adomnán also latinized the first name: as *ferreolus*, 'man of iron', on the assumption that Ernene was a diminutive of the Irish word *iarn*, 'iron'. Márkus also pointed out that this translation of a personal name into Latin by Adomnán was unique, and wondered what was so significant about it to have warranted such special treatment? See '*Adiutor Laborantium*', p. 153.

19 M. Stansbury, 'The Schaffhausen manuscript', pp 70–89, 84. He also (p. 83) refers to other assessments of the age limits of a *iuvenis*, up to 46 or even 50 years of age.

word here Adomnán was simply referring to the fact that he had heard the story before he left Ireland to go to live on Iona when, like Columba, he was also already in his forties, at least.

Druim Tuama is now Drumhome in Mullanacross townland, very close to the shore of Donegal Bay. It was mentioned as a late sixth- and early seventh-century Cenél Conaill border church in the last chapter. The surface remains there now include a graveyard with the ruins of a late medieval church.[20] It is probable also that Adomnán's *Druim Tuama* can be equated with the church in this general area referred to by Tírechán in the *Collectanea* as *Sirdruimm*.[21] However, for reasons that will be discussed more fully below, it seems unlikely that this was the area in which Adomnán was born, although there is a somewhat greater probability that he may have spent some of his 'youth' there. We will return to the issue of the connection between Adomnán and *Druim Tuama* below but, for the present, we can say that there is no evidence that he was born there. As we will see, his birthplace is much more likely to have been in the territory of his mother's people near Raphoe, which, as a result of various separate coincidences, would later become the chief church dedicated to him.

We have two slightly different genealogical traditions for Adomnán both claiming that, as with Columba, he belonged to Cenél Conaill.[22] The latter, as we have seen, was an aristocratic and royal dynasty that emerged before the early sixth century on the excellent agricultural land lying along the lower valley of the River Finn in east Donegal. In the early nineteenth century the Irish Ordnance Survey noted that in winter the floods from the River Finn – just like the significant flooding of the River Nile in Egypt – left behind deposits of fluvial mud that greatly improved the fertility of the land. Over thousands of years that mud enriched the soil in the area and, as a concomitant, the wealth of those who farmed the land along its banks. That was almost certainly the economic basis for Cenél Conaill's great political and cultural achievements. The land there is still recognized for its superior value and it was this richness that led to the area being intensively 'planted' or colonized by English settlers in the seventeenth century. The consequent huge population change and concurrent cultural dislocation at that time led to an enormous loss in the archaeological monuments of the area and in the understanding of its ancient historical lore and traditions.

20 B. Lacy, *Archaeological survey*, p. 284. The general site at Drumhome has been the subject of intermittent geophysical surveying and test-trenching since 2013. The results reveal the existence of considerable archaeological deposits including enclosures, structures and artefacts, and evidence for antler- and metal-working. Remains of other well-defined features such as possible wooden trackways and/or jetties have been identified in the adjacent wetlands. I am grateful to Mick Drumm of Wolfhound Archaeology for information on this work in advance of further study and publication.

21 B. Lacey, 'Tírechán's Sirdruimm', passim.

22 B. Lacey, 'Adomnán and Donegal', pp 20–4.

One version of Adomnan's genealogy (Table 6) is found in the opening section of the Raphoe recension of *c*.1000 of the *Cáin Adámnáin*.[23] Two late medieval manuscript copies of this survive (see chapters 4, 8 and 10 below), which apparently, ultimately derived from the now lost 'Old Book of Raphoe'.[24] The more general nature and influence of that text will be dealt with below; here we are just concentrating on Adomnán's pedigree. This, of course, claims to show Adomnán's descent just through the male line. His mother, named Ronnat, is said to have come from a different people, Cenél nÉnnai, of which more below.

> There were five ages before the birth of Christ: from Adam to the Flood, from the Flood to Abraham, from Abraham to David, from David to the captivity in Babylon, from the captivity of Babylon to the birth of Christ. Women were in servitude and in oppression during that time, until there came Adomnán son of Rónan, son of Tinne, son of Áed, son of Colum, son of **Lugaid**, son of Sétna, son of Fergus, son of Conall, son of Níall.[25]

Table 6: Adomnán's (false) Síl Lugdach genealogy

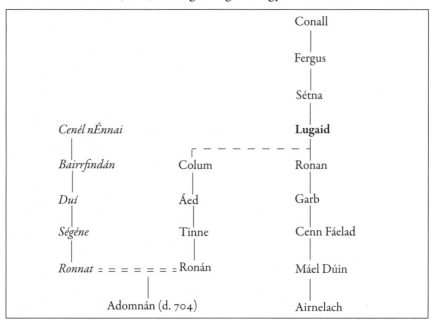

23 As will be explained more fully below in chapters 4 and 8, the title *Cáin Adomnáin* is used here to refer to the original text of the Law of Adomnán promulgated in 697, as defined in J. Houlihan, *Adomnán's* Lex Innocentium, p. 128. The title *Cáin Adámnáin* (*sic*) refers to the *c*.1000 recension of the former with various additional sections composed in or on behalf of the church of Raphoe (see below).

24 M. Ní Dhonnchadha, 'Birr and the Law of the Innocents', p. 16.

25 G. Márkus, *Adomnán's 'Law'*, p. 8. Emphasis on **Lugaid**, by this author.

Table 7: Early Cenél Conaill II

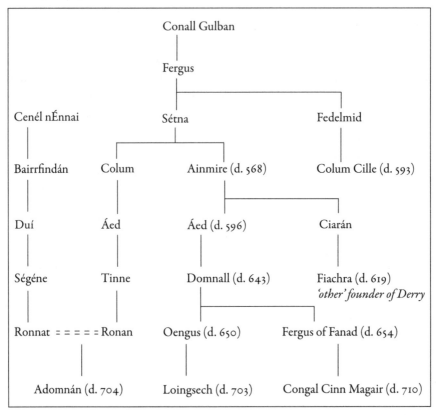

That pedigree is also partly repeated in verse form in the later genealogies of the saints,[26] but in that version *Colum* son of Lugaid is omitted, possibly because if it had been included the line would be one generation too long. To my knowledge these two medieval manuscripts derived from the 'Old Book of Raphoe' are the only places where Adomnán's pedigree is traced through Lugaid son of Sétna.

Lugaid is the alleged eponymous (although manifestly fictional) ancestor of the Síl Lugdach of north-west Donegal, the area represented now by the Gaeltacht parishes of Cloch Cheann Fhaola and Gaoth Dobhair. In this pedigree the Síl Lugdach are also shown (wrongly) to be connected to Cenél Conaill. In fact, Síl Lugdach was originally a quite separate kingdom, the name of which derived from some totemic devotion to or association with the 'Celtic' god Lug or Lugh Lámhfhada who was widely known and revered throughout western Europe.[27] The *Cáin Adamnáin* of *c*.1000 is clearly, at least in part, a Síl Lugdach

26 P. Ó Riain, *Corpus genealogiarum*, p. 186: 733.1.
27 Lacey, *Lug*, passim.

propaganda document, which seeks to claim, incorrectly as will be seen below, that Adomnán was one of their own. Adomnán's alleged connection with the Síl Lugdach goes against all the evidence of the other genealogical traditions. In what might be called the more reliable versions, Lugaid's name does not occur, and Colum is shown directly following on from Sétna son of Fergus, as in the normal Cenél Conaill genealogy (Table 7).[28]

However, having asserted Adomnán's fictional Síl Lugdach credentials (and Síl Lugdach's fictional connections with Cenél Conaill) the c.AD 1000 additions to the 697 *Cáin Adomnáin* (that is, the separate text characterized here as the *Cáin Adamnáin*, with a middle 'a') goes on to reinforce them by describing a solemn covenant that is alleged to have been made between his father's and his mother's people.

> Then Ronnat [Adomnán's mother] went to Brugach mac Dega and got a chain from him. She put it around her son's breast under the bridge of the Swilly in Cenél Conaill, the place where the covenant had been made between his mother's kindred and his father's kindred, i.e. between the Cenél nÉnnai and [Síl] Lugdach ...[29]

The covenant mentioned here seems to be connected with quite separate political events in the eleventh century, which will be examined below in chapter 8.

Apart from these false propagandistic references, there appears to be no genuine evidence that the historical Adomnán belonged to the Síl Lugdach. We do not know specifically when the latter began to develop the fictional link between themselves and Adomnán. But there must be a strong possibility that the impetus came from the 'historians' and genealogists of the Columban monastery at Kilmacrenan when the Síl Lugdach took over the territory in which that church was situated, about 800. That takeover occurred arising from what looks very much like Síl Lugdach's participation alongside Cenél nÉogain in the Battle of Clóitech (Clady, Co. Tyrone) in 789.[30] This was the Armageddon battle that saw the massive defeat of Cenél Conaill and their withdrawal from north Donegal to their lands south of Barnesmore. Síl Lugdach acquired much of the surrendered (or conquered) Cenél Conaill territory, including the lands around Kilmacrenan, Gartan and Raphoe. From then on they seem to have deliberately cultivated the false impression that they were actually relatives of the defeated (but previously powerful) Cenél Conaill and its illustrious clerics: Colum Cille and Adomnán.

28 P. Ó Riain, *Corpus genealogiarum*, p. 54: 340; p. 81: 662.15. See also additional twelfth-century notes in W. Stokes, *Martyrology of Óengus*, pp 210–11.
29 Adapted from G. Márkus, *Adomnán's 'Law'*, p. 10.
30 Lacey, *Lug*, pp 43–6, 67–9.

Raphoe, which was later a major centre of the cult of Adomnán, definitely came under the control of the Síl Lugdach around that time (see below chapter 8). It is not clear when that association began exactly. One hint may be discernable in the very first reference in the annals to the church of Raphoe in the year 817 when: 'Máel Dúin son of Cenn Fáelad, superior of Ráith Both, a member of Colum Cille's community, was slain'.[31] Although not identified in any more detail by the annalist, almost certainly Máel Dúin belonged to the Síl Lugdach (see table 4).[32] His father, Cenn Fáelad (although this was a relatively common name in Ireland in early medieval times), was probably the person of that name who was the son of Airnelach and grandfather of Dálach the son of Muirchertach, 'killed by his own people (*a gennte sua*)' in 870.[33] From his position in the pedigrees, the *floruit* of that Cenn Fáelad must have been around the year 800. An earlier Síl Lugdach Cenn Fáelad, the son of Garb and listed in the same pedigree,[34] would have lived at too early a date (around 700) to have been the father of Máel Dúin, the superior of Raphoe. It might be noted in this context also that the general area in which the Síl Lugdach originated is nowadays known in English as Cloghaneely, that is, Cloch ['stone of'] Cenn Fáelad.

In what we might call the regular genealogies Adomnán is shown very definitely as belonging to the Cenél Conaill proper (table 7). Traditionally, Cenél Conaill have been said to have been part of the 'Uí Néill of the north', allegedly the northern 'cousins' of the great southern Uí Néill ruling dynasty. But it seems now that this claim can no longer be accepted at face value.[35] In fact, Adomnán himself seems to throw considerable doubt on it with reference to his relative, Columba. Adomnán makes only one specific reference to the Uí Néill in the *Vitae Columbae* written close to 700.[36] The name of the dynasty is introduced in a story said to have happened after the Convention of Druim Cett when Columba met the abbot Comgall near the fortress of Cethern (the Giant's Sconce?), in what is now north Co. Derry. Water for washing their hands was brought to the two holy men. According to Adomnán, Columba then prophesied that the well from which the water had been drawn would be 'defiled' at a future time, when Comgall's kinsmen, the Cruithin, and the *Nellis nepotes*, 'the Uí Néill', would fight a battle in a nearby fortress. One of Columba's 'kindred will be slaughtered in the above-mentioned well', rendering it polluted.

The exact reference to the kindreds of the two saints is slightly unusual and, almost certainly, revealing. The original Latin text of the oldest surviving

31 AU 817.7.
32 Lacey, *Lug*, pp 43–4, passim.
33 AU 870.3; M. O'Brien, *Corpus genealogiarum*, p. 164: 144f8.
34 Ibid., 144f11.
35 Lacey, *CC*, pp 145–67.
36 Anderson & Anderson, *Adomnan's Life of Columba*, pp 316–17.

version in the Schaffhausen manuscript has: *Nam mei cognitionales amici, et tui secundum carnem cognati (hoc est Nellis nepotes et Cruthini populi) ...* Richard Sharpe translated this as: 'For my near kindred and your kinsmen according to the flesh (that is the Uí Néill and the Cruithin) ...'[37] However, the Andersons rendered this sentence somewhat differently: 'For my friends by kinship, and your kinsmen according to the flesh (that is to say the descendants of Néll [Niall], and the peoples of Cruthen) ...' The word *cognitionales* is clearly difficult to translate but Adomnán, in the phrase *nam mei cognitionales amici*, definitely seems to have been making some kind of significant distinction between the Cruithin who were kinsmen of Comgall 'according to the flesh', whereas Colum Cille's people were, in the Anderson's phrase, only 'friends by kinship' with the Uí Néill, or some variation of that idea. Adomnán's phrase seems to be of the utmost importance in the discussion about whether or not the Donegal kingdoms were related by blood to the Uí Néill. One possible explanation is that Adomnán may have been attempting to render in Latin a reference to the type of Irish alliance/kinship treaty known as a *cairde* (literally, 'friendship') that existed between Columba's people, Cenél Conaill, and the Uí Néill.[38] Thomas Charles-Edwards has discussed the manner in which the Uí Néill made use of this system of *cairde* in conjunction with their manipulation of the genealogies.

> The political order established by the Uí Néill and their allies was based upon consent more than military power. This consent was expressed in contractual form, in treaties of *cairde* between the principal kingdoms ... Contractual language was all-pervasive ... The political order was, therefore, one of contractual lordship, but it was also a complex pattern of lineages related by real consanguinity, by fictional consanguinity and by non-consanguineal kinship of foster-parents and foster-children.[39]

It seems that Adomnán's use of the phrase *cognitionales amici* may have been hinting at, in Prof. Charles-Edwards's phrase, Columba's (and, hence, Cenél Conaill's) 'fictional consanguinity' with the Uí Néill.

There is, of course, other evidence that also throws doubt on the alleged blood links between Cenél Conaill and the Uí Néill.[40] However, the important thing in this context is that Cenél Conaill, whatever their true genealogical and dynastic origins, were based in east Donegal, in the lower valley of the River Finn. In time, they, or more correctly the people who would describe themselves

37 R. Sharpe, *Adomnan of Iona*, p. 151.
38 Dr Edel Bhreathnach made this most interesting suggestion in a personal communication to me about 2005, when I was writing the book *Cenél Conaill and the Donegal kingdoms, AD 500–800*.
39 T. Charles-Edwards, *Early Christian Ireland*, pp 584–5. See also: pp 104, 113, 530 and 593.
40 The full arguments are set out in Lacey, *CC*, passim.

as Cenél Conaill, came to dominate the whole of Donegal, particularly in the post-Norman period in the guise of what were really the Síl Lugdach families of Uí Domnaill and Uí Dochartaigh. But from the perspective of Adomnán's time, all that was well in the unforseeable future.

Although we have no specific evidence for it, we can assume that Adomnán was educated into the Christian faith from early in his life. Neither do we have any direct evidence for where and when he acquired that basic education. But Christian churches and monasteries existed in many parts of the Cenél Conaill kingdom into which he was born. We know the names of the principal ecclesiastical establishments that had been founded before Adomnán's birth: Derry, Domnach Mór Maige nItha, Drumhome, Ráith Argi,[41] Ráith Cungi and Ráith Maige Aenaig, and there were probably several others. Despite the late traditions of its foundation by Colum Cille and its various claimed connections with Adomnán, it will be argued in chapter 8 below that the church of Raphoe did not exist in the lifetime of either of those clerics, and that it was not established until at least 200 years after the death of Colum Cille and about one hundred years after the death of Adomnán.

Adomnán seems to have spent some time close to and probably at the monastery of Drumhome in south Donegal. He was certainly familiar with that monastery and some of the people who belonged to it. As we saw above, writing as an old man he narrates a story in the *Vita Columbae* about miracles that are alleged to have happened a hundred or so years earlier on the night of Columba's death. An account of those miracles was told *milhi adomanano illo juveni in tempore*, 'to me, Adomnán, then a young(?) man', by Ernéne of the family of mocu Fir-roide who had seen them.

> [Ernéne] (himself a holy monk) lies buried among the remains of other monks of Saint Columba, and awaits the resurrection with the saints, in the ridge of Tóimm [*Dorsum Tómme, Druim Tuama*, Drumhome].[42]

Adomnán tells us no more about Drumhome or his links with its monastery but it is a reasonable assumption that in mentioning it, one of the very few places in Ireland that he does mention, that he is indicating some sort of personal connection with it. We know that Drumhome was a Cenél Conaill border church from sometime around the 590s when the area was captured by king Áed mac Ainmerech, up to the mid-640s when Cenél Conaill pushed their border even further south to the Erne (see chapter 1 above). The later stages of that period coincided with the time when Adomnán's was 'then a young man (?)', or

---

41 Although we do not know specifically where Ráith Argi was located it seems to have been at or close to where the later Cistercian abbey of Assaroe was constructed.

42 Anderson & Anderson, *Adomnan's Life of Columba*, pp 532–5.

at least in his teens. But since Drumhome was the burial place of 'monks of Saint Columba' at least in Adomnán's time, it is evident that it was also part of the *Familia Columbae* of which he would become head in 679. It is therefore quite possible that at least some of Adomnán's studies and preparations for his life as a cleric were undertaken at Drumhome.

One of the principal monasteries of the Columban confederation was at Dairmag (Durrow, Co. Offaly), in the Irish midlands far away from Columba's own homeland in the north-west. Despite later legendary claims for many other places, in fact Durrow is the only monastery founded by Columba in Ireland for which we have definite evidence. It has been argued, most particularly by Alfred Smyth, that Adomnán had a special connection with the monastery at Durrow and that before he left Ireland for Iona he spent a lot of time there.[43] Adomnán's several mentions of Durrow in the *Vita Columbae*, with specific references to buildings and other physical features, is offered as proof of his detailed personal acquaintance with the place. Professor Smyth rightly maintained that Adomnán's later written works indicated that his studies in the Christian Latin literature available at the time must have been comprehensive and that those studies had to have been undertaken at a place (or places) where there was a relatively extensive library, as there may have been at Durrow. The survival of the splendid Gospel manuscript, the Book of Durrow, is presented as confirmation of this. However, there is no certainty as to where the Book of Durrow was made, nor is there consensus about its date which may have been as late as the early eighth century, sometime after the death of Adomnán.[44] Smyth also argued that not alone did Adomnán study at Durrow but that he was a teacher there as well and that, perhaps, his most prominent pupil was the young Aldfrith who would later become a famous king of Northumbria. Aldfrith is known to have had mixed Irish-Northumbrian parentage. His connections with Adomnán will be examined in chapter 3.

Professor Smyth's speculations are very interesting, and they would certainly help to fill the large gap we have regarding Adomnán's life before he became abbot of Iona in 679. However, we have no actual evidence that Adomnán was ever in Durrow – although it does seem very likely – and that he studied or taught there. In cautioning us about reading too much into Adomnán's references to Durrow, Richard Sharpe wrote: 'the broad interpretation of the [circumstantial] evidence is preferable to the narrow'.[45] The speculations by Smyth and others about Adomnán and Durrow might well be a reflection of what had happened but we cannot confirm them!

43 A. Smyth, *Celtic Leinster*, pp 118–22.
44 See, for instance, B. Meehan, *The Book of Durrow*, pp 17–22.
45 R. Sharpe, *Adomnán of Iona*, p. 46.

One of the points Alfred Smyth made in support of his arguments about Adomnán studying at a place so remote from his home in Donegal is that, if he did so, he would have been following the example of his hero, Saint Columba. Adomnán himself tells us that Columba: *adhuc juvenis diacon in parte Lagenensium divinam addiscens sapientiam conversaretur*, 'still a young deacon, was living in the region of the Laigin [Leinster], studying divine wisdom'.[46] Adomnán even tells us the name of Columba's master at the time, the 'aged Gemman'. The story in which these references occur was important for Adomnán personally as it involved a miracle in which the slayer of a girl or young woman – *innocentium jugulator*, 'a killer of innocents' – died soon afterwards himself, through a miracle of Columba. As we will see Adomnán would be the author and sponsor of the *Lex Innocentium*, a law for the protection of innocent people such as the girl in the story. If Adomnán also pursued his Christian studies in Leinster, in the east or the midlands of Ireland, then we have no contemporary evidence for it. There is, however, a late anecdote preserved in the so-called Fragmentary Annals that does locate him as a student in that general region. The Fragmentary Annals is a peculiar document combining factual annalistic entries along with fictional saga material. It was probably compiled in the interests of the Osraige (from the area represented now, more or less, by modern Co. Kilkenny) and probably in the middle of the eleventh century.[47] The story in question here is entered at the year 677 but combines references to Adomnán both as a young and an old man so that date does not appear to be particularly relevant.

The main character in this relatively long story, in which Adomnán plays only a small part, is Finnechta Fledach, a real historical person from the Uí Néill, Síl nÁedo Sláine dynasty, who reigned as king of Tara from 675 to 695 (although he withdrew briefly in 688 before returning to office).[48] The kingship of Tara was the most widely respected and influential kingship in Ireland at the time, although not quite the overall-ruling monarchy that it is often claimed to have been. In fact, Adomnán in various references in the *Vita Columbae*, and almost certainly elsewhere also, was one of the principal apologists who argued that the king of Tara should be named and treated as the 'king of Ireland'.[49] Finnechta's reign coincided

46 Anderson & Anderson, *Adomnan's Life of Columba*, pp 382–3.

47 J. Radner, *Fragmentary Annals of Ireland*, pp xxv–xxvi. It might be worth pointing out that there are several Columban connections with the territory of the Osraige, and Prof. Pádraig Ó Riain has even suggested controversially that perhaps their principal saint, Cainnech, from whom Cill Chainnigh or Kilkenny is named, is actually just an alternative name for Columba himself (see P. Ó Riain, 'Cainnech *alias* Colum Cille').

48 E. Breathnach, *The kingship and landscape of Tara*, pp 201–3.

49 For instance, he refers to Áed Sláine as predestined by God for 'the kingship of all Ireland' and Áed's father Diarmait was 'ordained by God's will as king of all Ireland' (R. Sharpe, *Adomnán of Iona*, p. 122, p. 138). Both Áed Sláine and Diarmait were kings of Tara. See also M. Enright, *Prophecy and kingship*, passim.

with much of Adomnán's rule as abbot on Iona and head (comarba) of the Columban federation in both Britain and Ireland. As it happens, later in both their lives Finnechta and Adomnán did have real connections that are well documented (see chapter 3 below). But at the outset of the Fragmentary Annals story they are both relatively young, only at the beginning of their respective careers.

The following is a synopsis of the relevant parts of the story. Finnechta, not yet a king, was travelling with a horse-troop (*marcshluag*) to visit his sister. His party encountered Adomnán who, in trying to get out of the way of the horses, stumbled and broke a borrowed jug full of milk that he was collecting for his colleagues, three noble scholars (*trí meic leighinn maithe*, that is, teachers) and two fellow students. Finnechta said he would pay for the jug and invited Adomnán and the other five to dine with him that night. They went as invited to Finnechta's 'ale-house' (*teach leanna*) and when they got there Adomnán's tutor (*aite*) who had 'the spirit of prophecy' made the following prediction.

> Budh Aird Rí Eireann ... an fear da ttugadh an fleagh sa; & budh ceand crábhaidh & eagna Eireann Adhamhnán, & budh e anmchara Fionnachta, & bíaidh Finnachta i feachtnaighe mhóir coro oilbhemnigh do Adhamhnan.

> The man who has given this banquet will be High King of Ireland, and Adomnán will be the head of piety and wisdom of Ireland, and he will be Finnechta's confessor, and Finnechta will be in great prosperity until he gives offence to Adomnán.[50]

The story continues with Finnechta becoming king of Tara after an interval. Later through the trickery of St MoLing, a famous Leinster saint, Finnechta remitted or cancelled the *Bóroma*, a major levy that the south Leinstermen were obliged to pay to the king of Tara. Adomnán was not pleased by that and went to see Finnechta. But the latter would not leave the game of *fidchell* he was playing in order to talk to the cleric. Adomnán made a number of threats against the king but it was not till he made the third of them, that is, that Adomnán would pray that the king would 'not reach the kingdom of heaven', that Finnechta came to talk to the cleric. Adomnán reproached the king about cancelling the *Bóroma* tribute and then *ro raidh an láoidh* ('sings the lay') *Aniu ge chenglaid chuacha* which continues the reproach. This is a thirteen-quatrain poem in Middle Irish, attributed to Adomnán but his authorship, or its contemporaneity with him (or even some earlier version in Old Irish), is not likely. The following are the first two verses.

50 J. Radner, *Fragmentary Annals of Ireland*, pp 24–5.

Aniu ge chenglaid chuacha	Although the withered, gray-haired toothless king
an rí crínliath gan déda,	arrays himself today,
an búar do mhaith do Moling	he does not obtain the cattle – proper to the king –
– dethbir don cing-nis féda.	that he remitted to MoLing.

Damadh misi Fionnachta	If I were Finnechta,
[i]s gomadh mé flaith Temhra	and I were lord of Tara,
go bráth nocha (a)ttibherainn;	I would never give it [the remission];
ni dingenainn a nderna.	I would not do what he has done.

The story is concluded at the end of the poem with the following sentence.

Ro thairinn tra iar sin Fionnachta a cheann a n-ucht Adhamhnain, & do righne aithrighe 'na fhiadhnaisi; & ro logh Adhamhnan dó maitheamh na Boroma.

After that Finnechta laid his head in Adamnán's bosom, and he did penance in his presence, and Adamnán forgave him the remission of the *Bóroma*.[51]

There is no other evidence of Adomnán's unlikely involvement with the issues surrounding the *Bórama* (whether real or fictional) or, indeed, why this story links the cleric and king. In a later chapter we will see Adomnán, after he had become abbot of Iona, genuinely involved with Finnechta on a totally different matter. However, there is one other tentative link that might be reflected in this story. Although not referred to in the synopsis above, Finnechta is assisted and advised in his rise to power by the king of Fir Rois, a people who lived in what is now Co. Monaghan. In the *Vita Columbae* Adomnán tells a miracle story in which Columba predicts the mutual killing by each other of two noblemen *haut procul a monasterio quod dicitur Cell-Rois in provincia Maugdornorum*, 'not far from the monastery that is called Cell-Rois in the province of the Maugdorni', that is, the church of the Fir Rois now Carraig Machaire Rois, Carrickmacross, Co. Monaghan.[52]

Adomnán would have been in his mid-to-late thirties at least at the time of the Synod of Whitby in 664. This was the occasion when the Columban churches in Northumbria (and to some extent in eastern Scotland) suffered a massive blow because of the judgement against them on the issue of the calculation of the date of Easter and the traditional tonsure which they wore as monks. Adomnán himself was not present at the synod nor is there any evidence of his involvement

---

51 J. Radner, *Fragmentary Annals of Ireland*, pp 27–33. This story is repeated in the longer tract known as the Bórama saga. See J.F. Kenney, *The sources for the early history of Ireland*, p. 444 and S. O'Grady, *Silva Gadelica*, vol. I, pp 387–8; vol. II, p. 423.
52 E. Hogan, *Onomasticon Goedelicum*, p. 210.

behind the scenes in connection with it. But the matters discussed there (as we will see further below) would continue to haunt him for the rest of his life, most especially when he took over as abbot of Iona and leader of the *Familia Columbae*.

We know virtually nothing, really, about Adomnán's life until he took over that leadership role in 679. He would have been by then already over fifty years of age and a very 'senior citizen' in the context of the time. Obviously, his adult life had been spent in a monastery (or monasteries) somewhere in an Irish, and almost certainly in a Columban, context but we have no real evidence as to where that might have been. There is no evidence that he was even ever on Iona until the period of his predecessor's Failbe's abbacy, when he would have been already well over forty years of age. But wherever he pursued his youthful and middle-aged preparations for his later life as an abbot, the Life of Columba that he wrote later shows that he must have studied a wide range of Latin texts as well as the Scriptures and the commonly used liturgical works.[53]

To conclude this chapter, we can say that there is no reason to believe that Adomnán belonged to the Síl Lugdach of Donegal but every reason to believe that he did belong to Cenél Conaill. Neither is there any reason to doubt the tradition that his mother belonged to the Cenél nÉnnai of east Donegal. It is probable that he was born in east Donegal, possibly close to Raphoe, but that is not the primary origin of his later alleged association with the church there. The monastery at Raphoe, as we will see, does not seem to have been founded until around a century or so after Adomnán's death. His father's people (and thus his own), Cenél Conaill, were originally the rulers of a small but wealthy kingdom based along the lower River Finn. But for at least fifty years before he was born, under a series of powerful kings, Cenél Conaill had been expanding and conquering their neighbours, including his mother's people. By the time Adomnán was born, the kingdom of Cenél Conaill extended from Derry in the north to Drumhome in the south, the two border churches he would mention specifically in the *Vita Columbae*. During his teens and early manhood the kingdom expanded again, as far south as the Erne and northward into Fanad and the adjacent areas. Finally, as will be examined in detail in chapter 8 below, from the ninth century onward – seemingly culminating in the tenth- or early eleventh-century Raphoe text known as the *Cáin Adamnáin* – a separate Donegal people, the Síl Lugdach, exploited and distorted the traditions about Adomnán's origins for their own propaganda purposes, just as they did also with the traditions of his predecessor and relation, Columba.

---

53 See, for example, R. Sharpe, *Adomnán of Iona*, pp 57–9.

CHAPTER THREE

The ninth abbot of Iona

Shortly after the decease of his predecessor Failbe in 679, probably on 22 March (his feastday), Adomnán became the ninth abbot of Iona. Failbe had been abbot for the previous ten years. We know from mentions that Adomnán inserted in the *Vita Columbae* that both men knew each other; indeed, Failbe had been one of Adomnán's informants for some of the stories he would write up in the *Vita* about twenty years later. Adomnán must have appeared to the monks on Iona as, literally, a Godsend. Until recently many modern authors claimed that it was the common practice for the abbots of Iona to be chosen from the saint's kindred, Cenél Conaill. That claim was based on the acceptance of the veracity of the late and fabricated Uí Néill genealogical framework. But recent work by this author suggests that neither that framework nor the claim about the genealogical origins of the abbots of Iona can be taken at face value. In fact, since Columba's death in 593 only one abbot, his immediate successor and close relative Baithín who died in 596, can be shown with certainty to have belonged to Cenél Conaill.[1]

But, as we saw in the last chapter, Adomnán most definitely belonged to Cenél Conaill. His relationship with the founder Columba, however distant (see table 7), plus the talents he was to exhibit in his incumbency – and which evidently must have been obvious in some form before that – must have marked him out as a gift from the God they all believed in and in whose work they were assiduously engaged.

No specific record of how or when Adomnán took up the office of abbot has survived in the annals as they have come down to us, other than the notice of the death of his predecessor. Neither, apart from the speculations on the matter by various modern scholars, have we any precise information as to how his appointment came about: what, if any, formal selection process existed or qualifications were thought necessary. Evidently he was a very suitable candidate and, for the next twenty-five years till his death, he proved to be an enormously successful and influential incumbent.

He was in his early fifties, at least, by then. By the standards of his day that made him a venerable old man. We know from a variety of sources that clerics

---

1   The 3rd, 5th, 7th and 8th abbots belonged, apparently, to Cenél Duach; the 4th may have been British or belonged to Cenél mBogaine; the origin of the 6th is not known but it has never been suggested that he belonged to Cenél Conaill (B. Lacey, *Saint Columba*, pp 86–102). For the non-Cenél Conaill origins of Cenél Duach and Cenél mBogaine see Lacey, *CC*, passim.

were among the longest-living public figures at the time, something that must have added to their reputation for being especially favoured by God, not to mention their 'ability' to work miracles. They were elders and *seniores*, wise and learned from their life experiences and scholarly studies. Their relatively longer lives must have resulted in part from the organized and disciplined monastic regime they embraced, which would have included disciplined access to healthy food and medical resources, as well as the more 'peaceful' careers they enjoyed in comparison with their secular contemporaries. The latter – especially the aristocrats, many of them relatives of the senior clerics – would have experienced and participated in various forms of violence during their often much shorter lives.

We don't know when Adomnán went to live on Iona but despite referring to them on occasions in the *Vita Columbae* he shows no evidence of having a personal acquaintance with any of his predecessor abbots, except Failbe who took over in 669. Some authors have suggested that during the years 673 to 676, when we know that Failbe was visiting and travelling around Ireland, Adomnán, who was possibly still living there at the time, was identified as a suitable candidate for the abbacy of the chief Columban monastery on Iona.[2] The holder of that position was *ex officio* comarba, 'heir', of Columba and head of the whole Columban *familia* or confederation of churches throughout Ireland and Scotland, and, for some time at least, also a few churches in the north of England.

We have very little hard evidence to show us what the ordinary work of the abbot of Iona was, as distinct from his normal religious duties as a monk and priest. But knowledge of what daily life was like in the monastery on Iona in Adomnán's time can be gleaned from two sources. Adomnán's own *Vita Columbae* provides us with some contemporary documentation about the monastic way of life. It was certainly not part of his deliberate intentions to give us a description of the monastery on Iona or how it functioned in his own time. But in the *Vita Columbae* the incidental details mentioned as part of the various stories he tells about Columba (and, occasionally, about himself) do give us some impression of what it was like for Adomnán and his monks, and about their surroundings, while he lived and worked there.

In addition, various forms of archaeological investigations on the island have helped to build a picture of the material culture there at the time. The main problem with the archaeology of Iona is that there has not been, and because of the existence of the restored abbey there it is unlikely that there ever will be, total or even significant excavation of the site of the original monastery. There have been 'excavations' of a kind on the island since at least the end of the nineteenth

2   E.g., M. Herbert, *Iona, Kells and Derry*, p. 47.

century and, in the twentieth century, these became increasingly more scientific. But even the later excavations have been piecemeal and sporadic and necessarily dependent on modern development requirements at the site rather than part of any overall integrated research plan.[3] No doubt future work and improved technology will resolve many but clearly not all of those difficulties.

Very few traces of the earliest monastery survive to the present above ground, but it is certain that it was located on the gently sloping land on the eastern side of the island. The site is now dominated by the restored Benedictine abbey, originally founded about 1200. The only standing stone structures that survive from before the construction of that abbey are themselves relatively late and certainly do not go back to the times of Columba or Adomnán. We do know from Adomnán that the original monastery was at least partly surrounded by a vallum or 'boundary' of some sort, which seems to have included elements of both bank and ditch. Exceptionally, some evidence for this vallum still survives and indicates that it enclosed a somewhat square-shaped space about eight acres in extent which appears to have been open on the eastern or shore side. Until recently the shape of that enclosure was considered problematic by archaeologists, as what appear to be contemporary early ecclesiastical sites in Ireland were almost invariably circular or subcircular in plan. Also until recently, studies of sections of the surviving bank and ditch seemed to indicate that at least parts of that enclosure were older than the monastery and may have dated to the previous Iron Age. The suggestion was that an abandoned enclosure, already quite ancient, had been re-used by the monks in the mid-sixth century as the site of their monastery. However, the most recent radiocarbon dates 'dismiss this, confirming that the ditch was dug in the seventh/eighth century' and that the shape of the enclosure may have been 'based on English or Continental prototypes, whose monasteries derive[d] their form from Roman forts, towns or villa plans'.[4] There may also have been, as we will see below, a deliberate connection with the perceived layout of the area surrounding the Church of the Holy Sepulchre in Jerusalem.[5]

Adomnán mentions several of the monastic buildings, of which the most important was the church. This would have been built from timber in what Bede called the 'Irish manner'. Some of the required wood would have had to be brought over from Mull or, possibly, further from the Scottish mainland. Jean-Michel Picard drew attention to the fact that Adomnán himself appears to have

3   For a review of the excavation history on Iona up to the end of the twentieth century see J. O'Sullivan, 'Iona: archaeological investigations, 1875–1996'. For ongoing work see the website of the Iona Research Group based in the Centre for Scottish & Celtic Studies at the University of Glasgow. And see now, especially, Campbell & Maldonado, 'A new Jerusalem'.
4   Campbell & Maldonado, 'A new Jerusalem', pp 61–2.
5   Ibid.

taken part in the hard physical work involved;[6] he did not confine himself just to administrative and intellectual tasks. In incidental information he gives – when describing two occasions when the wind 'miraculously' changed as a result of Columba's intervention – it is clear that Adomnán was involved with the physical work himself: certainly on the second occasion and most likely on the first.

> On the first of these [two occasions], pine and oak trees had been felled and dragged overland. Some were to be used in the making of a longship [*longae navis*], and besides ship's timbers there were also beams for a great house to be brought here to Iona. It was decided that we should lay the saint's [Columba's] vestments and books [*vestimenta et libros*] on the altar, and that by fasting and singing psalms and invoking his name, we should ask St Columba to obtain for us from the Lord that we should have favourable winds. So it turned out, that God had granted it to him; for on the day when our sailors [*nautae*] had got everything ready and meant to take the boats and curraghs [*scafis ... et curucis*] and tow the timbers to the island [Iona] by sea, the wind, which had blown in the wrong direction for several days, changed and became favourable. Though the route was long and indirect, by God's favour the wind remained favourable all day and the whole convoy [*navalis emigratio*] sailed with their sails full so that they reached Iona without delay.
>
> The second time was several years later. Again oak trees were being towed by a group of twelve currachs from the mouth of the River Shiel to be used in repairs to the monastery. On a dead calm day, when the sailors were having to use oars, a wind suddenly sprang up from the west, blowing head on against them. We put in to the nearest island called *Airthraig*, intending to stay in sheltered water. All the while I complained of this inconvenient change of wind, and began after a fashion to chide our St Columba ... Hardly a minute had passed when the west wind dropped and, strange to say, a wind immediately blew from the north-east. Then I told the sailors to hoist the yards cross-wise, spread the sails and draw the sheets taut. In this way we were carried by a fair, gently breeze, all the way to our island in one day quite effortlessly, and all who were with me in the boats, helping to tow the timbers, were greatly pleased.[7]

It is probable also that as the monastery developed over the centuries other additional churches or chapels were built, possibly outside the vallum and in other parts of the island. The huts where the monks worked and lived are

6   J.M. Picard, 'Adomnán and the writing of the "Life of Columba"', p. 5.
7   Trans. from R. Sharpe, *Adomnán of Iona*, pp 200–2, with some minor changes; Latin words from Anderson & Anderson, *Adomnan's Life of Columba*, pp 452–4.

mentioned by Adomnán and at least some of those were made from wattle.[8] We read in the *Vita Columbae* of wattles being procured for precisely that purpose. Most likely there was a special scriptorium and library in the monastery. Various studies have attempted to list the books available on Iona before the beginning of the eighth century in addition to those that were actually composed there. That matter will be returned to below. Rather than on shelves as at present, the books were probably kept in satchels hanging from pegs in the wall. Various sheds and barns are referred to, some of which may have been outside the main enclosure. Traces of a circular wooden structure, although not necessarily a 'roofed building', were found by archaeologists inside the enclosure fairly close to the present abbey building. The location of the latter is always taken as a general guide to the whereabouts of the core of the Columban monastery. There is a supposition that the abbey church, although much bigger, may have been located in the same general area as the ancient monastic church, although there is no definite archaeological evidence to prove that yet.

The circular structure was composed of two concentric circles of posts, with an overall diameter of about 18 meters. Its date is not clear, but it seems to have been built in the early medieval period. The nature of that structure is highly problematic as it would have presented a relatively enormous engineering problem to have covered it over with a roof; nevertheless, such a possibility cannot be discounted. There seems to have been a smithy for iron-working and a disused millstone was used subsequently as the base for a cross. Adomnán tells us that crosses were set up at sites connected with special events in Columba's life. We do not know what material those crosses were made of, but they were probably wooden. The surviving finely sculpted stone crosses date to much later times, from the middle of the eighth century onwards. Those stone crosses seem to have been the end of an evolutionary process that started with wooden crosses, included crosses made of stone pillars with wooden transoms as an intermediate stage, and ended with the full stone cross. The evidence also suggests that Iona was something of a centre for experimentation and innovation in that regard, but most of that would have occurred well after Adomnán's death.

There was, of course, also a burial ground. Finbar McCormick has argued that the original monastic graveyard was probably on the site now known as Reilig Odhráin, 'Oran's Graveyard', which seems to have been separated from the core of the monastery by a deep ditch. More recently, Tomás Ó Carragáin has suggested that the alleged site of Columba's own grave under the small shrine chapel adjacent to the west wall of the late medieval abbey church, somewhat

---

8   Burnt wattle from a building on Tòrr an Aba – possibly Columba's writing hut – produced radiocarbon dates 'centring around AD 600' (Campbell & Maldonado, 'A new Jerusalem', pp 50–2).

away from Reilig Odhráin, may have been in the principal monastic graveyard.[9] That site was almost certainly close to the original church building.

Detailed archaeological evidence for diet and agricultural practices in the early monastery is much better than that for the buildings. Various dumps of discarded food refuse, especially animal bone, have been found and pollen from a part of the vallum ditch has been very useful in this regard also. The pollen evidence seems to show that there was still fairly extensive covering of oak and ash woods on the island at that time, especially close to the monastery. Cereal, probably barley, was cultivated nearby. Adomnán tells us that Columba himself checked the grain store shortly before he died and was pleased that the monks had enough for the coming year despite the fact that it was only early June, well before the harvest of that year. Evidence for the cultivation of cereals close to the monastery declines as time goes by, indicating perhaps that these crops were later planted elsewhere on the island; probably in the western *machair* area. In other words, the earliest monks may have been sufficiently catered for by the crops grown close to the monastery itself but as time went by, and presumably as the number of monks increased, it was necessary to expand the amount of farmed land to other parts of the island.

It seems from the finds of millstones that there was definitely a watermill for processing the cereal on the island from early in the history of the monastery. Indeed, a millstream (Sruth a Mhuilinn) still passes close to the abbey on its northern side, although we do not know how long it has had that name. Excavation at a kink in that stream revealed a large 'basin' (a pond?) that may have formed part of the workings of the mill. Unfortunately, no dating evidence was found there.

The deposits of bones that have been found show that cattle were the dominant animal species, although Adomnán also mentioned sheep and goats and some bones of those animals were found as well. The Schaffhausen copy of Adomnán's *Vita Columbae*, which was almost certainly made on Iona (see below, chapter 5), was written on cured goatskin as were, probably, many other manuscripts that have not survived. Pig bones were also found although whether these animals were actually raised on Iona remains an open question. As Finbar McCormick pointed out they could have been given to the monastery as donations. We know from the *Vita Columbae* that horses were used as farm animals. Puzzlingly, horse bones with clear evidence of butchering marks were found indicating that, on at least some occasions, horseflesh seems to have been eaten.

There was also evidence for wild animals being hunted and eaten: bones of red deer, roe deer and seals were found. Adomnán specifically mentions a breeding

9   F. McCormick, 'Excavations at Iona, 1988'; T. Ó Carragáin, 'The architectural setting', p. 168, n. 59.

colony of seals that seemed to have been recognized as actually 'belonging' to the monastery and which were being, as it were, 'farmed' by the monks. McCormick suggests that the deer must have come from the adjacent but much larger island of Mull where the monastery may have had some sort of off-site estate. The presence of badger, fox, wild-cat and otter bones in the collection has been interpreted as evidence that the skins of those animals were used by the monks. Traces of a fairly wide range of inshore and deep-sea fish as well as of fowl and wild bird bones were also found, indicating that those food sources were also exploited, to some degree at any rate.

We know that by the middle of the eighth century at the latest, Iona was the centre of a school of excellent artists who could work in a variety of media. There is archaeological evidence of metalworking, copper and tin (bronze), and of glassworking such as has been found on other contemporary high-status sites elsewhere in Scotland and Ireland. Evidence for woodworking was also found, with samples of stave-built and lathe-turned objects. The lathe-turned bowls seem to have been made mainly from alder but evidence for the use of willow was also found. Some of these wooden bowls seem to have been modelled on ceramic exemplars imported from the Continent, probably as part of the wine-trade. We know that there were carpenters among the monks and, unsurprisingly on an island, there is some evidence of boat-building: both timber-built vessels and skin-covered currachs. Excavation of part of the ditch produced remains of other kinds of woodworking in the monastery too, with evidence for the use of alder, ash, birch, fir, hazel, oak, pine, poplar and willow.

The ditch also produced evidence for leatherworking, especially shoemaking. Several shoes were decorated and some could be paralleled with those worn by the figure of Saint Matthew illustrated in the Book of Durrow, an undoubtedly Columban manuscript! The range of hides used included: cattle, horse, red deer, seal, and goat or 'hairy sheep'. But no evidence was found for the specialized production of prepared calfskin for vellum as has been found for instance at the monastic (and possibly Columban) site at Portmahomack[10] in north-eastern Scotland. Some evidence of pottery-making was found, as well as evidence for exotic imported ceramics from as far away as the Mediterranean. The latter may have been imported as much for their contents, olive oil and wine, as for the vessels themselves. It would have been necessary to have imported wine, for instance, for use in the Eucharistic liturgies as well as oil for various anointing ceremonies.

The Scottish archaeologist Aidan MacDonald has made Adomnán's *Vita Columbae* yield up a great deal of evidence about the monastery on Iona by subjecting the text to detailed close reading and scrutiny.[11] He has commented

10 Portmahomack is an anglicization of *Port mo Cholmóc*, 'port of my young (or 'dear') Colm'.
11 See, for instance, A. MacDonald, 'Adomnán's monastery'.

that for Adomnán the whole island of Iona seems to have been regarded as a sacred space. Indeed, Dr Jennifer O'Reilly suggested that for Adomnán Iona was another 'holy land'.[12] Adomnán frequently identifies the monastery with the entire extent of the island; not just the buildings or the area enclosed by the vallum. As with other early Irish church sites there seems to have been on Iona a gradation of spaces in terms of their perceived, progressively inward increasing degree of holiness. We know that, following biblical examples, early medieval ecclesiastical sites were often subdivided into distinct zones that were categorized as: *locus sanctus*, *locus sanctior* and *locus sanctissimus*, that is, 'holy', 'holier' and 'holiest' places. Those divisions of space would have had various practical consequences, such as rules for restricting the admission of lay people, maybe especially women, to the areas demarcated in that way.

For MacDonald the coastline of the whole island represented the outer boundary of this sacred space; the middle boundary was represented by the vallum; while a line of some kind enclosing the church and perhaps the space around it demarcated the innermost sanctuary. The space enclosed by the inner boundary may have been open only to clerics as well as, possibly, to select groups of the lay faithful who would have been admitted 'under strictest supervision'. Indeed, MacDonald suggests that at the earliest stages of its history, as distinct from the practice much later, the Iona monks may have wished to discourage lay people from visiting the island. MacDonald stresses that Columba's and Adomnán's Iona, and its contemporary counterparts in Ireland and Scotland, were 'proper' monasteries, quite unlike the heavily secularized and possibly semi-urbanized ecclesiastical settlements which some of those places evolved into in later centuries.

> 6th- to 7th-century Iona, and many other Irish monastic churches of the time, were originally regular cenobitic monasteries of a kind or kinds that would have been familiar enough in the late Roman world, East and West, or in contemporary Europe and (from the 7th century) Anglo-Saxon England. In other words, they were more or less enclosed and integrated religious communities living a common life under common discipline and authority, whether or not such communal organization was articulated explicitly in a written rule. While [the monks] acknowledged an interdependent relationship with the lay world around them, they lived secluded lives as detached as possible from that world for the sake of their proper spiritual goal – the contemplative search for God.[13]

12 J. O'Reilly, 'Reading the Scriptures', p. 86.
13 A. MacDonald, 'Adomnán's monastery', p. 25. We must also remember that the monastery would have evolved over time, perhaps even having been remodelled to some extent by Adomnán 'as an earthly manifestation of the heavenly Jerusalem ... [and] that the [perceived]

We do not know how many monks were living in that community at any one time, but the *Vita Columbae* and other evidence shows that its members were drawn from all the ethnic groups or 'nations' that inhabited Britain and Ireland at the time: Britons, Picts, Northumbrian Anglo-Saxons and both Scottish and Irish Gaels. The impression is given that at least some of the monks seem to have moved continually between Iona and its associated or dependent monasteries, both in the north of Britain and in Ireland.

The communal living style of the monks would have been reflected in the disposition of the various buildings within the monastic enclosure and in the internal arrangements of those buildings. Within the enclosure there was what Adomnán calls the *plateola*, a 'courtyard' or central open space. This may have been paved or otherwise surfaced in order to keep it dry. The major communal buildings of the monastery were probably arranged around this space. The most important building would have been the church, perhaps on the east side of the *plateola*. This was a wooden building although there is no reason to assume that it was also primitive. Great buildings in timber are known from Irish contexts as far back as the Iron Age and before. Neither is there any reason to assume that the building was not richly decorated. Carvings, painted walls and ceilings, tapestries, draperies and mats of various forms could have been used to embellish the church in the way we read about in the roughly contemporary descriptions of Saint Brigid's church at Kildare.

The Iona church would have been aligned in a general east-west direction and probably had a door at its west end, possibly opening out onto the 'courtyard'. There may have been a porch around this doorway. There was probably a window of some kind at the east end above the altar and possibly others, almost certainly at a high level, along the side walls, maybe particularly on the south side so that the best light could enter. MacDonald shows us that there was a small extra chamber opening off one side of the church, probably towards the east end, but it is not clear whether this was on the south or the north side of the main building. This additional chamber may have had no proper door but could have been screened off by a curtain or other temporary partition from the main part of the church. The *exedra* as Adomnán called that chamber was itself internally partitioned, and a lockable door led from the outer to the inner compartment. The outer part of this chamber may have served as a small chapel while the inner section may have been a sacristy.

Perhaps opposite the church on the west side of the *plateola* was the 'great house'. This seems to have been a relatively large building and was also built

layout of the structures associated with the Church of the Holy Sepulchre [in Jerusalem] was a more influential model at Iona.' Campbell & Maldonado, 'A new Jerusalem', p. 37; and see chapter 6 below.

of timber. It could have been rectangular or curvilinear, even circular, in plan. Adomnán seems to suggest that an equivalent building in Durrow was round. As we have seen above, there is archaeological evidence for a large circular wooden structure on Iona although the precise nature of that building has not been established, and it was located to the south-west rather than west of the church. The 'great house' may have functioned as a general living space for the indoor activities of the monks such as assembly, study, teaching and recreation. It is not clear if it was also used for dining. Wherever the monks ate there had to be also a nearby kitchen, although whether that was a separate building is not clear. Fire was a particular hazard in medieval times and measures to protect the main buildings, all of which would have been constructed of timber, would have been uppermost in the minds of the monks.

MacDonald suggests that the main meal of the day would have been eaten around three in the afternoon. There was probably an earlier meal on most days, except on the two weekly fast days – Wednesday and Friday (*Céadaoine* and *Aoine* 'first fast day' and 'fast day') – and perhaps during Lent, Advent and other times of special penitence. On Sundays and feastdays there seems to have been an additional meal. However, monks who were engaged in heavy work could have extra food and rest if they needed it. The arrival of guests sometimes interrupted the normal monastic eating regime. In terms of food, Adomnán mentions only bread, fish, fruit and milk. A baker is mentioned on one occasion, as is a gardener who may have supplied the monastery with fruit, vegetables and herbs. The latter, of course, would have been used for medicinal purposes as well as food flavouring.

As we have seen above meat bones were found in the excavations and the killing of animals is described occasionally by Adomnán. However, he does not mention meat being eaten as a normal part of the monastic diet and it is possible that it was allowed only to guests or perhaps to those monks who were ill or aged. Based on the general communal nature of the monastery, MacDonald has argued that most of the monks would have slept on beds in a dormitory of some sort, perhaps singly in cubicles opening off a larger communal space. That building could have been either circular or rectangular and may or may not have been identical with the 'great house'. It seems, however, from Adomnán's words that Columba himself may have slept in a separate cell, what is called the *hospitiolum*, implying a small space of some kind. Perhaps all, or at least some, of the subsequent abbots including Adomnán followed that practice, sleeping apart from the ordinary monks. Nearby was the *hospitium* or 'guest-house'. Various guests, both lay and clerical, are mentioned as visiting the monastery. Hospitality was an important duty, as it was also in Irish secular society at the time. It may be, based on references found widespread in medieval Irish literature, that there was an obligation to offer guests a minimum of three days and three nights of hospitality. The guest-house, which may have been a little more comfortable than the monks' own quarters, may have functioned also as an infirmary. Aidan MacDonald also thought that it was where new postulants would have been received.

MacDonald has shown us that Columba did not adopt a major pastoral or a missionary role, and this was likely the case in Adomnán's time also. At least as depicted by Adomnán, MacDonald argued that Columba was 'only conventionally an ascetic ... and in no sense a solitary.' There is a late text known as the 'Rule of Colum Cille' but rather than making regulations for the behaviour of a monastic community like that on Iona the rule is addressed to a hermit such as Virgno, whom we hear of living for twelve years at the beginning of the seventh century 'in the place of the anchorites, in *Muirbolc Mar*', on the unidentified island of *Hinba*.

> Be alone in a separate place near a chief monastery, if your conscience is not prepared to be in common with the crowd. Be always naked [metaphorically?] in imitation of Christ and the Evangelist ... A few religious men to converse with you of God and his Testament; to visit you on days of solemnity; to strengthen you in the Testaments of God and the stories of the Scriptures ...[14]

The principal daily duty of the monks, of course, was the worship of God through participation in liturgical observances, together with private meditation and prayer. Mass seems to have been said only on Sundays and feastdays rather than daily. Singing, especially of the Psalms, is mentioned repeatedly by Adomnán. Study and writing were also of great importance although possibly not for all members of the community.

The monks had to provide, of course, for their own domestic needs, erecting the various buildings and cultivating the fields. There are numerous references in the *Vita Columbae* to boats and boating as we would expect for island-dwellers. The monks themselves, their animals, visitors to the island, bulky building materials and other supplies would have had to be transported across the sound from neighbouring Mull or from the Scottish mainland, which was even further away.

In addition to leading the monastery on Iona itself, as abbot Adomnán also had responsibilities as comarba (sometimes anglicized as 'coarb') of the founder saint and thus leader of the widespread *Familia Columbae*. By Adomnán's time this was a confederation of monasteries and associated churches (and perhaps other 'institutions') spread across Ireland and in the Gaelic and Pictish parts of Scotland. In Scotland, besides Iona, Columba and his monks had established

14 Full text with translation printed in W. Reeves, *Acts of Archbishop Colton*, pp 109–12.

a number of dependent centres and churches on some of the other Hebridean islands and on the adjacent parts of mainland Scotland. One of these was at a place called *Campus-* or *Mag-Luinge* on Tiree, where there were at least two further monasteries, *Artchain* and *Bledach*. There was a monastery on the unidentified island of *Elena* and another at *Cella Diuni* near Loch Awe on the mainland. A monastery which figures several times in the *Vita Columbae* was on the unidentified island of *Hinba*; this seems to have been associated particularly with penitents or lay people who came to shrive their sins by living according to a particularly strict regime under the supervision of the monks. As well as the main monastery on *Hinba* there was also a hermitage nearby, at the place called *Muirbolc Mar*, as mentioned above. In the *Vita Columbae* we read of frequent comings and goings by boat between all these places as well as to others in Ireland and Britain. Visitors from these places seem to have come frequently to Iona as well.

Columban monks travelled fairly widely among the western islands and on the Scottish mainland, going to Skye, Eigg and Ardnamurchan; journeying to the other side of the highlands across the *Druim Albain* or 'Spine of Britain' up the Great Glen into the lands of the Picts and seemingly to the vicinity of Inverness, as well as further north to the Orkneys.

In Ireland, Durrow, Drumhome and Derry (as well as other centres) were definitely part of the *Familia Columbae* by Adomnán's time. We know that Adomanán made visits to at least some of those places during his abbacy. Other major churches that would be included in the confederation later – such as Kells, Raphoe and Tory – had yet to be founded or attached. But the formerly strong authority of the confederation in Northumbria had effectively collapsed following its major defeat on the Easter question and related matters at the Synod of Whitby in 664. Churches in the north of England and the Scottish border country, such as Lindisfarne and Melrose, had more-or-less lost their connection with the *Familia Columbae* (but, apparently, not their devotion to Columba himself) after the decision of the Synod. But, as we will see, Adomnán seemed to be intent on revitalizing at least some aspects of that earlier influence.

Apart from his regular duties as priest, monk, abbot and comarba we know that Adomnán undertook what could be described now as special projects. His attendance at, and probable organization of, the Synod of Birr in 697 is a major example of such an undertaking (see chapter 4 below). We also know that it was during his time as abbot that he wrote three of the texts attributed to him with certainty: the *Cáin Adomnáin*, *De Locis Sanctis* and the *Vita Columbae*. It is no wonder that in the final paragraph of *De Locis Sanctis* he asks its readers, but probably rhetorically, to excuse his writing 'in a lowly style, though beset by laborious and almost insurmountable ecclesiastical business from every quarter.' Each of those 'projects' will be dealt with in separate chapters below.

One of his not-so-widely-known activities, however, seems to have been a serious involvement in recording, writing about and even researching the past, what we would now call the practice of 'history'. We will see evidence of that interest again later when we come to look at his major written work, the *Vita Columbae*. But Adomnán also appears to have been involved personally with the compilation of the (partially) lost work that we now call the Iona Chronicle which, up to about the year 740, lies behind the earlier portions of the later Irish annals. The Iona Chronicle, as quoted in the later annals, is the principal source for the detailed history of Ireland and Scotland for that period.

From very early in the history of Iona, almost certainly as far back as Columba's own time, a record of significant contemporary events had been kept in the monastery. At some point other retrospective records of events prior to its foundation, based on even earlier records all of which are now lost, were also entered into this evolving chronicle. Various attempts have been made to deconstruct the surviving annals with a view to re-constructing the story of the development of the earlier versions. The leading authority on the subject, Dr Daniel Mc Carthy, for instance points out that the story began with events in continental Europe. He has drawn our attention to:

> a hitherto-unknown chronicle ... compiled by Rufinus of Aquileia between AD403 and 410, a work that had been slightly extended in *c*.420 by Sulpicius Severus in Gaul and then transmitted to Ireland ... In the later sixth century St Columba had used this text as the basis for his compilation of the Iona Chronicle wherein he extended the chronicle up to his own time ...
>
> This chronicle was maintained and continued in Iona after Columba's death, but at a date not long after the Paschal [calculation] reform in 716 this text was revised ... This reformed chronicle was removed from Iona to Ireland *c*.740 ...[15]

Iona may or may not have been the earliest centre in an Irish context for the compilation of such records, that is, for the beginnings of the 'written' history of Ireland, but it is certainly the earliest such place for which we now have substantial evidence. The Iona Chronicle grew over time and, as Dr Mc Carthy pointed out, by the 740s a copy had been brought to Ireland where it continued to evolve and be developed. Dr Mc Carthy has demonstrated that texts such as the Annals of Ulster (AU) and more particularly the Annals of Tigernach (Tig) and the *Chronicum Scotorum* (CS) retain major portions and the accurate (although now somewhat obscured) chronology of the original Iona text(s).

15   D. Mc Carthy, 'The original compilation of the Annals of Ulster', pp 84–5. See also Mc Carthy, *The Irish Annals*, passim.

From the later surviving annalistic texts, it is possible to reconstruct at least part of what was contained in the earliest strata of the Iona Chronicle. Columba and his successors on Iona seem to have played an enormously important role in the initiation and development of those types of records. But some modern authors have noted that from the 670s and 680s entries in the annals become 'more frequent' and 'much fuller'.[16] The significant connection is that Adomnán became abbot of Iona in 679.

His visits to Northumbria and its king, Aldfrith, in 687 and 689 are other examples of what I am calling here Adomnán's special projects. Given the conditions and travel limitations at the time, the journeys to and return from Northumbria would have taken huge amounts of time and effort. Adomnán was over sixty years of age at the time, an old man by early medieval standards. Strangely perhaps, despite his personal involvement with the compilation of the Iona Chronicle, the first time that his own activities as abbot are mentioned in the annals is that 687 journey to and from Northumbria, about eight years after his succession. In that year he returned to Ireland bringing with him the sixty captives who had been held prisoner by Ecgfrith, king of Northumbria, since they had been taken in a raid on Brega (roughly equivalent with Co. Meath) in 685. Ecgfrith died shortly after this raid and was succeeded as king by his half-brother Aldfrith whose relationship with the Irish, as we will see, was of a very different kind.

Aldfrith was an important ruler of Northumbria who reigned over his kingdom during a rich period in its history. His relationship with Adomnán was significant for both Britain and Ireland. As we will see below Aldfrith seems to have spent a lot of time as a younger man in Ireland or with the Irish, and we know that Adomnán's visits to him in Northumbria had various historical consequences. The apparent sources for these visits, consisting of the Irish annals, Adomnán's own mentions in the *Vita Columbae*, and a reference in the Venerable Bede's (his younger contemporary's) *Historia Ecclesiastica*, have caused not a little confusion as to how many times Adomnán visited Northumbria and king Aldfrith:

1   AU describes one visit;
2   Tig describes two (but the second may be just a duplicate of the first);
3   Adomnán, himself, explicitly refers to two in the *Vita Columbae*;
4   Bede refers only to one.

This may appear at first to be an abstruse matter of very little consequence but, in fact, quite a number of important things hang on our proper understanding of

16   For example, K. Hughes, *Early Christian Ireland*, p. 118.

it. David Woods in a brilliant article, that among other things tries to resolve the anomalies surrounding these visits, argues in favour of three: the two mentioned by Adomnán himself plus the one visit mentioned by Bede, which Woods argues was not one of the earlier journeys mentioned in the other sources.[17] As calculated by Woods, the latter visit would have taken place after the writing of the *Vita Columbae*; that is *c*.702.[18] That matter will be dealt with in detail below, based on Woods' chronology.

But to go back a few decades, AU recorded that in 685 'the Saxons laid waste to Mag Breg, and many churches, in the month of June'. A fuller account of this event is provided by the Venerable Bede (writing *c*.731) who tells us that:

> King Ecgfrith of the Northumbrians sent an army into Ireland under the command of Berctred, which brutally harassed an inoffensive people who had always been friendly to the English, sparing neither churches nor monasteries from the ravages of war. The islanders [that is, the Irish] resisted by force as well as they could, and implored the merciful aid of God ...[19]

Ecgfrith, in a battle famous in British history, was defeated and killed by the Picts in the following year, at Dún Nechtain or Nechtansmere in Scotland. Bede insisted that Ecgfrith's defeat had been at least in part punishment from God for the attack on the Irish in the previous year. But why Ecgfrith had specifically attacked Brega and taken the captives from there is not immediately understandable.[20] One possibility was that the attack was to discourage Irish (or, more properly, the ruling Uí Néill) support for the Pictish and Dál Riata opposition to Ecgfrith's aggrandizing policies in Scotland.[21] The seventeenth-century Annals of Clonmacnoise, a translation to English from an older text in Irish, says that it was because the Irish had an alliance with Ecgfrith's enemies the 'Brittaines', that is, the ancient pre-Anglo-Saxon inhabitants of Britain. Those 'Brittaines' could certainly have included the Picts.

The king of Tara at the time was Finnechta Fledach (mentioned above) who belonged to the Síl nÁedo Sláine. He must have been furious at Ecgfrith's assault on his authority, especially as it occurred in his own home territory of Brega.

17 D. Woods, 'On the circumstances of Adomnán's composition'.
18 C. Ireland, in an as yet unpublished article, suggests that Adomnán may have made a visit to Lindisfarne during one of his journeys to Northumbria in the 680s, and that it was on this occasion that he was converted to the 'Roman' ('Dionysiac') calculation for the date of Easter and related matters. I am grateful to Dr Ireland for allowing me to read his paper in advance of publication. See 'Lutting of Lindisfarne' (forthcoming).
19 Adapted from Bede, *A history*, p. 257.
20 See J. Fraser, *From Caledonia to Pictland*, p. 201.
21 See H. Moisl, 'The Bernician royal dynasty', p. 123.

It was almost certainly Finnechta who requested or encouraged Adomnán to travel to Northumbria as an emissary to the newly installed king, Aldfrith, with a view to obtaining the release of the Brega captives. Finnechta must have known that Adomnán and Aldfrith were at very least old friends. Some authors, both ancient and modern, have suggested that Aldfrith was actually staying on Iona at the time that the Brega captives were abducted, and when Ecgfrith was killed subsequently at Nechtansmere. In fact, adding to that connection, later sources claimed that the dead Northumbrian king's body was taken to Iona for burial. Ecgfrith was followed as king by Aldfrith. It may have been as some have argued that Adomnán was involved in the political manouevrings leading to Aldfrith's somewhat unexpected succession.[22] Whatever about that, the abbot of Iona would most certainly have welcomed the new arrival on the Northumbrian throne.

Aldfrith and Ecgfrith were sons of an earlier Northumbrian king, Oswiu, but they had different mothers. Sometime, possibly during the years 616 to 633 when Oswiu himself was a refugee from the intrigues of Northumbrian politics in Ireland (or among the Irish),[23] or maybe in the following decade when he disappears from the historical record altogether,[24] Oswiu is said to have become intimate with a daughter of the Irish Cenél nEogain king Colmán Rímid. Aldfrith

22 See B. Yorke, 'Adomnán at the court of King Aldfrith', pp 36–9. Aldfrith was illegitimate in English, though not in Irish, law and it certainly looks as if, prior to becoming king, he was being educated for a life as a clerical scholar (see below).

23 The complexity of the inter-relationships between the constituent kingdoms of Britain and Ireland and their rulers at this stage is mind-boggling. But one existential rule predominated: 'the enemy of my enemy is my friend'. This rule was almost never broken, although the resulting alliances might fade into the background temporarily. But some changes in circumstances might occasionally give the appearance of the rule being abandoned, such as, as often happened, when rivalries occurred within royal families and a member of an enemy dynasty might opportunistically become a 'friend'. The Donegal Cenél Conaill kingdom had a longstanding alliance with the Scottish Gaelic kingdom of Dál Riata. As indicated by Adomnán, Columba was one of the initiators and guarantors of that alliance. Dál Riata's enemies, the Picts, almost certainly had a counterbalancing alliance with Cenél nEogain, the Donegal enemies of Cenél Conaill, at least for a while. The cross-slab at Fahan, Co. Donegal, in Cenél nEogain territory may be a monument dating from the period of that particular alliance (B. Lacey, 'Fahan, Tory, Cenél nEogain'). But Dál Riata and the Picts had a sometime mutual enemy in Northumbria, which dragged the Donegal (and other Irish) kingdoms into opposition with it, except when they were able to exercise influence there such as through 'friendly' kings such as Oswald (634–42), Oswiu (642–71) and Aldfrith (686–704). The establishment of the Columban monastery on Lindisfarne in 635 (with relations and connections to other churches in the region) had also been a major source of positive Irish influence in Northumbria until that considerably lessened following the defeat on the Easter and related questions at the Synod of Whitby in 664.

24 C. Ireland, 'Where was king Aldfrith of Northumbria educated?', p. 32. The various articles by Dr Ireland on Aldfrith and related topics have informed much of what is written on the subject here.

was their resulting son. Aldfrith would be considered later, in Bede's word, a *nothus* or 'bastard' in England, but contemporary Irish law had no such concept and treated a variety of sexual relationships as legitimate. Aldfrith also had (or was later given) an Irish name, Flann Fína, Fín or Fína being possibly his Irish mother's name.[25] He knew the Irish language and is credited with the authorship of a number of written works in it, including some poetry and a wisdom text.[26] Indeed it has been suggested that he may have been 'more culturally Irish than ... Anglo-Saxon and more fluent in Gaelic than ... in Old English'.[27]

Although specific evidence is scarce and ambiguous, many authors claim that Aldfrith spent a lot of his time in Ireland or among the Irish before becoming king of Northumbria. His first stint among the Irish may have been as a baby and perhaps as a small boy. He certainly lived with the Irish again when he was older. Bede, who would have had definite information about him, tells us that he studied among the Irish as well as the English. Some late sources claimed that he had been one of Adomnán's students, even giving him the epithet *Dalta Adomnáin*, Adomnán's 'pupil', or 'foster son'. Alfred Smyth argued strongly that their master and pupil relationship must have occurred at the Columban monastery of Durrow,[28] but that is pure speculation and has been queried by

25 Dr Elva Johnson has pointed out, however, that in most of the references to him by that name 'Flann Fína is a figure of romance who bears only a tenuous relationship with the historical [Aldfrith]' (*Literacy and identity*, p. 105). It has to be admitted that we have no direct documentary evidence for Flann Fína/Aldfrith's mother at all. She only ever appears in the sources as a genitive of someone else: i.e., the genitive of her son or of her father. Aldfrith alias Flann Fína, of course, had to have a mother: the only question is about her identity. As Colin Ireland has told us, Flann is a name which means 'red – specifically blood-red', and it is often found in poetic contexts 'as a masculine noun meaning "blood"'. The second part of his Irish name, Fína, is understood in most sources as the genitive form of his alleged mother's name, the nominative form of which would probably have been Fín; but there are some linguistic problems with this. Dr Ireland points out that there are reasons to doubt that the word Fín was used as a personal name at so early a period as the early to mid-seventh century when Aldfrith's mother would have been alive. Fín from Latin *vinum* can literally mean 'wine'. There is also a related Irish word *fíne* that means 'vine'. A possibility that we cannot overlook is that Fína in this instance is an epithet or nickname of some sort, for example, meaning 'Flann of the wine'. Wine often occurs in the contemporary literature as a symbol of sovereignty, of virtue and of various other positive characteristics that were widely attributed to Aldfrith both in Britain and Ireland. Colin Ireland says that the name Flann Fína can be understood literally as 'Blood of wine', a symbolic indication of nobility and virtue drawing on parallels with the attributions of Jesus (C. Ireland, 'Aldfrith of Northumbria and the Irish genealogies', pp 70–2).

26 R. Sharpe, *Adomnán of Iona*, pp 350–1. See also: P. Henry, *Saoithiúlacht na Sean-Ghaeilge*, pp 96, 98 and 217 and further references cited there; C. Ireland (ed.), *Old Irish wisdom attributed to Aldfrith of Northumbria: an edition of* Bríathra Flainn Fína maic Ossu (Tempe Arizona, 1999). Although it should be said here that there are problems of identification, particularly of dating, with each of the texts in Irish attributed to Aldfrith.

27 B. Yorke, 'Adomnán at the court of King Aldfrith', p. 44.

28 A. Smyth, *Celtic Leinster*, p. 120.

several other authors. Adomnán had certainly become a friend of Aldfrith at some stage before the latter became king. As we have seen, Aldfrith, whom James Fraser claimed was a monk at the time,[29] was actually staying at the monastery on Iona and was possibly a clerical student there in the same year that Ecgfrith had abducted the Irish captives.

The Irish genealogies purport to explain Aldfrith/Flann Fína's Donegal family connections. Although the Laud genealogies are not contained in the oldest manuscript, they may transmit the oldest relevant information, dated to about AD 800. As it happens, the information for Flann Fína there is the same as that in the oldest manuscript, the early twelfth-century Rawlinson B. 502. They both more-or-less say, in a characteristic mixture of Irish and Latin:

> *Colmán Rímid athair Fína, máthair íside Flaind Fína meic Ossu regis Saxonum.*

Colmán Rímid, father of Fín/Fína, that is, the mother of Flann Fína son of Oswiu king of the Saxons.[30]

Colmán Rímid, king of Cenél nEogain, died in 602. Later Cenél nEogain propaganda tried to show that he had reigned as king of Tara also. That is very doubtful, but the matter is not important here.[31] What is certain is that Colmán was a powerful Cenél nEógain aristocrat, whatever that meant at the time.[32]

If Colmán was the father of Aldfrith's mother and, therefore, the Northumbrian king's Inishowen grandfather, then that was not his (Colmán's) only possible connection with the northern English kingdom. AU for 659 records the death of a bishop Finnán son of Rímid. A Finán son of Rímid is allotted the 6 January as a feastday – that is, as a 'saint' – in the early ninth-century *Martyrology of Tallaght*, and a Finán son of Colmán is listed in the corpus of saint's genealogies.[33] The interval between the death of Colmán in 602 and of bishop Fin[n]án in 659 might seem a bit long for them to have been father and son but, as outlined above, we could expect that a bishop would lead a relatively untroubled and, therefore, comparatively long life.

---

29 *From Caledona to Pictland*, p. 257.

30 M. O'Brien, *Corpus genealogiarum*, p. 135: 140a39/40. K. Meyer, 'The Laud genealogies', p. 294: 24–5.

31 Lacey, *CC*, pp 205–10.

32 Incidentally the second word of his name *Rímid* means 'counter', as in the children's rhyme 'the king was in his counting house, counting all his money'. *Rímid* is an ancestor of the word in modern Irish *ríomhaire* meaning 'computer'. We don't know why Colmán acquired the epithet *Rímid*. Could it imply that he had some scholarly attributes himself, perhaps in the general area of mathematics or computistics? A number of his relatives as we will see were honoured as scholars. Or perhaps the opposite is the explanation. Maybe his name was a joke and he couldn't count at all!

33 P. Ó Riain, *Corpus genealogiarum*, p. 146: 707.446.

The only bishop Fin(n)án we know of around this time from other sources is the Finán who was bishop at the Columban monastery of Lindisfarne off the Northumbrian coast. He acquired that position in immediate succession to Aidán, the founder of that church, who died in 651, that is, well before the decisive Synod of Whitby in 664. Bede described the Lindisfarne Finán as 'a hot-tempered man whom reproof made more obstinate and openly hostile to the truth'. Rather than an objective general assessment of Finán's character, however, that remark by Bede (who couldn't have known Finán) specifically referred to his obstinate (or just plain 'loyal') adherence to what is usually called the Celtic position in the controversy about the dating of Easter, which will be dealt with more fully below.

While we cannot be certain about the matter it is very possible that bishop Finán of Lindisfarne was the son of the Cenél nEógain king, Colmán Rímid. If so, he would have been also a sort of brother-in-law (in Irish law at least) of the Northumbrian king Oswiu. Oswiu, of course, was father of Aldfrith, making the latter therefore a nephew of Finán (see table 8)!

Bishop Finán's name is a hypocoristic or endearing diminutive form of the name Fin, meaning something like 'little' or 'dearest Fin'. This is slightly different but very close to the alleged name of Aldfrith's mother Fín or Fína. As pointed out by Colin Ireland, ancient Irish families often favoured names that were etymologically or alliteratively related.[34] Thus a brother called Fin (or Finán) with a sister called Fín (or Fína) makes absolute sense in contemporary Irish terms.

Aldfrith's posthumous reputation in Ireland was so great that he, or rather Flann Fína, was honoured as a saint. Although he himself is not listed in the text known as the corpus of saints' genealogies, a text which is found in various manuscripts from the twelfth century onwards, his alleged mother, Fína or Fín, is included in the list of the 'mothers of saints'. However, a relatively obscure quatrain in the *Martyrology of Óengus* for 15 December[35] has recently been re-translated, and recognized by Colin Ireland as referring to Flann Fína/Aldfrith:[36]

> The invocation of blessed Faustus[37]
> with the fine clergy of his church
> at the feast of Flann the honourable emperor[38]
> the enduring heir of Bangor.[39]

34 C. Ireland, 'Aldfrith of Northumbria and the Irish genealogies', p. 74.
35 W. Stokes, *Martyrology of Oengus*, p. 251. The Martyrology of Óengus is now dated by Pádraig Ó Riain to between 829 and 833, a little over a century after Aldfrith's death (*Feastdays of the saints*, pp 97–8).
36 C. Ireland, 'Where was king Aldfrith of Northumbria educated?', pp 63–74.
37 St Comgall of Bangor.
38 Adomnán described Oswald, Aldfrith's uncle, as *totius Brittaniae imperator*.
39 St Comgall's monastery, now Bangor, Co. Down.

Aldfrith is referred to in Irish sources in Latin as a *sapiens* or its Irish equivalent, *ecnaid*, such as in the AU entry on his death. The title *sapiens*, given to those who were specially venerated for their learning, seems to imply that at least some of them were trained in an ecclesiastical context but did not necessarily continue the rest of their lives as clerics. We know of course from separate contemporary sources, such as those written by Bede and Aldhelm in England and the posthumous Irish references to him, that Aldfrith's reputation for learning, and specifically for Latin Christian learning, was very high. Indeed, as Dr Elva Johnson and other authors have suggested, as the younger son of king Oswiu, Aldfrith may have been intended originally for a life as a cleric.[40]

Colin Ireland addressed some of the chronological difficulties inherent in the alleged relationship of Aldfrith with the Cenél nÉogain through Fín/Fína and Colmán Rímid. Oswiu, Aldfrith's undoubted father, died in 670 at the age of fifty-eight, giving him a birth date of about 612. If Colmán Rímid died in 602 or thereabouts then a daughter of his could have been born no later than 603, thus she would have been at least nine years older than Oswiu, her alleged consort. As Colin Ireland says, 'this does not create an insurmountable chronological problem, particularly in light of the often-transient sexual liaisons acceptable to the early Irish.'[41] We know from other sources that Oswiu and his brothers spent the years *c.*617–33, as it were, 'on the run' among the Irish and the Picts, that is, between his age of five years and twenty-one years. Oswiu became king of Northumbria in 642 and Dr Ireland suggests that it was during the decade 633 to 642, when as an Northumbrian prince he is largely missing from the historical record but might have continued his stay among the Irish, that he fathered Aldfrith. Comparing Aldfrith's age with his contemporary and friend Aldhelm, Dr Ireland suggests that Aldfrith was born in the late 630s when his father would have been in his late twenties and Colmán Rímid's daughter, if she was his mother, would have been at minimum in her late thirties. If that is the case, then Aldfrith would have been about ten-to-fifteen years younger than Adomnán who, as we have seen, is often portrayed as one of the former's teachers and mentors.

There is a political context that might have provided the opportunity for an encounter between the Northumbrian Oswiu and a Cenél nÉogain woman. We know that Oswiu had connections with, and may have even fought for, the Dál Riata, the Gaels of south-western Scotland. In 639 the Dál Riata had an alliance with Cenél nÉogain in the events surrounding the important battle of Mag Roth. That episode was famously referred to in a quotation from an earlier book by Cumméne Find added in a peculiar manner to the Schaffhaussen manuscript

40 E. Johnston, *Literacy and identity*, pp 104–5.
41 C. Ireland, 'Aldfrith of Northumbria and the Irish genealogies', p. 75.

of Adomnán's *Vita Columbae* (see below, chapter 5). Could that alliance have been the context in which Oswiu encountered a Cenél nÉogain aristocratic woman, whose name may or may not have been Fín or Fína and who may or may not have been the daughter of Colmán Rímid?[42]

There is certainly a tradition as we saw above, at least in the literature but probably reflecting real life, that when the time came for the mothers of significant Donegal figures to give birth, they would travel back to their own home place for the baby's delivery; the birth would not happen in the father's home. That would support the idea that Aldfrith may have been born in Cenél nÉogain territory, the Inishowen peninsula. Again, citing the contemporary Irish law of fosterage, Colin Ireland shows that the Northumbrian Oswiu, the father, would have been identified by the Irish as a *cú glas*, 'a foreigner from across the sea'.[43] In Irish law this meant that responsibility to foster and educate the child fell totally on the mother's wider family. Thus, if Aldfrith did have an Inishowen mother, Irish law and tradition would almost certainly have ensured that he be born, brought up and educated among his maternal Donegal family. Although we can have no certainty, all the circumstantial evidence points to a senior branch of the Cenél nÉogain as that family (Table 8).

Table 8: Family of Colmán Rímid, Aldfrith and Cenn Fáelad

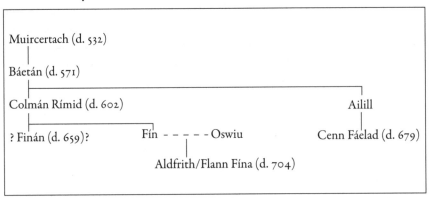

One other point arises: where did Aldfrith obtain his excellent scriptural and Latin learning? As Elva Johnson says, the compliments he later received for

42   The battle of Mag Roth was important in several ways but one of the reasons it was remembered was that it was an occasion when the alliance between Dál Riata and Cenél Conaill broke down and the former allied instead with Cenél nÉogain. There were probably several reasons why the story was included in the *Vita Columbae* but, by introducing the quotation about this episode from a different book, was Adomnán (or the scribe of the text, Dorbbéne) adverting deliberately to the context of Aldfrith's conception? See below, chapter 5.

43   C. Ireland, 'Where was king Aldfrith of Northumbria educated?', pp 31 and 54.

that learning 'do not seem to have been mere sycophantic flattery'.[44] There were many places in Ireland where Aldfrith could have received that sort of schooling, in fact the system of education then was most definitely peripatetic; students would travel around to the locations of the most famous scholars. Although most authors until recently have assumed that the Irish part of his education was at least mainly in a Columban milieu (Drumhome, Durrow and Iona are frequently mentioned as likely locations), Colin Ireland, using the quatrain quoted above, has suggested that Bangor in Co. Down was a likely location for at least some of Aldfrith's studies.[45] It might be worth noting that there is some inconclusive evidence in the early sources for a connection between Cenél nÉogain (Aldfrith's maternal family) and the Dál Fiatach of Co. Down.[46] Bangor was situated in Dál Fiatach territory. Between about 610 and 671 Cenél Feradaig – said to have been a segment of Cenél nÉogain – were in the ascendant among the latter. But there are at least hints of a genealogical connection between Cenél Feradaig and Dál Fiatach.[47] Such links could at least partially explain why a young man born in Inishowen might have been educated in Bangor. The two places would, of course, have been easily linked by boat around the north-eastern coast of Ireland.

If Aldfrith's mother was a daughter of Colmán Rímid then, as well as having an uncle (Finán) who was probably bishop of Lindisfarne, but before Aldfrith became king of Northumbria, he was also related to what appears to have been one of the greatest Irish scholars and intellectuals of the time, Cenn Fáelad mac Ailello (Table 8). Cenn Fáelad died in 679 and, like Aldfrith himself, was given the title *sapiens* in his death notice in the annals. Unfortunately, very little of Cenn Fáelad's *oeuvre* survives except perhaps a few fragments of verses attributed to him that are scattered as marginalia in the annals. Two legal poems claimed to be by him really date to about half a century after his death, and there is no certainty about the date of the Old Irish grammar *Auraicept na nÉces* ('The scholar's primer') traditionally said to have been authored by him.[48]

Cenn Fáelad may have been Aldfrith's first cousin once removed and although we have no date for his birth the likelihood is that he was a lot older than Aldfrith, certainly old enough to have acted in some kind of mentoring or tutoring capacity for his nephew of mixed Irish-Northumbrian origins. We have very little contemporary evidence for his life but Cenn Fáelad is noted in many later Irish texts as a poet and, very unusually, as an exponent of both native

44 *Literacy and identity*, p. 104.
45 'Where was king Aldfrith of Northumbria educated?'.
46 Lacey, *CC*, pp 91, 162–3.
47 Lacey, *CC*, pp 162–4, 259–60.
48 D. Ó Cróinín, *Early medieval Ireland*, p. 194. See also C. Ireland, 'What constitutes the learning of a sapiens?: the case of Cenn Fáelad'; and C. Ireland, 'Aldfrith of Northumbria and the learning of a *sapiens*', pp 68–71.

Irish and Christian canon law. Whatever the historical truth, he was particularly remembered in Irish tradition for being one of the persons most responsible for bringing together and combining the study and exposition of *fénechas*, native Gaelic law; *filidecht*, Gaelic poetry and native lore, legends myths etc; and *léigend*, Latinate ecclesiastical learning including church law.

Cenn Fáelad belonged to the Cenél nÉogain of Inishowen. After 671, although with a Cenél Feradaig interlude between about 681 and 700, there followed the restoration of another branch of Cenél nÉogain, Cenél Maic Ercae, and the reigns of three exceptionally powerful Cenél nÉogain kings: Máeldúin mac Máelfithrich who died in 681; his son Fergal who died in 722 as king of Tara, and the latter's son Áed Allán, also a king of Tara, who died in 743. Those three kings were the initiators of the real political success of Cenél nÉogain: (i) its extension beyond the bounds of Inishowen; (ii) its occasional taking of the overlordship of Donegal and the kingship of Tara; and (iii) its ultimate defeat in 789 of Adomnán's (and Columba's) people, Cenél Conaill. That was the Irish political, dynastic and cultural background from which the future king Aldfrith of Northumbria had emerged.

In 687 Adomnán was in Northumbria, probably sent specifically as an ambassador[49] of the king of Tara, Finnechta Fledach, to King Aldfrith to seek the release of the Brega prisoners captured for King Ecgfrith in 685. The Annals of the Four Masters (at the incorrect year 684) describe this as follows (in John O'Donovan's translation):

> [Adomnán] went to Saxon-land to request [a restoration] of the prisoners which the North Saxons had carried off from Magh-Breagh the year before mentioned. He obtained a restoration of them, after having performed wonders and miracles before the hosts; and they afterwards gave him great honour and respect, together with a full restoration of everything he asked of them.

As mentioned already, Adomnán must have been about sixty years of age if not older when he undertook that extraordinarily arduous journey from Iona (or Ireland?) across the borders of Scotland and Northumbria to the other side

---

49 In a letter sent by Ceolfrith abbot of the monastery of Wearmouth/Jarrow near Newcastle-upon-Tyne to king Nechtan of the Picts about 710 there is a reference to 'Adomnán, a renowned priest and abbot of the Columbans, who when he was sent on an embassy for his nation to King Aldfrith ...' (Bede, *History*, p. 326). Bede, who preserved that letter for us, in his own text, also refers to Adomnán 'sent by his nation on a mission to Aldfrith'. The chronology of these references suggests that they do not refer to events in 687 but to another occasion *c*.702 (see below) but they certainly indicate that Adomnán was recognized in Northumbria as an Irish ambassador, perhaps the first such official 'legate' in our history.

of the north of England. Once there, as many authors have suggested, he would have had little trouble persuading his friend King Aldfrith to release the captives. There is a very good chance that they communicated in Irish. According to AU, Adomnán himself brought the sixty released prisoners back to Ireland. He probably crossed the Irish Sea from a port in the Carlisle area directly to a harbour in Brega. The Annals of Tigernach says that he repeated that journey and for a similar purpose in 689 but that is almost certainly an erroneous repetition of the 687 entry. However, in 689 (or thereabouts), he did in fact return to Northumbria. We know that because in the *Vita Columbae* he says so, referring to 'my first visit, [sometime] after Ecgfrith's battle [at Nechtansmere] and on my second visit two years later'.[50]

The annals (AU and CS) say that in 692, 'in the 14th year after the repose of Failbe [previous abbot of Iona]', Adomnán visited Ireland again. This was most likely a formal visitation of the Columban churches throughout the country, similar to that made on several occasions by his predecessors. He may have had to deal with the sort of problem adverted to by Tírechán who as mentioned above, writing about the same time, indicates that there was a dispute between the communities of Colum Cille, of Patrick in Armagh, and of Eógan of Ardstraw (Co. Tyrone), about the control of the monastery of Ráith Cunga in south Donegal. Ráith Cunga was very close to the Columban church at Drumhome. Whatever tasks he undertook in Ireland on this occasion, Adomnán is likely to have returned to Iona for the following year when we are told that the king of the Picts, Bruide son of Bile, the victor over Ecgfrith at Nechtansmere, was buried on that island. Two short ironic verses allegedly commemorating this event are attributed, probably inaccurately, to Adomnán. The first is as follows:

Mór do ingantu do-[g]ní	Great wonders are worked
in rí génair ó Muire,	By the king born of Mary,
betha Scuabán I mMuilí,	To Scuabán on Mull he gives life,
écc do Bruide mac Bile	But death to Bruide mac Bile.[51]

The reference in the verse to Scuabán, which has been taken here as a personal name, is slightly problematic and will be considered further in chapter 10 below. But the connection with Bruide suggested in these verses is further evidence of Adomnán's excellent diplomatic relations as abbot of Iona with the diversity of kings and polities in both Ireland and northern Britain during his lifetime. Below we will see more evidence of Adomnán's continuing good relationship

---

50   That is, two years after the first visit, not after the battle. R. Sharpe, *Adomnán of Iona*, p. 203.
51   M. Herbert & P. Ó Riain, *Betha Adamnáin*, p. 58. The loose translation here by this author is based on the more literal version by the latter editors.

with the Pictish kingdom when its then ruler, Bruide son of Derile, endorsed, as a so-called 'guarantor', Adomnán's Law for the protection of innocents in time of war.

Later traditions, however, imply (whether factually or fictionally) that Adomnán did not always have positive relations with every one of those who supported the promulgation of his Law. For instance, the Fragmentary Annals has an unlikely story about Adomnán that links him with Írgalach son of Conaing, the Síl nÁedo Sláine king of Knowth or north Brega (Co. Meath) who died in 702. The story suggests hostility between the two men but, in fact, Írgalach was another of the so-called 'guarantors' who endorsed Adomnán's Law in 697. One possible source of tension between them may have surrounded Írgalach's wife Muireann who some sources suggest had been previously married to Loingsech mac Óengusa the king of Tara, Adomnán's distant cousin. In the story 'enmity arose' between the two men for the king (that is, Írgalach) had 'flouted Adomnán by killing his own kinsman, Niall, in spite of Adomnán's protection.' Adomnán fasted every night without sleeping, standing in cold river water, in order to shorten Írgalach's life. Each night Írgalach would quiz Adomnán about what he was going to do and then, to counteract the intentions of the cleric, he would do the same thing himself. To deceive Írgalach, one night Adomnán put his own clothes on one of his household clerics and got him, as it were, to stand in for him. The cleric told the king, who assumed he was talking to Adomnán, that he would spend that night feasting and sleeping, 'for it was easier for Adomnán that one of his people should lie than himself.' The king feasted and slept in the assumption that Adomnán was doing likewise but the latter, outwitting the king, had really fasted and stood in a vigil in the River Boyne until morning. The king actually dreamt about what Adomnán was up to and awoke with a fright. His wife, who 'was humble and obedient to the Lord and to Adomnán', was afraid that the cleric's curse would affect the child she was carrying in her womb. Adomnán then came and told Írgalach that he would die presently and go to Hell.

> When Írgalach's wife heard that, she came before Adomnán and lay at his feet, and besought him for God's sake not to curse her child, the infant that was in her womb.

> Adomnán said, 'The infant in your womb will be king indeed, but one of his eyes is now broken as a result of the cursing of his father,' And that is how it was. The boy was born immediately after that, and he was half blind.[52]

52 J. Radner, *Fragmentary Annals of Ireland*, p. 49.

Later, at the year 728, the same annals record: 'In this year Cináed Cáech ['the one-eyed'] son of Írgalach was killed, and none of his descendants took the kingship of Ireland [after him]. Flaithbertach son of Loingsech [mac Óenguso] killed him.'

As can be appreciated, at this remove over thirteen hundred years later, it is difficult to be absolutely precise about when specific events occurred. But one of the dates we are most confident of in the life of Adomnán is 697 when he organized the Synod of Birr (Co. Offaly) and, in the words of AU, 'gave the *Lex Innocentium* ['the Law of the Innocents'[53]] to the people.' Both the formulation and composition of the Law, the organization of its endorsement by almost one hundred prelates and kings from both Ireland and Britain, and the organization of the synod itself where it was enacted, were triumphs for Adomnán and a highpoint of his career in the public domain. Both the text of the law and the circumstances surrounding it will be dealt with in detail in chapter 4.

Likewise, Adomnán's composition of the Life of his illustrious predecessor Columba, the *Vita Columbae*, was a triumph of contemporary literature, scholarship and 'history'. The research for and writing of the Life must have taken several years, and scholars have debated when precisely that might have happened. In the *Vita* he mentions although does not name, very briefly and characteristically very modestly, what is most likely the Synod of Birr in 697. We can be fairly sure, therefore, that at least some, and perhaps most, of the work on the book was carried out between 697 and his death in 704. In early medieval terms that is as close to accurate pinpointing as we can expect to get. The book and the circumstances surrounding its composition will be dealt with in chapter 5.

Apart from the issue of the Brega captives we know that a number of other controversial matters were of interest and concern to Adomnán. These included the differences over the shape of the monastic tonsure and, most importantly, the ongoing controversy over the correct method for the calculation of the date of the moveable feast of Easter. Dr Daniel Mc Carthy has produced extensive evidence, including the visual evidence from the Columban manuscript known as the Book of Kells, to show that the conservative Irish tonsure required that the head be shaved from the forehead to the crown. This resulted in a triangular or Delta shape with the wide part to the front,[54] rather than the approved 'Roman' manner in which the crown of the head only was shaved in the form of a disc.

From our perspective these would seem to have been such relatively unimportant matters that it is hard to believe now that they generated such argument and conflict in early medieval times. But whereas, in so far as we are interested in them at all, those matters are more or less agreed for us now, the

53 This would later be known also as the *Cáin Adomnáin*, 'Adomnán's Law'. See below, chapter 4.
54 D. Mc Carthy, 'Representations of tonsure in the Book of Kells'.

achievement of such agreement involved issues of mathematics, astronomy, history and tradition, not to mention theology and study of the Bible. For most of the seventh century these were major questions of debate in Britain and, seemingly to a slightly lesser extent, in Ireland. The resolution of the Easter controversy had been decided for Northumbria at the Synod of Whitby in 664. What might be called the Iona or Columban position on the matter lost the argument on that occasion.[55] That controversy had its origins centuries before in the debate about the future of Christianity's links with Judaism, and specifically whether or not the celebration of the Resurrection should be linked with the Jewish celebration of Passover.

As I am writing this, on 19 April 2020, the news media is telling us that 'today' is Easter Sunday according to the Orthodox rite. However last Sunday was Easter according to most of the rest of the Christian world, a week in the difference this year. But we do have general global consensus now (despite some surviving cultural differences) after centuries of debate and argument about such matters as: the date and beginning of the year, the date of solstices and equinoxes, the number of days and months in the year, and that it is at midnight locally that each new day begins, etc. These were not matters that were agreed unanimously across and between cultures in ancient times.

Throughout prehistoric and earlier historic times before the rise of academic science it was the priesthoods of various cultures that assumed responsibility for measuring the passing of time and the marking of festivals and anniversaries. Separate cultures had their own way of doing that but for the most part those matters were based on the 'movements' of the sun and the moon as observed from the different parts of the earth, and the changing seasons for plant and animal life.

But there was no global agreement, for instance, on at what time a day changed. For us, as universally agreed now, it is unquestionably the moment of local midnight. But here in Ireland, even now, a festival day is still often understood as beginning on the evening before the day in question, the 'eve of' the big day such as Halloween, the 'eve of all hallows', Christmas eve etc. In ancient times such matters depended on local beliefs and practices, and new days were often understood as beginning at local sunsets or, alternatively, local sunrises etc.

Easter is the most important festival of the Christian religion but it has slightly odd pre-Christian and even non-Christian features.[56] Unlike most if not all of the other Christian festivals, the date of Easter is related to the movements

55 The two competing views are often characterized by modern authors, somewhat inaccurately, as the winning '*Romani*' or 'Roman' view and the losing 'Celtic' or 'Iona' view.

56 Now calculated (mainly) as the first Sunday, after the first full moon, after the Spring Equinox. Unlike Christmas, which is always 25 December no matter what day of the week that falls, Easter is always celebrated on a Sunday and not on any presumed 'date' of the resurrection, which would of course fall on differing days in different years.

of the moon rather than specifically to the relationship of the earth to the sun. Easter takes some of its aspects from: (i) the universal celebration of the arrival of Spring; (ii) the Spring equinox; (iii) from its antecedent in the Jewish festival of Passover and, of course; (iv) from a calculation of when the crucifixion and resurrection of Jesus is likely to have taken place. But its calculation still presents questions of a general nature such as: at what time does the day change; what is the date, at least the conventional date, of the Spring equinox etc?

When Christianity arrived in Ireland part of its cultural package included the mathematics or computistics necessary for the correct calculation of Easter as then known and practiced in the universal church. Traditions were established and handed on. Conservatism set in and when it was learned that new ideas about that calculation had developed at the heart of church, in Rome or elsewhere, there was reluctance among the clergy here at the edge of the earth to surrender the practices inherited from their own saints and founding fathers. In 630, the then pope wrote to the Irish church remonstrating with them for not keeping up to date on this matter and, as a result, churches in the south of Ireland conformed to the newer system. The north proved more recalcitrant but by 688 at the latest Armagh and the churches associated with it had yielded to the new calculations.[57] It appears that only the *Familia Columbae* led from Iona held out, loyal to the system bequeathed to them by their founder, Columba. The subject must have come up for discussion, at least, when Adomnán made his two visits to Northumbria in 687 and 689. There are hints in the *Vita Columbae* – probably largely written within the following decade but, no doubt, already beginning to be formulated in Adomnán's mind (see chapter 5) – that, although he was abbot and comarba on Iona, at very least he had doubts about that community's conservatism on the matter.[58] Personally, he must have been at

---

57 T. Charles-Edwards, *Early Christian Ireland*, pp 428–9. In fact, as pointed out by Clare Stancliffe as well as other authors, by then there had been a revision of the earlier revised system. In 630 the so-called system of Victorius of Acquitane was in use. By the 680s Rome was advocating the so-called Alexandrian or Dionysian system (C. Stancliffe, 'Charity with peace' p. 51). The precise calculations employed in these systems are complex and highly technical. A succinct explanation is given in C. Stancliffe, 'Charity with peace', pp 57–9, and a fuller account by T. Charles-Edwards, *Early Christian Ireland*, pp 391–415. Stancliffe shows that in 689 the two systems – 'Celtic' and 'Roman' – gave the same date for Easter, 11 April, but from then to beyond the end of Adomnán's life in 704 they gave different dates. Also, 690 was the beginning of a new cycle of Easter dates according to the Irish system. On the basis of these and other coincidences, but ignoring the possible later visit to Northumbria c.702 suggested by David Woods, Stancliffe argued that Adomnán probably yielded to the new system in time for Easter 690, i.e., shortly after his second visit to Northumbria. The major problem with this, although she attempts to deal very cleverly with it, is that it leaves Abbot and Comarba Adomnán in conflict with his own monks on a relatively major issue for almost fifteen years. Whereas Woods' chronology does not. See below, and chapters 6 and 7.
58 See C. Stancliffe, 'Charity with peace', pp 53–4.

least pondering whether a change was desirable. He must have known that it was surely inevitable, at some stage.

A letter of about 710 from the Northumbrian abbot Ceolfrith to king Nechtan of the Picts outlines a discussion he is said to have had with Adomnán on the subject of the tonsure.[59] Ceolfrith was the abbot of the very important monastery at Wearmouth/Jarrow, near modern Newcastle-upon-Tyne.

> Adomnán, a renowned priest and abbot of the Columbans, who when he was sent on an embassy for his nation to King Aldfrith and chose to visit our monastery, displayed remarkable wisdom, humility, and devotion in his ways and conversation.
>
> I said to him in the course of discussion: 'Holy brother, you believe that you are on the right road to receive the crown of life that knows no term. Why then, I beseech you, do you wear on your head the image of a crown which, in a fashion that belies your faith is terminated [i.e. the tonsure shape abhorred by the *Romani*]? And if you seek the society of blessed Peter, why do you imitate the tonsure of the man whom Peter cursed?[60] Why do you not do everything in this life to show that you love to imitate him with whom you desire to live in blessedness for ever?'
>
> He replied: 'My dear brother, rest assured that, although I wear Simon's tonsure after the custom of my country, I wholeheartedly abominate and reject all simoniacal wickedness. So far as my frailty permits, I wish to follow in the footsteps of the most blessed Prince of the Apostles.'
>
> I then said: 'I am sure that this is so. Nevertheless, you should give some indication of your inward esteem for whatever derives from the Apostle Peter by displaying openly whatever you know to be his. For I think that your wisdom clearly appreciates that it would be better for you, who are vowed to God, to alter your outward appearance from any resemblance to a man whom you wholeheartedly detest, and whose hideous face you would loathe to see. On the other hand, since you wish to follow the example and teachings of Peter, it would be fitting for you to conform to the outward appearance of him who you desire to have as your advocate in the presence of God.'

59 The letter was possibly drafted by Bede. But it may be that in the copy he preserved in the *Historia Ecclesiastica* he deliberately distorted what the letter had actually said or, indeed, the nature of the original exchange between Adomnán and Ceolfrith. The words put into Adomnán's mouth look somewhat suspicious!

60 The so-called Celtic tonsure was insultingly characterized as that of Simon Magus, a first century Samaritan religious figure known as the 'sorcerer' or 'magician'. He had converted to Christianity, but the Acts of the Apostles reports his clash with St Peter. The negative word 'simony' derives from his name. In later times those believed not to be obeying all the rules of the church were sometimes insultingly described as followers of that Simon.

Such, then, were my words to Adomnán, who showed how greatly he had profited by seeing the observances of our Church; for after he had returned to Scotia [in this case meaning Ireland and the Gaelic parts of modern Scotland], he won over large numbers to the Catholic [the *Romani*] observance of Easter by his preaching. But although he was their lawfully constituted head, he was unable to persuade the monks of Iona to adopt a better rule of life. Had his authority been sufficiently great, he would surely have taken care to correct the tonsure also.[61]

Bede, whose copy of this letter as an appendix to his own *Historia Ecclesiastica* is the only version that has survived, is often accused by modern writers of telescoping the events reported and adverted to in it. Because of the opening reference to when he was 'sent on an embassy' many authors have interpreted this to imply that the conversation that followed took place during Adomnán's first visit to Northumbria in 687. But because of the closing references concerning his failure to convince the Iona monks to adopt the new rules, others have opted for the second visit in 689, seemingly his last visit. However, necessarily, if either of those dates was correct it would imply, very improbably, that Adomnán was in dispute with his monks on Iona for much of his abbacy, from at least 689 to 704.

In the main text of the *Historia Ecclesiastica*, Bede gives his own account of Adomnán's struggle with these issues.

At this period, by the grace of God, the majority of the Scots [Irish] in Ireland, together with some of the Britons [P-Celtic-speaking people] in Britain, conformed to the logical and canonical time of keeping Easter. Adomnán, priest and abbot of the monks who lived on the Isle of Iona, was sent by his nation on a mission to Aldfrith, King of the English [Anglo-Saxons of Northumbria] and remained in his province for some while, where he observed the rites of the Church canonically performed. He was earnestly advised by many who were more learned than himself not to presume to act contrary to the universal customs of the Church, whether in the keeping of Easter or in any other observances [such as the tonsure], seeing that his following was very small and situated in a remote corner of the world. As a result he changed his opinions, and readily adopted what he saw and heard in the churches of the English in place of the customs of his own people. For he was a wise and worthy man, excellently grounded in knowledge of the Scriptures.

On his return home, he tried to lead his own people in Iona and those who were under the jurisdiction of that monastery into the correct ways

61   L. Sherley-Price, *Bede: A history*, pp 326–7.

that he himself had learned and wholeheartedly accepted; but in this he failed. Then he sailed over to preach in Ireland, and by his simple teaching showed its people the proper time of Easter. He corrected their ancient error and restored nearly all who were not under the jurisdiction of Iona to Catholic unity, teaching them to observe Easter at the proper time. Having observed the canonical Easter in Ireland, he returned to his own island [Iona], where he vigorously pressed his own monastery to conform to the Catholic observance of Easter but had no success in his attempts. Before the close of the next year he departed this life. For God in his goodness decreed that so great a champion of peace and unity should be received into everlasting life before the time of Easter returned once more, and before he should be obliged to enter upon more serious controversy with those who refused to follow him in the truth.[62]

Regarding the chronological difficulties raised by these two quotations and more specifically by the interpretations put on them by modern scholars, David Woods brilliantly resolved the problem by postulating that the visit reported here, both by Ceolfrith and Bede, was in fact a third, otherwise undocumented, visit, that took place c.702. According to Woods's interpretation, Adomnán must have visited Northumbria c.702. It was on that occasion that he finally changed his own mind on the tonsure and Easter questions. He then returned home to Iona but failing to convince the monks there he travelled on to Ireland where he had a lot more success and 'observed the canonical Easter' there in 703 or 704. He then returned to Iona well before the next Easter of 705 but died, probably on 23 September 704, in his own monastery.

As part of his assessment of Adomnan's abilities and integrity, Bede also mentioned the latter's composition of the book about the Holy Land, *De Locis Sanctis*. That matter will be addressed in chapter 6 below.

The chronology of what we can know about Adomnán's last two years or so as recalculated and reinterpreted by David Woods makes eminent sense, especially in terms of the abbot's differences with his own monks on Iona. Those would have lasted then for no more than roughly two years, from 702 until his death in 704, much of which time he was absent from Iona in Ireland anyway. Woods's interpretation also absolves Bede from the accusation frequently made against him that, either accidentally or deliberately for his own propaganda purposes, he distorted the chronology of these events, reducing about sixteen years of Adomnán's life into one year.

Adomnán died in 704, most likely on 23 September the date commemorated as his feastday, his *die natalis*, literally 'birthday', the day he was born into his

62 L. Sherley-Price, *Bede: A history*, pp 299–300.

new life in the hereafter.[63] Unlike Columba, for whom Adomnán gives an account of the end of his life, his death and burial (whether real or, as we have reason to suspect, in part fictional), we have no account of Adomnán's final days and passing. The annals claim that he was seventy-seven years of age at the time but this does not tally with some of the information noting his birth. As we have seen earlier, Pádraig Ó Riain suspects that seventy-seven is a fictional figure, used in this instance to indicate numerical perfection as part of the growth of Adomnán's hagiographical depiction as a saint himself.

63 But for some confusion about the date of the feastday, see chapter 8 below.

CHAPTER FOUR

The canons of Adomnán and the
Lex Innocentium

Several written texts are attributed to Adomnán. The evidence for his authorship or even his personal connection with each of those varies. In a later chapter the more ambiguous texts will be looked at. Here Adomnán's reputation as a rule-maker and law-maker is examined.

One very interesting text attributed to him is a set of twenty canons in Latin regulating the consumption or otherwise of clean and unclean food. This set of instructions is similar to and obviously ultimately drawn from cognate material in the Mosaic laws. The argument for the attribution to the abbot of Iona consists principally in the title *Canones Adamnani* being assigned to them in the surviving manuscripts 'none of which is earlier than the ninth century',[1] a hundred years at least after Adomnán's death. Adding to the doubt about who composed them, their editor Ludwig Bieler thought that the text bears little resemblance to the writing style of the author of *De Locis Sanctis* or the *Vita Columbae*.[2] Bieler suggested that maybe 'these canons were enacted on the authority of [Adomnán] although their wording is not his'.[3] He drew attention for example to references in several of the canons to an external anonymous male source who was evidently the original authority for these instructions before they were, as it were, committed to writing.

Canon 16 looks to be somewhat out of place, both in terms of its physical location in the text and also because it deals with a very different matter to the other nineteen canons. Paradoxically, however, it adds some support for the attribution of the text to Adomnán. It refers to two matters with which we know Adomnán was definitely involved: issues about the status of women and the theological differences between the so-called *Romani* and the *Familia Columbae*.

---

1   L. Bieler, *The Irish penitentials*, p. 9, and pp 176–81, for the Latin text and translation into English, from which all quotations below are taken. See also P. Ó Néill & D. Dumville, *Cáin Adomnáin and Canones Adomnani*.

2   But it has to be said that other commentators have suggested that there is not much resemblance to each other in the writing style of the latter two works which, undoubtedly, were written by Adomnán.

3   But for a more positive opinion on the attribution to Adomnán, see now J. Houlihan, *Adomnán's* Lex Innocentium, p. 103 and references cited there.

Of a wife who is a harlot, thus the same man [that is, the external authority? – Adomnán?] explained, that she will be a harlot [*meretrix*], who has cast off the yoke of her husband, and is joined to a second husband or a third. Her husband shall not take another (wife) while she lives. For we do not know whether that verdict which we read in questions of the *Romani*[4] was attested by acceptable or false witnesses.

In the notes to his translation Bieler commented that he was not certain that the Latin text has been transmitted accurately in the manuscripts and suggested a meaning of the second half of the paragraph along the following lines: 'A husband deserted by his wife, who wishes to marry again, must establish the death of his former wife by reliable witnesses'. The *Romani* mentioned here are of course those clerics in the seventh century who championed the cause of the 'non-Celtic' calculation of the date of Easter and other related matters. Thus Canon 16 refers to two issues that we know were among Adomnán's real concerns: matters connected with the legal rights of women and the so-called *Romani*/Celtic controversy of the seventh century. It is not definite proof of Adomnán's authorship but it is a clear link with matters that we know were of interest and concern to him.

The rest of the canons are mainly matters of commonsense. Some relate for example to the flesh of animals that are found dead rather than ones that are hunted or deliberately killed in farming. Distinctions are made between good meat and flesh that is carrion (putrefied or with blood still inside). Interestingly animals that are half alive because they were attacked by other animals can be eaten by 'bestial men', *bestialibus hominibus*, although the damaged bits are to be cut off and fed to the dogs. Flesh of a dead animal half-eaten by other animals is totally unclean. Likewise, 'the marrow of the bones of stags' [*medullas ossuum ceruorum*] eaten by wolves is to be rejected. Canon 20 forbids the eating of stags killed in a trap if only their legs were injured and only a small amount of their blood had flowed out leaving most of it inside their bodies. Those must be rated as carrion:

> For since the Lord has forbidden the eating of flesh with blood, what was lacking is not the cooking of the flesh but the draining of the blood; and what has been said above must be understood also of beasts that have died in extreme weakness after the cutting off or (simple) cutting of an ear. Their fat, however, and their hides we shall have for diverse uses.

4   The text has *Romanorum* which Bieler translated as 'Romans', but I have used *Romani* here as an indication of a category of opinion. The people concerned were not 'Romans' but the supporters of the 'Roman' position on the Easter etc. issues.

Swine that have eaten carrion are to be rejected unless 'this has been ejected from their intestines'. An animal that tastes the flesh or blood of, or kills, a man is to be rejected. This latter is true also of hens and their eggs, both unclean, but their chicks (*foetus*) 'may lawfully be preserved since the uncleanness of their mothers does not pollute them.' A cistern (*puteus*) that is found to have a dead animal or human in it is to be thoroughly cleaned before being used again.

> That which is contaminated by swine [defecated on?] is to be cooked, and distributed to unclean men [*inmundis hominibus*]. For swine eat things clean and unclean; but cows feed only on grass and the leaves of trees.

Anything contaminated by a defecating crow in flight (and presumably, by extension, by any flying bird) or by a leech is to be rejected. Cattle seized in a raid and offered to Christians, whether in trade or as a gift, are to be rejected: 'for the weeping of the robber's victim would seem to make void [the Christians'] alms'.

Canon number 1 sensibly says:

> Marine animals cast upon the shores, the nature of whose death we do not know, are to be taken for food in good faith, unless they are decomposed.

But Canon 14 makes the distinction that:

> Things [land animals] drowned in water are not to be eaten, since the Lord hath prohibited the eating of flesh that contains blood. For in the flesh of an animal drowned in water the blood remains coagulated. This the Lord prohibits, not because in those [biblical] days men ate raw flesh, since it would be none too sweet, but because they had been eating drowned and carrion flesh. And the Law written in metrical form says: 'Thou shalt not eat carrion flesh'.

James Houlihan warns that these injunctions are not just about 'culinary hygiene' but that they are also concerned with matters of 'spiritual pollution'. He argues that in these regulations 'Adomnán' was attempting to define 'the boundaries between man and animal ... [and] the Christian as distinct from the non-Christian [possibly the 'bestial' or 'unclean men']'.[5]

For the year 697 the Annals of Ulster has the following entry: *Adomnanus ad Hiberniam pergit & dedit Legem Inocentium populis*, 'Adomnán proceeded to Ireland [from Iona] and gave the Law of the Innocents to the people'.[6] The Law

5 *Adomnán's* Lex Innocentium, p. 104 and references there.
6 As it has come down to us the Law is written in Old Irish but the title *Lex Inocentium* used in the (admittedly fully Latin) annal entry prompts the question as to whether it might have

of the Innocents was also known from the outset as the *Cáin Adomnáin*, 'the Law of Adomnán' or 'Adomnán's Law'.[7] The law was designed to protect non-combatants – that is females, clerics and male youths – from violence and to take its enforcement under the protection and moral authority of the monastery of Iona and the *Familia Columbae*.[8] James Houlihan argues that in the Law Adomnán 'instituted a new category of person, the non-combatant' and that:

> It is reasonable to conjecture that only a significant shock, resulting from a first-hand personal encounter [with violence] ... would be sufficient, in the first instance, to instil in Adomnán his singular awareness of innocents and, second, to motivate him to undertake the exceedingly onerous task of their protection.[9]

Not too exaggeratedly, the Law of the Innocents is sometimes described as an early precursor of the Geneva Convention; nothing like it would be known from anywhere else in Western Europe for several more centuries.[10] Several modern authors have suggested that it may have been significant that the Law of Adomnán was proclaimed at a synod held in 697, what then may have been thought of (but most likely incorrectly) as the centenary of Columba's death.[11] However that is far from certain.

been composed in the latter language. As will be seen below one of its 'guarantors' was the king of the Picts suggesting that it must have been translated also into Pictish in some form, either written or (at minimum) orally.

7   It is so described multiple times in the Law itself, at least in the text as it has come down to us (see J. Houlihan, *Adomnán's Lex Innocentium*, pp 195–7) and is referred to as the *recht* [also 'law of'] *Adamnáin* (*sic*) in the early eighth-century law tract *Crith Gablach* (D. Binchy, *Crith Gablach*, p. 21).

8   M. Ní Dhonnchadha, 'Birr and the Law', pp 13–32. However, sometime later and certainly from the eleventh century the *Cáin Adomnain* (or, strictly-speaking, the *Cáin Adamnáin*) came to have a slightly different emphasis that was largely concerned with women, effectively excluding the other non-combatants – clerics and boys, who were dealt with elsewhere, as demonstrated in J. Houlihan, *Adomnán's Lex Innocentium*, passim. See chapter 8 below.

9   *Adomnán's Lex Innocentium*, pp 188–9. He suggests that Adomnán's experience must have been somewhat similar in affect to that of Henry Dunant who went on to establish the Red Cross in the 1860s.

10   J. Houlihan, *Adomnán's Lex Innocentium*. Ewan Campbell suggested recently that it was also a precursor of the UN Universal Declaration of Human Rights ('Peripheral vision', p. 24).

11   Until recently 597 was understood generally to be the year of Columba's death. D.P. Mc Carthy's revision of the chronology of the Irish annals, however, would now date that event to 593. Several modern authors have assumed that Adomnán was aware of the alleged significance of 697 as a centenary year. That claim is based to some extent on a story in the *Vita Columbae* (R. Sharpe, *Adomnán of Iona*, p. 202 and p. 346, n. 341; and see below) where Adomnán describes himself rushing back from the Synod of Birr in Ireland to be on Iona for the saint's feastday on 9 June. But the story only confirms Adomnán's awareness of the significance of the 9 June date, not that of the year.

Early medieval Ireland had a highly developed traditional native system of law and custom through which, in general, society was regulated and organized. For the most part this was similar to our modern civil law in that breaches were resolved and imbalances restored through systems of compensation rather than by punishment *per se*. Legal specialists of the time were highly regarded members of the professional and learned classes, who consequently had important status in society along with various social privileges. The arrival of Christianity, of course, introduced new forms of legal thinking, processes and law – canon law – such as the very important early eighth-century *Collectio canonum Hibernensis*.[12] A very extensive set of native law tracts – texts for the teaching and setting out of the law rather than the equivalents of the modern enactments of parliaments or suchlike – survives. The manuscripts date to the later Middle Ages but the texts of the laws themselves date from the seventh and eighth centuries.[13]

But from time to time special new laws (in the context of emergencies or newly arising issues) that were not part of traditional legal teaching were promulgated – often by clerics – that would then be approved, guaranteed and enforced by the relevant ecclesiastical and secular authorities. In Irish these laws (and, indeed, the related fines that arose from them) were known as *Cáin*.[14] Several are known or, though now lost, are known to have existed such as the: *Cáin Dar Í, Cáin Domnaig, Cáin Drochit, Cáin Éimíne Báin, Cáin Fhuithirbe, Cáin ÍarRáith, Cáin Inbir, Cáin Lánamna, Cáin Pátraic* and the *Cáin* of Aduar.[15] At the year 753, AU records that the *Lex Coluim Cille* had been promulgated by the king of Tara, Domnall Mide, and the same annals also refer to *Lex Ailbhi, Lex Brendani, Lex Ciarani, Lex Comain & Aedain* and *Lex aui Suanaich*. We know which aspects of life some of these Laws dealt with. According to the late twelfth-century commentary[16] attached to the Martyrology of Óengus, Patrick's Law dealt with the killing of clerics, Adomnán's Law (in its revised

---

12 R. Flechner, *A study, edition and translation of the Hibernensis*. The *Collectio* had an undoubted Iona connection and at least benefited from Adomnán's influence if not his actual involvement in its compilation. See M. Ní Dhonnchadh, 'Birr and the Law', p. 31.

13 The complete texts but without translation are published in the 6 vols of D. Binchy, *Corpus iuris Hibernici*. The best general introduction to the laws is F. Kelly, *A guide*, where (pp 68–79) he gives a very good description of this traditional law as it applied to women, including the *Cáin Lánamna*, which was concerned with formal marriages and cognate relationships.

14 The equivalent word in Latin is *Lex*. *Cáin* is the word used in modern Irish for 'tax'. The compound Old Irish word *síthcháin* (literally, 'peace-regulation') gives us the modern Irish *síocháin* meaning 'peace', an interesting association between the payment of taxes and the maintenance of social harmony. See M. Ní Dhonnchadha, 'Birr and the Law', p. 20.

15 M. Ní Dhonnchadha, 'The Law of Adomnán', p. 54; M. Ní Dhonnchadha, 'The guarantor-list', p. 178; E. Bhreathnach, *Ireland in the medieval world*, p. 284. For the *Cáin* of Aduar see P. Ó Riain, 'A misunderstood annal', pp 561–6. See also J. Houlihan *Adomnán's Lex Innocentium*, passim.

16 P. Ó Riain suggests this was compiled in Armagh c.1170–1174 (*Feastdays of the saints*, p. 202).

understanding) with the killing of women, Daire's (Dar Í's?) Law, apparently, dealt with the killing of cattle, and the Law of Sunday proscribed travel on the Sabbath.[17] These latter four Laws are elsewhere described as the *cethri primchána na Herend*, 'the four chief laws of Ireland'.[18] The eighth-century secular law tract *Crith Gablach*, which deals mainly with matters of secular status, tells us that the *Cáin Adomnáin* (actually *recht Adomnáin* (*sic*), Adomnan's 'law' or 'ordinance') is the kind of law that it 'is proper for a king to bind on his people', characterizing it as: 'a law of religion that inspires'.[19]

The occasion of the 'giving' of the *Lex In[n]ocentium* 'to the people' was a great gathering known as the Synod of Birr. We know that this assembly was certainly attended by the senior clergy of the country including Adomnán himself but the question of whether or not there were important lay people present also has not been decided. Several authors have pointed out that the clergy in early medieval Ireland were extremely reluctant to allow lay people attend their meetings. On the other hand, the main item for decision at Birr was going to affect lay people to a considerable degree. Along with the clerics, the list of so-called 'guarantors' of the Law includes some of the most important lay people in Ireland at the time – headed by the king of Tara – along with the king of the Picts in Scotland. But whether that reflects their attendance at the synod is not known. Notwithstanding that, Richard Sharpe characterized the event, not improbably, as a 'national assembly'.[20] However, James Houlihan provides strong arguments that the list of lay guarantors (which was apparently originally compiled without their titles or political affiliations being cited) is a roll-call of those laymen that actually did attend the gathering.[21]

Birr is in modern Co. Offaly, more-or-less in the middle of Ireland. In early medieval times it was on or close to the border between the two 'halves' (or alleged subdivisions of political interests) of Ireland known as Leth Cuinn, 'Conn's Half' to the north and Leth Moga, 'Mug's Half' to the south. It was thus a convenient and politically astute place to hold a meeting at which a matter would be discussed and a decision made relating to the whole island of Ireland, and, indeed as we will see, to the northern part of Britain.[22]

The occasion almost certainly involved various elaborate liturgical celebrations as well as secular social events, in addition to the serious religious, political and

17 W. Stokes, *The Martyrology of Oengus*, pp 210–11.
18 See J. Houlihan, *Adomnán's* Lex Innocentium, pp 157–8.
19 D. Binchy, *Crith Gablach*, p. 21.
20 R. Sharpe, *Adomnán of Iona*, p. 346.
21 J. Houlihan, *Adomnán's* Lex Innocentium, pp 117–18 and 125.
22 M. Ní Dhonnchadha, 'Birr and the Law', p. 14 and references therein, especially for that area of the midlands as the location of several other royal secular assemblies, *rígdála*. See also J. Houlihan, *Adomnán's* Lex Innocentium, pp 116–17, for additional reasons as to why Birr was an appropriate choice.

legal discussions. Where exactly in or near Birr it took place is not known but
we should probably envisage a specially erected settlement with tents and other
temporary structures such as we know to have been created for other major
ad hoc gatherings and one-off events of the sort. Birr is about 45kms from the
important monastery at Durrow, which was part of the *Familia Columbae* of
which Adomnán was the head (comarba). In fact, as outlined by Adomnán in
the *Vita Columbae*, Durrow is the only monastery in Ireland for which we have
definite evidence of its foundation by Columba. Birr was the site of an important
monastery too, said to have been founded by the very early cleric St Brendan who
is also mentioned by Adomnán in the *Vita Columbae*. In noting this reference
Pádraig Ó Riain said that it is clear from Adomnán's account that St Brendan
of Birr 'was held in high esteem by the community on Iona ...'[23] For instance
Adomnán refers to St Brendan in a story about Columba having been improperly
excommunicated 'on a charge of offences that were trivial and very pardonable',
by a synod at Tailtiu (Teltown, Co. Meath) shortly before he left Ireland for
Iona. When Columba came to the assembly (*congregationem*), however, Brendan
'rose quickly and bowed his face, and he kissed Columba reverently'. Some of
the elder clerics (*seniores*) present remonstrated with Brendan but the latter
defended Columba and claimed to have seen visions that demonstrated God's
great approval of him. The result was that the excommunication was abandoned
and, instead, Columba was 'honoured with great reverence'.[24]

We cannot be sure that it was Adomnán himself who chose Birr as the location
of the 697 synod but, if so, there must have been some allusion to poetic justice
for Columba and Brendan in the choice of venue. There may have been another
such poetic allusion to the excommunication event in terms of the timing of the
synod. In the *Vita Columbae* Adomnán tells how Columba who was on Iona at
the time became aware miraculously of the moment of Brendan's death in Birr.
That day would be commemorated from then on as his feastday, his *dies natalis*.
There is some confusion as to the exact calendar date but as Padraig Ó Riain
points out two dates in early-to-mid May are connected with Brendan: 9 and 16.
The date of the Synod of Birr may have been selected to coincide with (or at least
be close to) Brendan's feastday. It certainly seems to have taken place around that
time, in a general sense at least. A hint as to a late spring or early summer timing
may exist in the *Vita Columbae*. Richard Sharpe highlighted a story told there by
Adomnán about himself and his companions when they were returning to Iona
'in the summer season, after the meeting of the Irish synod'.[25] Almost certainly
from the context we can take it that the synod in question was the Synod of
Birr. Having reached the unidentified Scottish island of *Saine* somewhere in the

23   P. Ó Riain, *A dictionary*, p. 114.
24   Anderson & Anderson, *Adomnan's Life of Columba*, pp 468–71.
25   R. Sharpe, *Adomnán of Iona*, p. 202.

territory of Lorne, contrary winds forced them to halt their journey. They were on *Saine* on 8 June, the eve of Saint Columba's feastday, but were very anxious to be back on Iona for their founder's festival on the following day. Adomnán prayed to his predecessor and, on rising at first light on the next morning, 9 June, he found that the wind had dropped so that he and his companions could set sail back to Iona safely, arriving in time for the liturgical celebrations (for the actual text, see below). Adomnán clearly believed that the timely change in the weather had been a miracle wrought through the intervention of Saint Columba. If those events occurred on 8 and 9 June, on Adomnán's way back from the synod in Ireland, then a suggested date for the latter in mid-May, around Brendan's feastday, would not be problematic. Normally that time of year would be better for sea travel anyway.

Máirín Ní Dhonnchadha points out that one of the so-called 'guarantors' of the Law of the Innocents, St Moling, the founder of the monastery of St Mullins (Co. Carlow), whose feastday was 17 June (his death date?), died that same year.[26] It is not certain that the 'guarantors', at least all of them, were actually present at the synod. But the fact that St Mullins is only about a hundred kilometers from Birr would make it likely that St Moling was indeed present. Presumably, at the very latest, the synod had to have occurred before his demise later the same year.

The annals tell us very little other than that the Law was introduced by Adomnán in 697. A text of the Law survives in a later expanded version but, seemingly, the later material can be separated reasonably well from the original (see below). Two manuscripts survive: one from the fifteenth or sixteenth century and the other from 1627. The latter was copied on 31 March in that year by Mícheál Ó Cléirigh at the Franciscan house in Bundrowse in south Donegal from a copy made by his cousin Cúmhumhan Ó Cléirigh. Cúmhumhan's copy, which doesn't survive, ultimately derived from the 'Old Book of Raphoe', as did other texts relating to Adomnán. Mícheál Ó Cleirigh's copy is now preserved in the Bibliothèque Royale in Brussels while the earlier copy whose provenance is not clear is preserved at the Bodleian Library in Oxford.[27] A number of authors have attempted to disentangle and date the later additions from the original seventh-century text of the Law.[28]

The whole work as it has come down to us is made up of fifty-three sections or paragraphs. These were not numbered originally but were distinguished from each other by enlarged capitals and other orthographic features. The

---

26 Ní Dhonnchadha, 'Birr and the Law', pp 14–15.
27 See Ní Dhonnchadha, 'Birr and the Law', pp 15–16; J. Houlihan, *Adomnán's* Lex Innocentium, pp 119–20; and chapter 8 below
28 See, for instance, the studies cited in the bibliography by M. Ní Dhonnchadha, G. Márkus and P. Ó Néill & D. Dumville, but now superceded by J. Houlihan, *Adomnán's* Lex Innocentium, especially pp 121–39.

various modern editors and translators of the text, however, have introduced a paragraph numbering system to facilitate convenience of reference. That system will be followed here. As a complete entity the text dates to the Middle Irish period which extends roughly from 900 to 1200. Specifically, a date at the end of the tenth or beginning of the eleventh century, about 1000, has been assigned to it although it clearly draws on and reworks material of various earlier dates. It is also clear that it was composed on behalf of and probably in the Síl Lugdach church of Raphoe (see below, especially chapter 8). After detailed analysis, James Houlihan's recent research and book on the subject concludes that only sections 34 to 49 (inclusive) reflect the text of the original Law as prepared by Adomnán in 697. In addition, section 28, the list of so-called 'guarantors' of the Law and probably attendees at the Synod of Birr, is original except for the accompanying geographical and political identifications which were evidently added later (many of which are inaccurate, anachronistic or completely wrong).[29] In this chapter it is intended to deal only with the Law as originally promulgated in 697, that is, as James Houlihan expressed it, the Law 'emanating from the mind of Adomnán'[30] without the layers of accretions and associations it acquired in later centuries. The latter will be dealt with in a later chapter.

The provisions of the *Cáin* itself opens at section 34 with a formal statement:

> This is the enactment of the Law of Adomnán in Ireland and Britain: the immunity of the church of God with her *familia* [*Columbae?*] and her insignia [*a fethlaib*] and her sanctuaries [*termnaibh*] and all the property, animate and inanimate, and her law-abiding laymen with their legitimate spouses [*al-láichib dligthechaib cona cétmunteraib*] who abide by the will of Adomnán and a proper, wise and holy confessor.[31]

29 Until recently it was generally accepted that the text as we have it was composed of roughly three sections: (i) the original Law, (ii) the original guarantor-list (section 28) with the later addition of political identifications, and (iii) what was usually described as the opening Middle Irish Preface (sections 1–27). James Houlihan's analysis presents a much more nuanced division, particularly seeing sections 29 to 33 as later, as well as sections 50 to 53. These will be discussed in chapter 8 below. Houlihan's analysis also shows that along with being later these additions give the composite text a different emphasis focussing more or less on women alone (*Adomnán's Lex Innocentium*, passim). For convenience of reference the title *Cáin Adomnáin* is used here to refer to the original 697 Law and guarantor-list. *Cáin Adamnáin (sic)* refers to the later extended recension of around the year 1000.

30 Houlihan, *Adomnán's Lex Innocentium*, p. 202.

31 All the translated quotations used here and below are taken from J. Houlihan, *Adomnán's Lex Innocentium*, pp 202–5, which itself is a copy of M. Ní Dhonnchada's translation in 'The law of Adomnán', pp 57–68. The excellent translation by Gilbert Márkus has also been consulted frequently (*Adomnán's 'Law of the Innocents'*). Irish words and phrases are taken from J. Houlihan, *Adomnán's Lex Innocentium*, pp 195–7, which itself is a copy of K. Meyer, *Cáin Adamnáin*, pp 14–32.

The text continues saying that it seeks to protect 'clerics, and females, and innocent [male] youths until they are capable of [old enough for] killing a person, and of taking their place in the *túath*', that is, accepting their responsibilities as adult members of the kingdom or polity to which they belong. There then follow twelve sections or paragraphs of technical provisions for the fines and penances due for various breaches of Adomnán's Law with an indication as to where the fines must be paid.[32] Various types of killings, injuries and physical attacks (including attacks by animals) are mentioned. For example section 41 says that:

> The enactment of the Law enjoins that payment in [of?] full fines is to be made for every woman that has been killed, whether a human had a part in it, or animals or dogs or fire or a ditch or a building. For in *cáin*-law every construction [i.e., anything built that can cause injury] is to be paid for, including ditch and pit and bridge and hearth and step and pool [*lind*] and kiln and every hardship besides, if a woman should die on account of it.

Fines must be paid for the 'violent death of a woman ... including slaying and drowning and burning and poison [*neim*] and crushing and submerging and wounding by domesticated animals, and pigs and cattle'. Lesser fines are to be paid for 'non-mortal' injuries. The Law has provision for fines in the case of deaths from 'charms' [*epthai*] and in the event of the discovery of a body with 'dire mutilation and dismemberments' [*dubchrecha & chnáimchroí*] abandoned in nearby upland or wild terrain. The Law even envisages injuries inflicted by one woman on another such as 'woman-combat' (*banaugra*) and hair-pulling (*foltgabál*) between women with resulting consequent fines. But the judgment of a woman guilty of killing is to be left to providence. She is 'to be put in a boat of one paddle [*in-nói óin[s]lúaisti*] at a sea-marking ['buoy' or something along those lines?] out at sea, to [see if she will] go ashore with the winds. Judgment on her in that regard [belongs] to God.'

Not only victims and perpetrators are mentioned but witnesses and those with varying degrees of culpable responsibility. There is a provision that judges [*brithimain*] in the relevant cases are to be chosen by 'the *familia* of Adomnán' and there are rules for the feeding of the Steward [*rechtaire*] of the Law and his retinue as they travel about ensuring its enforcement and collecting the fines due to Adomnán and his successors. The Law also includes regulations concerning the holding of hostage-sureties by various monasteries and churches for guaranteeing the implementation of the Law by the secular authorities. This

32 J. Houlihan (*Adomnán's* Lex Innocentium, passim) fully examines and analyses the provisions of the Law from a legal perspective, taking into account contemporary Irish ('Brehon') law and international comparisons.

latter was a common phenomenon in other aspects of legal enforcement in early medieval Ireland. Sections 50 to 52 include provisions for dealing with different sorts of insults, sexual assaults and rape on females and denial of paternity but, as outlined above, those paragraphs date to much later than the original seventh-century *Cáin Adomnáin*.

The list of ninety-one 'guarantors' of the Law is an extraordinary roll call of virtually everyone of political importance, both clerical and lay, throughout Ireland and to a more limited extent in Scotland, at the end of the seventh century. Perhaps surprisingly it includes figures from both sides of that ultimate theological bugbear of the time, the dispute about the calculation of the date of Easter. Many commentators have pointed out that the role of Adomnán at the Synod of Birr, the enactment of the *Cáin*, and particularly the list of its supporters, is a stunning indication of the enormous prestige and eminence that he had achieved in both Irish and Scottish church circles as well as in the secular political spheres in both countries.

Máirín Ní Dhonnchadha has made a detailed study of the names included on the list and although she concluded that many, perhaps all, of the 'titles' of the individuals were added later, she could find no reason to deny that the list itself was a contemporary part of the original documentation and thus an accurate reflection of the widespread support for the law.[33] The later scribe who added the titles seems not to have been totally familiar with the history of the individuals concerned and introduces some anachronisms as well as outright errors. But, as Ní Dhonnchadha also shows, this is hardly surprising given that half of those who can be identified on the list were dead within eight years of the enactment of the Law. As we saw above, James Houlihan has recently gone even further arguing, with strong supporting circumstantial evidence, that the list is also almost certainly a record of those who attended the Synod of Birr in person.

As we have it the list is headed by Fland Febla, the sage-bishop (*suí-epscop*) of Armagh who was also comarba of Patrick and, as such, the claimant to be the head of the Christian church in Ireland. There follow the names of abbots, bishops and other clergy representing almost every, if not actually every, major church on the island: Bangor, Birr, Clonard, Clonfert, Clonmacnoise, Cloyne, Emly, Ferns, Kildare, Leighlin, Lismore, Lorrha, Lusk, St Mullins, Sletty and Terryglass, as well as some that are less well-known now. Perhaps surprisingly the churches of the *Familia Columbae* are not included but that was presumably because their support was inherent in the person of the author of the Law, Adomnán himself. Six ecclesiastics from Scotland are named. The list included the Anglo-Saxon bishop Céti or Coeddi from Iona. Two unidentified clerics who might have been Pictish are listed as is, among the secular guarantors, the king of the Picts, Bruide

---

33   M. Ní Dhonnchadha, 'The guarantor-list', passim.

son of Derile. Bruide's name is the very last of the ninety-one individuals on the list, so it is at least possible that it was added in later.

Those secular guarantors were headed by Loingsech mac Óenguso, Cenél Conaill king of Tara. He had acquired that position, the most powerful kingship in Ireland, only a year or two earlier. Several commentators have noted the significance that Adomnán's evident rise to prominence coincided with the reign of Loingsech. The king was a distant Donegal relative of Adomnán and must surely have played some role in the background manouevrings to the enactment of the Law of the Innocents and to the gathering of support for it.[34]

The list continues with the names of kings who were representative of effectively every part of Ireland. If there are gaps because some regions or individuals withheld their support, then it is very hard to see them now. All of Donegal was represented as we might expect, as were mid and east Ulster. The various constituent parts of north and south Leinster and of Munster are there, as are the midlands and Connacht. The kings of Dál Riata in both Ireland and Scotland are included as is, as we saw above, the king of the Picts. In effect the whole of Ireland, lay and clerical, was indicating its support for the promulgation of the *Caín Adomnáin*. The same was true for important representatives from much of modern Scotland.

As James Fraser pointed out, Adomnán's campaign for the protection of innocents and non-combants – women, clerics and children – on its own was not an indication that he was a pacifist or indeed a peacemaker in a modern sense.[35] Some modern commentators have tried to recruit his memory uncritically to that end. But Adomnán was a man of his time and a relative and friend of some of the most powerful (and, thus, probably most violent) kings in Britain and Ireland in his day. Indeed, he defended such kings although it seems mainly in a bid to promote order in society. Violence was an existential element of that society. Adomnán clearly accepted that reality, as indeed, at least in Adomnán's version, did his hero Columba, the Bible and, evidently, the God of that Bible that they preached about in their clerical lives.[36]

> Anyone who recognized the value of effective kingship to the extent that Adomnán did, as well as the notion that God occasionally deigns that the wicked should be killed, could not be comfortable with out-and-out pacifism as we would use that term today. After all, where God wishes for a state of war to exist in order to redress an injustice, the act of peace-mongering must become a questionable activity.[37]

34 J. Houlihan, *Adomnán's Lex Innocentium*, pp 118 and 143.
35 J. Fraser, 'Adomnán and the morality of war', especially pp 108–11.
36 See M. Enright, *Prophecy and kingship*, especially pp 157–84.
37 J. Fraser, 'Adomnán and the morality of war', pp 110–11.

In that sense the *Cáin Adomnáin* was an attempt to mitigate and constrain the violence which was, unfortunately, endemic in society in its author's time.[38] But however impressive it was in that regard, the *Cáin* was not the whole story of Adomnán. Despite the views expressed above, other aspects of Adomnán's career make it clear that he strove on many of the controversial issues of his day to find peace and harmony, and to reduce conflict. His greatest written work, the *Vita Columbae*, gives repeated proof of that. As Alfred Smyth said:

> [That] Life is an even greater witness to the gentleness of spirit and the sanctity of the writer [Adomnán] than it is for the miraculous powers of Columba.[39]

---

38 On this matter, see now also, most importantly, J. Houlihan, *Adomnán's* Lex Innocentium, passim.
39 A. Smyth, *Warlords and holy men*, p. 133.

CHAPTER FIVE

The *Vita Columbae*

As mentioned above, in the *Vita Columbae*,[1] the hagiographical Life he wrote about his predecessor and distant relative, Adomnán tells a story about his own return journey from Ireland to Iona by boat after the Synod of Birr in 697. The story is the third[2] in a sequence of anecdotes about the wind miraculously changing through the success of his prayers to St Columba.

> The third time this happened was during the summer, when I had been to the meeting of the Irish synod, and on the return journey found myself delayed for some days by contrary winds among the people of Cenél Loairn [Lorne, in south-west Scotland]. We had reached the [unidentified], island of *Saine* and the eve of St Columba's solemn feast [8 June] saw us still held up there. I was much disappointed by this, for I very much wanted to be in Iona for this joyful day. So, as on the previous occasion, I complained, saying:
>
> 'Is it your wish, O saint [Columba], that I should stay here among the lay people till tomorrow, and not spend the day of your feast [9 June] in your own church [on Iona]? It is such an easy thing for you on a day like this to change an adverse wind into a favourable one, so that I might partake of the solemn masses of your feast in your own church.'
>
> When night had passed and we rose at first light, we realized that the wind had dropped completely and we set out in the boats [*navibus*, so, apparently, not currachs, *curucis* (see above)] in still weather. Soon a south wind rose behind us, and the sailors shouted for joy and raised the sails. In this way God gave us a fast and fair voyage without the labour of rowing for St Columba's sake, so that we achieved our desire and reached the harbour of Iona after the hour of Terce [roughly 9 a.m]. So we were able to wash our hands and feet before entering the church with the brethren to celebrate together the solemn mass at the hour of Sext [12 noon], for the feast of St Columba and St Baithéne [Columba's cousin and successor as second abbot of Iona, whose feastday also fell on 9 June]. It was the same day that we had sailed all the way from *Saine* since early morning.

1   There are various editions and translations of the *Vita Columbae* most notably Anderson & Anderson, *Adomnan's Life of Columba*, and R. Sharpe, *Adomnán of Iona*. T. Charles-Edwards characterized the latter as the better translation. Below, all quoted translations are from Sharpe unless otherwise stated. Latin quotations are from Anderson & Anderson.
2   The other two are outlined above in chapter 3.

Adomnán really wanted to be back on Iona on 9 June 697. Some authors have suggested that he strongly believed that date to have been the one-hundredth anniversary of Columba's death.[3] However, the story quoted above, which is usually cited as the basis of that belief, certainly does not confirm such an understanding. We cannot be sure anyway that the custom of specially commemorating the centenary of the death of a saint was practiced by the Irish monks at that time, although it does seem likely. We know definitely that yearly anniversaries of their deaths were remembered, indeed, that was the origin and *raison d'être* of the feastdays of the saints. If Adomnán was particularly aware of the significance of the hundredth anniversary of Columba's death then the composition of the *Vita Columbae* may well have been another way in which he sought to commemorate that centenary. It was certainly written within a decade or so of 697 as its author would be dead before the end of 704 and seems to have been exceedingly busy on other matters in the final few years of his life. It is evident from the passage quoted above, however, that the text of the *Vita* was not yet finished on 9 June 697. We can be certain therefore that at least some, and perhaps most, of the work on the book was carried out between 697 and 704. The book may have taken quite a while, maybe even a few years, to complete; it certainly shows evidence of having been added to by the author subsequent to an earlier draft. Indeed, as we will see below, Mark Stansbury argues that the book was not finished by the time of the death of its author.

In an important article on the subject published almost forty years ago, Jean-Michel Picard finished by saying that 'Adomnán's primary aim [in the *Vita*] was to write what he saw as a faithful account of the life of Columba, which would serve as a model for the Christians of his [Adomnán's] time'.[4] If a centenary memorial was his intention, however, it was certainly not the only reason for writing the book; indeed there can be few books in ancient or modern times that were written for only one reason. In a slightly later article, Picard crystallized Adomnán's intentions in the *Vita* by saying that 'besides the spiritual message, its aim was to settle matters of ecclesiastical politics, namely to boost the confidence of Columba's *paruchia*, to answer Armagh's claims of supremacy [over the church in Ireland] and to defend Iona's position in Northumbria'.[5]

The very opening sentence of the book, in the first of its two prefaces, tells us that it was composed 'in response to the entreaties of the brethren', presumably in the first instance that meant the monks of Iona and the wider *Familia Columbae*

3 Although the original sources are slightly confusing, until recently 597 was accepted as the year of Columba's death. The work of D. Mc Carthy on the chronology of the Irish annals now suggests the year 593 instead.

4 See J.M. Picard, 'The purpose of Adomnán's *Vita Columbae*', p. 177 and T. Charles-Edwards, 'The structure and purpose of Adomnán's *Vita Columbae*'.

5 J.M. Picard, 'Bede, Adomnán and the writing of history', p. 60.

in Ireland and Scotland. As we will see below also, the oldest manuscript copy of the Life – now preserved in Schaffhausen in Switzerland and made shortly after the writing of the original – may have been prepared specifically for export to the Continent; most probably for the monks of the Irish monasteries connected with St Fursa in northern France and Flanders.[6] It was from that hub on the Continent also that some of the oldest material relating to St Patrick and St Brigid was in due course disseminated across western Europe. Perhaps Adomnán was aware in some way that the 'brethren' there would also welcome a Life of Columba, the third of the great Irish 'national' saints. By the end of the seventh century when Adomnán wrote the *Vita*, seminal 'Lives' of both Brigid and Patrick had already appeared: Cogitosus's Life of Brigid about 675–86, and two works about Patrick, the *Collectanea* of Tírechán dating to between 688 and 693 and Muirchú's more conventional chronological Life written about 695.[7] Columba could not be the only one of the three great saints not to have a major *Vita* composed about him.

Picard's 1982 article had already proposed a continental audience for the *Vita Columbae*. But he also stressed the importance for Adomnán of addressing the Christians of Northumbria, given the decline in that kingdom of the influence of the *Familia Columbae* following the decision against it on the Easter and tonsure questions at the Synod of Whitby in 664. Notwithstanding that, Adomnán certainly did not over-emphasize the Easter issue in the *Vita*. There is only one passing reference to the matter as follows:

> During the time that St Columba stayed as a guest at Clonmacnoise he prophesied many things by the revelation of the Holy Spirit. Among them was the great dispute that arose years later among the churches of Ireland concerning differences in the date of Easter.

Richard Sharpe said of this last sentence: 'it is especially interesting that he [Adomnán] does not put forward his own convictions [about the Easter issue]'.[8] According to Mark Stansbury, this reference to Easter in the *Vita Columbae* may have been added late in the production of the written text, and maybe even by someone other than Adomnán himself.[9]

Whatever Adomnán thought about the issue while composing the *Vita Columbae*, opposition to the monks of Iona – from where ironically Northumbria had originally acquired its Christianity – was maintained all through the latter's

6   J.M. Picard, 'Schaffhausen, Stadtbibliotek, Generalia 1', pp 66–9.
7   I am here following the dates for these texts as argued by T. Charles-Edwards, *Early Christian Ireland*, pp 438–40, with a summary on p. 440.
8   R. Sharpe, *Adomnán of Iona*, p. 262, n. 7; quotation from text p. 117.
9   M. Stansbury, 'The Schaffhausen manuscript', p. 73, especially n. 18.

abbacy and beyond, not least by the highly influential Venerable Bede. That opposition was often personified as criticism of the founder Columba. As Picard said: 'The *Vita Columbae* [was] Adomnán's answer to Northumbrian attacks on Columba.'[10] One translator went so far as to describe the *Vita* as nothing less than the 'Gospel of Colum Cille' written principally for the Northumbrians.[11]

One of the reasons why Picard and other authors have suggested that the *Vita* was definitely addressed to foreign audiences is because of what has been taken as an odd remark by Adomnán at the very beginning of the book. In the opening paragraph of the first preface, and writing in Latin, he apologizes for what will be his necessary use of Irish-language words and names in the text that follows:

> There are words here in the poor Irish [*Scotice*] language, strange names of men and people and places, names which I think are crude in comparison with the different tongues of foreign races.[12]

Picard noted that this apparent poor opinion of Irish was in direct conflict with Adomnán's actual use of the language where he 'appears to be proud of his native tongue'. I believe the phrase can be understood in two quite different, even contradictory, senses: (a) at face value but possibly sardonically, addressed to any reader not lucky enough to know the Irish language and (b) as a kind of tongue-in-cheek in-joke for his Irish readers.[13] In fact it quickly becomes apparent when proceeding to read the *Vita* that the very opposite is the real truth; Adomnán actually exults in his use of Irish, his own mother tongue.[14] In a few instances he latinized Irish words including his own name while respecting the appropriate grammar of both the Latin and Irish languages. Clearly, he could have done that more often if he really wished to exclude all the 'strange names of men and people and places'. But in a way that is very recognizably Irish, Adomnán evidently loved playing with unusual words and the variety of languages that were relevant to his theme. As Picard said:

10 'The purpose of Adomnán's *Vita Columbae*', p. 174.
11 J. Marsden, *The illustrated Columcille*, p. 181.
12 *Adomnán of Iona*, p. 103; *Adomnan's life of Columba*, p. 178.
13 The Irish have always known their place, most especially when addressing the English! The phrase has the ring of pure, distilled Irishness about it. And, of course, at that time writing in English was itself only in its infancy. Adomnán may have been rubbing in the latter point.
14 Irish would also have been the mother tongue of Dorbbéne the scribe of the oldest manuscript copy of the *Vita* and almost certainly also the language of the scribe of the original copy of the B tradition of manuscripts (see below). For the evolutionary changes in the Irish language relevant at the time as displayed in the text see A. Harvey, 'Some orthographic features', especially p. 96 and his fascinating exposition, as an example, of the context of the instructive gap left by Dorbbéne in the middle of the native name *Fech reg*.

The first preface is full of literary reminiscences which a learned insular public [in Britain and Ireland] would have recognized and which were also fashionable in monastic milieus on the Continent. At the beginning of the second preface he shows his erudition by displaying some knowledge of Greek[15] and Hebrew. These demonstrations of *urbanitas* go together with a pompous style [of language] where interlacing constructions such as 'praemisis multorum cyclis annorum' appear. This type of construction was a poetic device of classical elegiac origin which was favoured by insular authors. It was used by Columbanus [the Irish founder of such continental monasteries as Luxeuil and Bobbio, who died in 615] and Aldhelm [the famous English monk, who died in 709], especially in the letters where they wished to impress their opponents, and it was probably in the same spirit that Adomnán employed it in the *Vita Columbae*. He feels compelled to use the full battery of his art from the first pages of the *Vita* so that his [foreign] reader does not dismiss the book because of its Irish content ...[16]

Again, in the opening of the second preface and also in a very Irish fashion Adomnán can be seen to be playing with words; this time commenting on the variations of his subject's name in Hebrew, Greek and Latin: *Jona*, *Peristera* and *Columba*.[17] This section can be read as a kind of philological 'showing off' or, more positively, as Adomnán making some interesting linguistic points.

Clearly Adomnán had many reasons to write the *Vita Columbae*, a whole agenda of issues to be dealt with in its chapters. Throughout the book Columba

15 For other relevant examples of the use of that language it should be noted that on the final page of the Schaffhausen *Vita Columbae*, otherwise blank, the Our Father has been written in Greek. However, we don't know when or where it was added. Also, about 25kms north of the Raphoe area where Adomnán is likely to have been born and raised (see chapter 2 above) there is the early ecclesiastical site of Fahan where a celebrated cross-slab had a quotation in Greek carved along its northern edge. The inscription appears to be the oldest such use of Greek anywhere in western Europe. The date of the slab, which appears to have Pictish stylistic connections, is not agreed. It is sometimes suggested that it was made during Adomnán's lifetime, but it is more probable that it was carved within a few decades after his death. However, the inscribed doxology, 'Glory and honour to the Father, the Son and the Holy Spirit', was adopted at the Fourth Council of Toledo in 633. See B. Lacey, 'Fahan, Tory, Cenél nÉogain and the Picts'.

16 J.M. Picard, 'The purpose of Adomnán's *Vita Columbae*', pp 176–7.

17 The Hebrew form may have contributed to the later medieval error in the spelling of the name of Iona. As far as we know the island was referred to when Columba arrived there in the mid-sixth century by the simple name 'Í', a Gaelic word that meant 'tree' or perhaps 'yew-tree'. But when the monks began to write about the island in Latin they had to give it an adjectival form, something like 'tree island' or even 'tree-ey island'. In Latin that would have been 'Insula Iova'. At some stage an anonymous medieval monk miscopied the 'v' of 'Iova' as an 'n' and hence the erroneous name 'Iona' was born. It has remained Iona ever since, despite being evidently wrong!

is *sanctus*, 'holy' or 'saint' Columba. For Adomnán his predecessor and distant relative of a century earlier was unambiguously *Saint* Columba, on a par, at least, with the other great saints of the church such as Martin of Tours and even with some of the original apostles, not to mention some figures from the Old Testament (see below). The book gathers together all the evidence necessary for him to prove that, at least to his own satisfaction. In the *Vita Columbae*, Adomnán 'makes' the founder of Iona into one of the great saints of the universal Church, not just a local Irish or Scottish saint. Although Columba was clearly a highly influential and, most probably, a very holy man, memory of him might have faded were it not for the *Vita*. It was the *Vita*, more than anything else, which 'made' Columba into the saint that later generations would celebrate.

In the first preface of the *Vita* Adomnán forewarns his readers 'that many things worth recording about [Columba] are left out ... for the sake of brevity, and only a few things out of many are written down so as not to try the patience of those who will read them'. Nevertheless, very similarly to how a modern historian would work, the author appears to have collected, examined and referenced all the evidence available to him about his subject from both written and oral sources. If anything, he seems to have valued oral testimony more highly than written evidence, outlining in many instances the precise chain of transmission by which the various word-of-mouth stories had come down to him.

It is very unusual in the case of a medieval text that a copy more-or-less contemporary with its original time of composition has survived. This is even rarer when we know not only the identity of the author of the work but also the identity of the scribe whose copy has survived. But that is the case with the *Vita Columbae*. The oldest surviving manuscript of the *Vita* was transcribed by a cleric called Dorbbéne who asks us to pray for him in a little colophon attached to the end of the Life. He is usually identified as the Dorbbéne whose death as a senior cleric on Iona is recorded by AU for 28 October 713 (but see below, chapter 7). That Dorbbéne was a distant relative of Adomnán (and, thus also of Columba).[18] The copy that Dorbbéne made of Adomnán's *Vita Columbae* has been described as an 'almost wonderfully legible ... prestige manuscript'.[19] Dorbbéne could have made his copy while Adomnán was still alive and even have shown it to the author before his death in 704.[20] At any rate his copy was made extremely close in time to the date of the original composition of the text

18 See genealogical table 9 below.
19 A. Harvey, 'Some orthographic features', p. 90.
20 However, see M. Stansbury, 'The Schaffhausen manuscript', pp 86–7 and the diagram on p. 89, for a detailed reconstruction of how Adomnán may have worked on the text and how Dorbbéne and the contemporary initial scribe of the B tradition manuscript may have made their copies. Stansbury argues that the text of the *Vita Columbae* was not completed before Adomnán died.

of the *Vita*. The manuscript, which consists of 68 pages of goatskin parchment, each about 28cms by 21cms, is now preserved in the public library in the small town of Schaffhausen in Switzerland. That copy, and a ninth-century copy made of it, together with later briefer copies, are referred to as the A tradition manuscripts (see below, chapter 7). Three much later copies, the so-called B tradition manuscripts, also survive (see below).

The *Vita*, especially the Schaffhausen copy, is obviously a great source for the study of early medieval Latin but it also contains important evidence about the earliest written phases of the Irish language.[21] Apart from the archaeological study of the Schaffhausen manuscript itself as an object[22] there are a number of stories in the *Vita* that help us to understand how books were made and used at the time of its composition. Close study of the text tells us much about the earliest medieval involvements with writing culture and the making of texts and manuscripts. In addition to the composition of new works, such as the *Vita Columbae* and the annals, the copying of existing documents, especially biblical and liturgical texts, was one of the most important tasks in an early medieval monastery. Everything didn't always go smoothly. Adomnán tells a story about how a particularly clumsy visitor who on his arrival on Iona goes to kiss Columba and, in so doing and as predicted, upsets and spills the inkhorn that the saint was using. Another story points to the importance of proof-reading the new copies thus created, although in this instance as a result of a miracle, there was actually no need for such a check.

> One day Baithéne [Columba's successor as abbot of Iona] came to St Columba and said:
> 'I need one of the brethren to help me go through the text of the psalter I have copied and correct any mistakes.'
> The saint said to him:
> 'Why do you bring this trouble on us when there is no need? For in your copy of the psalter there is no mistake – neither one letter too many nor one too few – except that in one place the letter *i* is missing.'
> So it was. Having gone through the whole psalter, it was found to be exactly as the saint predicted.

We know that mistakes in copying were common enough in the medieval scriptoria. Many of the mistakes made then are actually extremely useful now, helping to show sometimes the relationships between separate copies and often

---

21   A. Harvey, 'Some orthographic features'.
22   For a page-by-page study, see E. Graff, 'Report on codex', pp 22–55. See also E. Campbell, 'The archaeology of writing'.

supplying information as to the date, or at least the date *post quem*, of a particular text. Adomnán himself seems to have been particularly aware of the danger of mistakes being made in the copying of manuscripts. The very last words of his text underline this:

> I beseech any who wish to copy these books [that is, the three sections or 'books' of the *Vita*], nay rather I call on them in the name of Christ, the judge of the ages, that when the copying has been done with care, they should then diligently compare what they have written with the exemplar and correct it, and they should add this injunction here at the end of what they have written.

Books would have been very valuable objects at the time and on Iona there was certainly a scriptorium for producing them and a library for containing and studying them. But a number of stories indicate that not all the books were treated with utmost reverence and ceremony, accessible only in the library or church. One story tells how a monk who was studying a book on Iona just tucked it under his arm when he got up to do some task and the volume fell into a 'butt full of water'. Another story tells how a young man fell off his horse into the River Boyne (Co. Meath).

> At the time of the fall he was carrying a leather [*pellicio*] satchel [*sacculo*] of books under his arm, which he was still clutching when the body was found so many days later. When his body was brought to the bank, the satchel was opened and the pages of all the books were found to be ruined and rotten except one page, which St Columba had written out with his own hand. This was found to be dry and in no way spoilt as though it had been all along in a book case [*scriniolo*].

The so-called B manuscripts of the *Vita* preserve a slightly different version of Adomnán's original work to that copied by Dorbbéne. The differences are minor but instructive, nevertheless. One suggestion is that Dorbbéne may have copied an early draft of the Life, whereas the B manuscripts represent a more developed later version, possibly one corrected by Adomnán himself. The best of the latter copies – B1, a late twelfth-century manuscript – came from the scriptorium of Durham cathedral where we know a devotion to Colum Cille survived into late medieval times. The other two, B2 and B3, are clearly related to B1 in terms of their text. All three are now preserved in the British Library in London. Durham cathedral from where they derive was in direct ecclesiastical descent from the formerly Columban monastery on Lindisfarne Island off the Northumbrian coast in the north-east of England. Durham inherited much of the lore and manuscript tradition of Lindisfarne. If Adomnán intended the *Vita* to be addressed, as almost certainly he did, to a Northumbrian audience then we do not know when the original exemplar of the B manuscripts arrived there. But it seems to have been after 731 when Bede's *Historia Ecclesiastica* was written. Bede shows no knowledge of the *Vita Columbae*. He makes no reference to it, even in sections of his *Historia* where almost certainly he would have used it as a source had he had access to it.

The *Vita*, which has been described as 'a stylistic and narrative experiment',[23] is set out in three sections or 'books', dealing respectively with examples of: (i) Columba's 'miraculous' powers, (ii) his 'prophetic foreknowledge', and (iii) his 'angelic visions'. Each book is divided into chapters with chapter headings that in some instances give us extra information not contained in the chapter itself.[24] Those headings were probably added at a late stage in the production of the book but were definitely Adomnán's own work. However, there are also slight differences in the headings between the A and B manuscripts.[25]

The text deals mainly with the saint's life in Iona and Scotland. Some events in Ireland are included but not to anything like the same extent. Although it certainly wasn't his intention, the incidental details of the various stories that Adomnán tells us are a rich source for understanding how daily life was carried on in the monasteries of the *Familia Columbae*.[26] Unfortunately, from our point of view, Adomnán did not write anything like a modern chronological biography or history. His only real concession to a logical timeline is in the concluding sections where he deals with Columba's death. Frustratingly he hints at topics we would like to know more about and avoids others we might consider to be of great importance. He may also have deliberately ignored any evidence that cast his subject in a bad light. Instead of a biography he compiled a work of hagiography (which, of course, was his main intention) to demonstrate, extol and venerate the spirituality of his subject. In doing so he also, evidently, demonstrated his own spirituality and even some of his political convictions and desires.

Adomnán rarely mentioned himself in the *Vita Columbae* except to communicate to his readers how he had acquired the information about a particular episode in Columba's life, or to express his belief in a 'miraculous' event that he himself had witnessed. A few such 'miracles' affecting the wind have been described already. In one episode that had occurred seventeen years before Adomnán wrote about it, he considered that Columba was responsible for the timely arrival of rain on Iona.

23   E. Graff, 'Report on the codex', p. 17.
24   For a list of these see M. Stansbury, 'The Schaffhausen manuscript', pp 76–80.
25   T. Charles-Edwards, 'The structure and purpose', pp 206–7.
26   These have been studied, in effect 'quarried', by Dr Aidan MacDonald in an extremely useful series of publications. See Bibliography and chapter 3 above.

Right through the spring a severe drought lasted unrelieved so that our fields were baked dry. It was so bad that we thought our people were threatened by the curse which the Lord imposed on those who transgressed … [We] debated what should be done and decided on this. Some of our elders should walk around the fields that had lately been ploughed and sown, carrying with them St Columba's white tunic and books which the saint had himself copied. They should hold aloft the tunic, which was the one he wore at the hour of his departure from the flesh, and shake it three times. They should open his books and read aloud from them at the Hill of the Angels, where from time to time the citizens of heaven used to be seen coming down to converse with the saint.

When all these things had been done as we decided, on the same day – wonderful to tell – the sky, which had been cloudless through the whole of March and April, was at once covered, extraordinarily quickly, with clouds rising from the sea, and heavy rain fell day and night. The thirsty ground was quenched in time, the seed germinated and in due course there was a particularly good harvest. In this way the commemoration of St Columba's name, using his tunic and his books, on that occasion, brought help to many districts and peoples in time to save their crops.

Adomnán tells another miracle story about his protection from plague, which is particularly relevant to the conditions in which we find ourselves in 2020 as this book is being written. Not only was he a witness to this 'miracle' wrought by St Columba but a personal beneficiary. He introduces the story by telling us that 'twice in our own time [the great plague] has ravaged a large part of the world.' The first time was in the 660s. The spread of that plague and the accounts of many of those who died from it are well documented in the Irish annals. The second time was in the 680s.

[T]he islands of the ocean, Ireland and Britain, have been twice ravaged by a terrible plague [*dira pestilentia*]. Everywhere [in those islands] was affected except two peoples, the population of Pictland and the Irish who lived in Britain [Dál Riata], races separated by the mountains of Druim Albain. Although neither of those peoples is without great sin [*grandia peccata*], by which the eternal judge is moved to anger, none the less to this date he has been patient and has spared them both. Surely this grace from God can only be attributed to St Columba [*gratia a deo conlata nisi sancto Columbae*]. For he founded among both peoples the monasteries where today he is still honoured on both sides …

[W]e often thank God that through the intercession of our holy patron [Columba] he has preserved us from the onslaughts of plague [*a mortalitatum invasionibus defendit*], not only at home among our islands, but also in England [*Saxonia*]. For I visited my friend [*visitantes amicum*] King Aldfrith while the plague [*pestilential*] was at its worst and many whole villages on all sides were stricken [*et multos hinc inde vicos devastante*]. But both on my first visit [in 687] ... and on my second visit two years later [in 689], though I walked in the midst of this danger of plague [*mortalitatis*], the Lord delivered me, so that not even one of my companions died nor was any of them troubled with disease [*nec aliquis ex eis aliquo molestaretur morbo*].[27]

The Schaffhausen manuscript of the *Vita* contains one lengthy quote from an older Irish source written by Cummeneus *Albus* (or Cummène *Find*, 'white').[28] The quotation is preceded in the main text by a story about how Columba had received a number of angelic visitations, and had received a blow from the angel, before being persuaded to 'ordain' Áedán mac Gabráin on Iona as king of Scottish Dál Riata. Although the exact nature of that ceremony, and whether or not it even actually took place, has been much debated by experts, some have argued that it is the earliest recorded instance in European history of the specifically Christian inauguration of a king. The story, at least, very much fitted Adomnán's agenda to see an ideal Christian kingship established in both Ireland and Britain.[29] The Cummène quote then continues with Columba prophesying that Áedán's descendants will have success as long as they do no evil to Columba or his kindred (Cenél Conaill). The 'evil' (*malum*) warned about did occur when the Dál Riata deserted their traditional allies, Cenél Conaill, for Cenél nÉogain at the battle of Mag Roth in 639. Apart from being a warning in general to kings who would read (or hear read) the *Vita*, the quote may have had a secondary purpose. As was pointed out above, the 639 alliance between the Dál Riata and Cenél nÉogain alluded to in the quote may have provided the circumstances in which king Aldfrith of Northumbria had been conceived by his Inishowen mother.

27 English translation from R. Sharpe, *Adomnán of Iona*, pp 203–4. Latin words and phrases from Anderson & Anderson, *Adomnan's Life of Columba*, pp 460, 462.
28 Cummène, who was abbot of Iona from 657 until 669, belonged to the west Donegal people, Cenél Duach, as apparently did two of his predecessors and his successor, Failbe (see table 5 above). The source of the quote is described as *in libro quem de virtutibus sancti Columbae scripsit*, 'a book that he [Cummène] wrote on the miraculous powers of Saint Columba'. Other than this quote that book no longer survives. Because the quotation does not appear in the B manuscripts it is difficult to know whether Adomnán himself intended its inclusion or if it was an addition by Dorbbéne on his own initiative. The quotation was entered in a smaller script late in the production of the manuscript, a suitable gap having been left for it when the general text was written earlier. See also M. Stansbury, 'The Schaffhausen manuscript', pp 72–6 and 81–5 for other noteworthy omissions and/or later additions possibly made by persons other than Adomnán.
29 M. Enright, 'Royal succession and abbatial prerogative in Adomnán's *Vita Columbae*'. Also M. Enright, *Prophecy and kingship*. For a critical view see R. Sharpe, *Adomnán of Iona*, pp 355–6.

Apart from the Cumméne quote, Richard Sharpe and other authors have pointed out how the Bible and existing Lives of several other great international saints were used in and clearly influenced both the way Adomnán structured the *Vita Columbae*, and in some instances his choice of language and the content of the narrative.[30] Among those models and influences were: St Benedict as depicted in the Dialogues of Gregory the Great; St Anthony as described in Evagrius's translation into Latin of Athanasius's account in Greek; and St Germanus of Auxerre as outlined in the writings of Constantius of Lyon. The greatest external literary influence on the *Vita Columbae* seems to have been the Life of St Martin of Tours written at the end of the fourth century by Sulpicius Severus. Sulpicius was influential in several other areas of early medieval Irish Christian life such as, for instance, the background to the beginning of the compilation of the annals.[31] He may even have been the real source behind one of Adomnán's less important firsts: the first appearance in history of what would become known as the Loch Ness Monster.[32] The 'monster' makes his debut in a story Adomnán tells about Columba travelling in the lands of the Picts and having to cross the River (*sic*) Ness. He saw some people burying the corpse of a man who had been savaged by a water beast. Columba astonished the onlookers by sending one of his companions to swim back across the river to fetch a boat.

> But the beast [*bilua*] was lying low on the riverbed, its appetite not so much sated as whetted for prey. It ... suddenly swam up to the surface, rushing open-mouthed with a great roar towards the man as he was swimming midstream ... [Columba] raised his holy hand and made the sign of the cross in the air, and invoking the name of God, he commanded the fierce beast [*bestiae*], saying:
> 'Go no further. Do not touch the man. Go back at once.'
> At the sound of the saint's voice, the beast fled in terror so fast one might have thought it was pulled back with ropes.

In the story the swimmer was saved, of course, and the pagan onlookers were so impressed by the miracle that 'they too magnified the God of the Christians'. A similar story to this is told about St Martin of Tours in the *Dialogi* by Sulpicius Severus. We could be forgiven for being suspicious that Adomnán didn't always think it necessary to re-invent the wheel!

Clearly any detailed consideration of the *Vita Columbae* would need to examine and assess that work's theological content. However, that is not within the competence of this author (but see chapter 12 below). Adomnán was

30 R. Sharpe, *Adomnán of Iona*, pp 57–9.
31 D.P. Mc Carthy, 'The original compilation of the Annals of Ulster', p. 84, and chapter 3 above.
32 J. Borsje, 'The monster in the River Ness'.

writing with a clear propaganda agenda and intent about his predecessor and the founder of both the monastery of Iona and the monastic federation – the *Familia Columbae* – over which he now found himself as leader. It is therefore very difficult to separate out what Adomnán himself thought about such matters from what he says were the attitudes of his subject, Columba. Are the thoughts and opinions expressed in the *Vita* really Columba's or are they, in fact, the ideas of Adomnán, or are they both – as it were indicating that Adomnán shared but wished to develop the opinions of his illustrious predecessor? For example, we might quote the very last words Columba is said to have addressed to his monks before he died, as put into his voice by Adomnán. As is evident from the words themselves, however, the first sentence of this statement, at very least, has been definitely 'edited' by the ninth abbot of Iona.

> I commend to you, my little children, these my last words: Love one another unfeignedly. Peace. If you keep this course according to the example of the holy fathers, God, who strengthens the good, will help you, and I dwelling with him shall intercede for you. He will supply not only enough for the needs of this present life, but also the eternal good things that are prepared as a reward for those who keep the Lord's commandments.

The comparison of the relationship between the ideas of Socrates and the writings of Plato, although perhaps a bit strained, has sometimes been quoted when discussing the discourse between Columba and Adomnán.

Perhaps the strongest statement about Adomnán's intentions in the *Vita Columbae* has been made by Michael Enright in his own 2013 book *Prophecy and kingship in Adomnán's 'Life of Saint Columba'*. Several other authors have pointed out how in the *Vita* Adomnán seeks to place Columba on an equal level to the great founding saints of the universal Church, and even with some of the Apostles. Enright goes further, arguing that Adomnán was really demonstrating in the stories he told that Columba was on a par with several of the great Prophets of the Old Testament, such as Moses, Samuel and Elijah. Moreover, that Adomnán was attempting to show that Columba was specifically and divinely chosen 'to impose God's will on the British Isles.' This was to be achieved by 'selecting, anointing and guiding' the kings and rulers in that society just as had been done in the case of the peoples of the Old Testament. Among the many benefits that would follow from Columba's (and or Adomnán's) guidance to those kings would be victory in battle. The Holy Land where the Old Testament narratives had been acted out was not some exotic foreign entity but, according to Adomnán, a familiar model for how life, especially kingship, should be organized in Britain and Ireland.

CHAPTER SIX

The writing of *De Locis Sanctis*

Sometime in the closing decade or so of his life, when he was already over sixty years of age at the most conservative calculation, Adomnán wrote the book *De Locis Sanctis*, 'concerning the holy places'. This is mainly an account in Latin of the sacred sites of Palestine in the early years after the Islamic conquest, together with some other related places. When he wrote the book Adomnán had been resident for a few decades already on Iona, a tiny island off a larger but still small island (Mull), off the west coast of Scotland, as 'remote' as anywhere could have been in western Europe at that time. Yet, as its editor Denis Meehan pointed out, *De Locis Sanctis* connects together elements from Celtic, Moslem, Byzantine and even Merovingian backgrounds and casts light on how people in the far Atlantic west may have imagined the world of the eastern Mediterranean from where their Christian faith had come originally. Ewan Campbell noted that:

> Adomnán was described by medieval commentators on the Continent as 'the Illustrious', the only Gael in the Middle Ages to achieve this distinction,[1] a testament to his learning which expressed itself in the *De Locis Sanctis*, which was repeatedly copied and was the standard work for many centuries (despite Adomnán never leaving these islands).[2]

The book purported to be an account of a pilgrimage to the holy places undertaken towards the end of the seventh century by a Gaulish – or, perhaps more correctly by that date, a Frankish – bishop whose name has come down to us as Arculf. The Holy Land had been conquered by the Moslems in the 630s and 640s, but no serious damage or destruction had been caused to the major Christian monuments. In addition, relatively good intercommunal relations, including a formal treaty in 678 between the Caliph Mu'awiya (named as Mauias in Adomnán's text) and the Byzantine emperor Pagonatus, facilitated continuing pilgrimage by Christians to the sacred sites. Arculf's whole journey could have taken as much as two to three years.[3] He is said to have spent about nine months in Jerusalem and perhaps another nine in Constantinople, as well as visits to other places *en route*. There have been various attempts to calculate the exact dates of his visit but, to some extent, these have been based on the

1   Campbell here references: T. O'Loughlin, 'Adomnán the illustrious', pp 1–14.
2   E. Campbell, 'Peripheral vision, p. 24.
3   D. Meehan, *Adamnan's* De Locis Sanctis, p. 19.

supposed dating of Adomnán's writing of the book, itself a matter not entirely resolved to this day (see below).

De Locis Sanctis is a fairly short book,[4] but it is also one of the relatively unfamiliar jewels of early medieval Irish culture. Not very widely known today, in fact it is one of the – if not actually *the* – oldest such works on its subject in existence, especially by an author from north-western Europe. Although the text of the book itself survives as well as some near contemporary commentary about it, nonetheless it has left a number of historical puzzles that have lasted to the present day.

The book begins:

> In the name of the Father, Son and Holy Ghost, I begin to write a book concerning the Holy Places.
>
> The holy bishop Arculf, a Gaul by race, versed in divers far-away regions, and a truthful and quite reliable witness, sojourned for nine months in the city of Jerusalem, traversing [visiting] the holy places in daily visitations. In response to my careful inquiries he dictated to me, Adomnán, this faithful and accurate record of all his experiences which is to be set out below. I first wrote it down on [wax] tablets: it will now be written succinctly on parchment.

The identity of Arculf, the 'Gaulish' bishop whom Adomnán named as his informant, has been the subject of much scholarly speculation and enquiry. The matter is still unresolved. He has been identified with a man called Arnulf or Arnoul who was bishop of Châlons-sur-Marne in northern France around the years 682–8, but this is not certain.[5] Some sceptical commentators have gone so far as to claim that Arculf didn't actually exist at all; that he was just a literary fiction invented by Adomnán to give his own imaginative account some structure and a basis of authority.[6] The latter extreme position that there was no real Arculf at all seems most unlikely as in the closing paragraph of *De Locis Sanctis* Adomnán appeals to its readers to pray for the elusive informant, definitely distinguishing the latter from himself.

> I beseech then those who will read these brief books[7] to implore divine mercy for the holy priest Arculf, who being a frequenter of the holy places, most willingly dictated to us his experiences of them. And I have set them

---

4   T. O'Loughlin has commented on *brevitas*, 'succinctness', as being a 'core value' of the 'intellectual culture' of the time ('The *De Locis Sanctis* as a liturgical text', p. 182).

5   See, however, D. Woods, 'Arculf's luggage'.

6   See, for instance, T. O'Loughlin, 'Palestine in the aftermath of the Arab conquest', pp 79, 88.

7   Adomnán divides his text into three *libellos*, 'little books'.

forth, albeit in a low style, though daily beset by laborious and almost insupportable ecclesiastical business from every quarter. Thus I admonish the reader of these experiences that he neglect not to pray [to] Christ the judge of generations on behalf of me, the writer, a wretched sinner.

A median position has been suggested also as we will see below; that is, that Adomnán read somewhere an account of travels in the eastern Mediterranean and, imaginatively, edited and rewrote it as fictional exchanges between himself and the author, the so-called 'Arculf'.

We know that at very least Adomnán did augment the 'Arculf accounts' with his own readings and extracts from other books that were available to him. In fact, the process of writing the book had at least three elements: (i) the making of notes and drawings on wax tablets from Arculf's account, whether that was spoken or written; (ii) the augmentation and sometimes the 'corrections' or alteration of the details in those notes with readings from other sources; and finally (iii) the creation of a fair copy on parchment.

The Venerable Bede, writing in his *Historia Ecclesiastica* about a quarter of a century after Adomnán's death, described how he understood the process through which *De Locis Sanctis* had come to be written.

> Adomnán also wrote a book about the Holy Places, which is most valuable to many readers. The man who dictated the information to him was Arculf, a bishop from Gaul who had visited Jerusalem to see the Holy Places. Having toured all the Promised Land, Arculf had travelled to Damascus, Constantinople, Alexandria, and many islands; but as he was returning home, his ship was driven by a violent storm on the western coast of Britain. After many adventures, he visited Christ's servant, Adomnán, who, finding him learned in the Scriptures and well acquainted with the Holy Places, was glad to welcome him and even more glad to listen to him. As a result [Adomnán] rapidly committed to writing everything of interest that Arculf said that he had seen at the Holy Places. And by this means, as I have said, he compiled a work of great value to many people, especially those who live at a great distance from the places where the patriarchs and Apostles lived, and whose only source of information about them lies in books. Adomnán presented this book [his *De Locis Sanctis*] to King Aldfrith, and through his [the king's] generosity it was circulated for lesser folk to read. The writer himself [Adomnán] was sent back to his own land richer by many gifts.[8]

---

8   L. Sherley-Price, *Bede*, p. 300.

Many modern commentators have read into Bede's account the ideas that Arculf was shipwrecked and ended up on Iona. But neither of those things was stated by either Bede or Adomnán. Following the statement quoted above Bede went on to include a couple of pages of extracts from Adomnán's book, incorporating them in the text of his own *Historia*. He concludes that section by saying:

> I have thought it useful to include these extracts from the works of the above author [Adomnán] for the benefit of those who read this history [*Historia Ecclesiastica*], and have retained the sense of his words but summarized them in a shorter form. Should anyone wish to know more about his book, they may either study it in the original form or read the abridgement containing short extracts which I have recently completed.[9]

Bede's ultimate compliment to Adomnán had been that he had made his own version and abridgment of the latter's book, also called *De Locis Sanctis*. Evidently that book by Bede had been written before the *Historia Ecclesiastica*. Denis Meehan described Bede's version as: 'really an epitome of Adomnán's work'. Bede later wrote very complimentarily about Adomnán. It is not certain but Bede may have even met the abbot of Iona when he himself was a young monk. Such a meeting could have occurred on one of Adomnán's visits to Northumbria, more specifically when he travelled to the monastery of Wearmouth/Jarrow as we know he did from a reference in a letter written by its abbot Ceolfrith about 710 (see above, chapter 3).

The principal modern editor and translator of the text of *De Locis Sanctis*, Denis Meehan,[10] unlike other commentators, was quite critical of Adomnán's Latin style[11] but was otherwise praising of the work.

> The finished product reveals its compiler as a man of relatively high critical standards, good scriptural scholarship, and painstaking accuracy in the manipulation of his material. He is careful to check Arculf's findings against the written sources at his [Adomnán's] disposal, shows a reasonably good initial acquaintance with the topography of the near east, and an enlightened interest in the significance of Greek and Hebrew nomenclature. One might naturally expect considerably more wonder and incomprehension in his descriptions of the elaborate Constantinian buildings than he actually displays. Such structures, one supposes, far transcended anything in his own physical environment or experience.

9 Ibid., p. 303.
10 Although, as is acknowledged by Meehan, Ludwig Bieler gave a lot of assistance, especially the section 'The text tradition', pp 30–4.
11 See discussion on p. 5, n. 2.

Yet, for the most part, he is remarkably matter-of-fact, and not without occasional touches of patronage.[12]

The text of *De Locis Sanctis* survives either totally or partially in over twenty medieval manuscripts scattered in various continental libraries but not, ironically, in any collection in Ireland. This relatively large number of surviving copies is an indication of the widespread reputation the text earned in the Middle Ages. Four of the manuscripts – in libraries in Brussels, Paris, Vienna and Zurich – were selected as sources for the preparation of the published text.[13] The presence of glosses in the Irish language, 'Hibernian' spellings, and other 'insular' features confirms the Irish origin for the transmission of the text. Through whatever circumstances, a copy of *De Locis Sanctis* reached northern France by the middle of the eighth century. That copy, itself later copied and recopied, is probably the origin of all the later versions that have survived.[14]

As mentioned above Adomnán's *De Locis Sanctis* is divided into three 'little books'. That division may be just a convenience, but it has been suggested that it also has symbolical meaning. Thomas O'Loughlin has pointed to the similarity with a tripartite division of the world in the Acts of the Apostles: 'in Jerusalem, in all Judea and Samaria, and to the ends of the earth'. He also highlighted the suggestion made by David Jenkins and others that early Irish monasteries were laid out like a Russian doll into areas of increasing importance and decreasing space: *sanctus*, *sanctior* and *sanctissimus* – holy, holier and holiest areas – in symbolical homage to the temple in Jerusalem.[15] We have already seen that putative division of space on the monastic island of Iona. The first book of *De Locis* is itself divided into twenty-nine short chapters[16] dealing with the city of Jerusalem and its surroundings. The second book of thirty short chapters deals with the wider Holy Land, Alexandria and the River Nile. The final book is divided into six short chapters and deals with Arculf's visit to the city of Constantinople by way of Crete, and a volcano island close to Sicily. Following a detailed study of the text, one researcher reached the conclusion that the first and third books were derived mainly from the accounts of Arculf, 'though recorded in the words of Adomnán', while the second book is based mainly on other literary sources.[17]

As well as Arculf's 'accounts', Adomnán certainly consulted other books both as a check on and to augment what he was 'told' by the Gaulish bishop.

12 On p. 6, n. 4, Meehan outlines some of what he says are displays of Adomnán's patronizing attitude.
13 L. Bieler, 'The text tradition' in D. Meehan, *Adamnan's* De Locis Sanctis, pp 30–4.
14 J.M. Picard, 'Adomnán's *Vita Columbae* and the cult of Colum Cille', p. 6.
15 'The *De Locis Sanctis*', p. 192; D. Jenkins, *Holy, holier, holiest*, passim.
16 There is some slight confusion about the division into and the number of these chapters.
17 R. Aist, 'Adomnán, Arculf and the source material', p. 163, n. 12 quoting Paul Geyer.

If his exchanges with Arculf were with a real person then there may have been other monks present as an audience as, in the text, Adomnán frequently uses plural pronouns about those occasions.[18] As he told us himself, he first wrote the accounts on wax tablets – presumably similar to those found in Springmount Bog (Co. Antrim) in 1914[19] – and later he transferred the text to parchment. Arculf is also said to have drawn rough sketch-plans of a number of the monuments for Adomnán, e.g., the round church built over the Lord's sepulchre and the Basilica on Mount Sion. Like Adomnán's notes, those plans were also drawn on wax tablets that were then reproduced in the original manuscript, with redrawn versions of the sketches included in subsequent copies.[20] Rodney Aist concluded that 'Adomnán's text stands out as the most substantial and descriptive pilgrim source [for Jerusalem] of the early Islamic period.'[21]

About one hundred sites are described or mentioned in the text. These include famous buildings, structures and relics, and natural features connected with the biblical stories. There are too many of them to rehearse here but although there are some omissions most of the main sites connected with the birth and life of Jesus, his crucifixion, burial and resurrection are covered, as also are other sites associated with biblical characters or stories from the early history of Christianity. In addition, there are some descriptions of ceremonies and natural events that were deemed to be 'miraculous'. Not all of the latter can be taken at face value. As an example, one such event is described as follows.

> On the twelfth day of the month of September, he [Arculf] says, there is an annual custom whereby a huge concourse of people from various nations everywhere is wont to come together in Jerusalem to do business by mutual buying and selling. Consequently it happens inevitably that crowds of different peoples are lodged in this hospitable city for some days. Owing to the very great number of their camels, horses, asses, and oxen, all carriers of divers merchandise, filth from their discharges [animal dung] spreads everywhere throughout the city streets, the stench proving no little annoyance to the citizens, and walking being impeded. Wonderful to relate, on the night of the day on which the said bands depart with their various beasts of burden, there is released from the clouds an immense downpour of rain, which descends on the city, and renders it clean of dirt by purging away all the abominable filth from the streets.[22]

18 D. Meehan, *Adamnan's* De Locis Sanctis, p. 12, n. 1.

19 The 6 Springmount tablets, dated roughly to *c*.600 and inscribed with sections of the Psalms, are held in the National Museum of Ireland.

20 Adomnán's book must be one of the earliest northern European works to use technical illustrations in this way. See D. Meehan, *Adamnan's* De Locis Sanctis, opposite pp 47 and 63.

21 R. Aist, 'Adomnán, Arculf and the source material', p. 166.

22 D. Meehan, *Adamnan's* De Locis Sanctis, pp 40–3.

Adomnán, who describes this downpour as the 'baptism of Jerusalem' (*Hierusolimitatanum baptizationem*), goes on to describe how the situation of the city on a slope meant that the floods cannot lie but are swept immediately out to the Kidron valley. The 'eternal father' would 'not suffer' Jerusalem to be dirty for long 'out of reverence for his only begotten son, who has the honoured places of his holy cross and resurrection within the compass of its walls.' The rain then stops as miraculously as it began.

As interesting as is this traveller's tale from Arculf, it is really based, as Rodney Aist has demonstrated,[23] on a misunderstanding of the events surrounding the festival of *Encaenia Ecclesiae* established to commemorate the original dedication on 13 September AD 335 of the church of the Holy Sepulchre. But Adomnán's account nowhere indicates that the event he partially and misleadingly describes was essentially a religious occasion. The real annual festival began on the evening of 12 September and lasted for eight days. Among its components were a market and the administering of the sacrament of baptism, otherwise normally reserved to the Christmas and Easter periods. Just as Adomnán said, the festival would certainly have had an international character as clergy, especially bishops, busy at home with services at Christmas and Easter, would have been free to travel to Jerusalem for the *Encaenia*, which was unique to that city. But the need for Adomnán's flood to follow gravity out of the washed and cleaned city forces him to make a number of mistakes about its physical layout. Notwithstanding these errors, Rodney Aist also points out that Adomnán's account has been used by those involved in the modern restoration of the Holy Sepulchre as well as (sometimes incorrectly) by those studying the archaeology of early Christian period Jerusalem.[24]

A similar indication of how it was believed that God bestows special favours on Jerusalem occurs in the story of a high column where a young man who had died came back to life.

> It is remarkable how this column (which is situated in the place where the dead youth came to life when the cross of the Lord was placed upon him) fails to cast a shadow at midday during the Summer solstice ... this column, which the sunlight surrounds on all sides blazing directly down on it during the midday hours (when at the Summer solstice the sun stands in the centre of the heavens), proves Jerusalem to be situated at the centre of the world ... that is Jerusalem, which is said to be in the centre of the earth and its navel [*umbilicus*].[25]

23 R. Aist, 'Adomnán, Arculf and the source material', pp 174–80.
24 R. Aist, 'Adomnán, Arculf and the source material', pp 162–2, especially notes 9 and 10.
25 D. Meehan, *Adamnan's De Locis Sanctis*, p. 57.

Adomnán is justly entitled to the reputation that he was the 'first' or the 'best' etc., in a number of different situations. Another such unexpected entitlement is that through the pages of *De Locis Sanctis* he may have been the first person to introduce to the English the character who became the patron saint of their country, St George of England. In the final 'book' of *De Locis* he recounts at somewhat greater length than normal Arculf's 'account' of hearing a number of stories, legends, in Constantinople about George the confessor. As Denis Meehan says the account by Adomnán:

> appears to be the earliest account of George in any northern [European] source; and it seems quite possible that the cult of the saint in Britain really begins with Celtic influence in Northumbria. Notice of George appears in other [later] Irish sources[26] ... it was doubtless pilgrims such as Arculf who popularized the cult ...
>
> The first indications of [the] George-cult in strictly English sources appear in Northumbria. He is not mentioned by Bede [in the *Historia Ecclesiastica*], but is commemorated in the early-tenth-century Durham Ritual ... The Council of Oxford in 1222 ordered the feast of St George be kept as a national festival; but it was not until the fourteenth century under Edward III that he became the official patron.[27]

We know from Bede that Adomnán gave a copy of his *De Locis Sanctis* to Aldfrith king of Northumbria 'through [whose] generosity it was circulated for lesser folk to read.' We also know that Durham cathedral mentioned above was the direct institutional descendant of the original Columban monastery on Lindisfarne and had inherited many of the latter's traditions, relics and manuscripts. If Ireland's patron saint, Patrick, was a 'gift' from the British, it seems only right that in return the English patron saint should be a 'gift' from the Irish. Adomnán may well have been the vehicle![28]

So where, when and why did Adomnán compose *De Locis Sanctis*, and when did he give the copy to King Aldfrith? Until recently those questions seemed relatively easy to answer although the main source used for that purpose, Bede's *Historia Ecclesiastica*, seemed to contain a number of puzzles that will be returned to below. We know from his own words in the *Vita Columbae* that Adomnán visited the king in Northumbria on two occasions: in 687 according to the annals and again two years later. So one or other of those visits must have been the occasion for his presentation of the book to the king and, obviously

---

26 Meehan lists several at this point; and see below for George among the lists of 'cursing' saints connected with Adomnán.
27 D. Meehan, *Adamnan's* De Locis Sanctis, pp 111–13, n. 1.
28 But if so, probably by way of the writings of 'Arculf'. See D. Woods, 'Arculf's luggage', and D. Woods, 'On the circumstances of Adomnán's composition'.

therefore, the text had to be written before that. In addition, Adomnán was abbot of Iona and that's where he lived from 679 onward at least. Iona was also most certainly where he composed the *Vita Columbae*; logically, that's where he most likely also composed *De Locis Sanctis*. So confident were several commentators about these matters that, among other things, they used the various additional literary references in that text as a guide to what books, besides those used for the *Vita Columbae*, might have been available in the monastic library on Iona in Adomnán's time.[29]

However, an article by David Woods (referred to previously) challenged all of the points made above.[30] Woods argued that although Adomnán did tell us about only two visits to Northumbria in the *Vita Columbae* up to the time of his writing of it, and that the Irish annals are slightly divided as to whether there was one or two visits, and that Bede tells us about only one visit, there is no need to assume that these reports were all referring to the same journeys or that these were Adomnán's only visits. On that basis and citing some other evidence, largely drawing on the chronology set out by Bede but which had been missed by most previous authors,[31] Woods concluded, as a few others had previously done more tentatively, that Adomnán must have made another visit to Northumbria a few years before his death in 704, probably about the year 702. Woods's interpretation, as well as other things, removes all the chronological difficulties, for example, as to how long Adomnán would have been in dispute with his own monks in Iona concerning the Easter question (see chapter 3 above).

Further, Woods argued that as *De Locis Sanctis* itself tells us nothing about the whereabouts or circumstances of its composition, but that as Bede is both familiar with and highly praising of the text, a monastic library in Northumbria may have been the place of its composition and a visit there by Adomnán about 702 the occasion. It follows then that it would have been also on that occasion that Adomnán presented a copy of the book to King Aldfrith. Finally, drawing on his previous publications on the subject Woods concluded that Adomnán never met Arculf (or whatever the latter's real name was) in the flesh. But he did do so in the form of reading a manuscript 'collection of topographical descriptions and miracle stories' by him which he, Adomnán, had found in a Northumbrian library. That manuscript, according to Woods, was Adomnán's

29 See, for instance, Clancy & Márkus, *Iona; the earliest poetry*, pp 211–22; T. O'Loughlin, 'The library of Iona'.

30 'On the circumstances of Adomnán's composition of the *De Locis Sanctis*'. See also D. Woods, 'Arculf's luggage'.

31 But see J.M. Picard, 'The purpose of Adomnán's *Vita Columbae*', p. 160, where he notes scepticism of the 'traditional' understanding of Bede by authorities such as William Reeves, Charles Plummer and Ludwig Bieler.

main source, to which he added additional material derived from other literary compilations.[32]

Finally, the purpose as to why Adomnán wrote *De Locis Sanctis* has been debated often. As has been seen above, as a set of traveller's tales it makes for what we'd now call a 'good read', like a sort of much earlier version of Marco Polo's travels. But early medieval texts almost always, if not always, had a purpose beyond the outlining of their ostensible subject. Thomas O'Loughlin in a series of articles and books has argued that *De Locis Sanctis* is principally a work of exegesis designed to help the readers of the Scriptures, especially in liturgical contexts, to understand and navigate their way through the topography of the Holy Land in order to reach a deeper appreciation of the Bible stories.

> We can read [*De Locis Sanctis*] as a liturgical text: a guide to those places where Christians can enter the world of the holy and whose *virtus* [grace?] can be extended to those who cannot physically visit them, by letting them hear of them and experience them at a distance. Just as a relic could become the bearer of the spiritual *virtus* of a place or object over physical and temporal distance; so within the liturgy a *narratio* [story?] can fulfill the same role and [*De Locis Sanctis*] contains many such *narrationes*.[33]

Notwithstanding this, David Woods, arguing that *De Locis Sanctis* was written in Northumbria around the same time as Adomnán's conversion to the 'Roman' system of dating Easter,[34] suggested a more personal reason for its composition.

> He [Adomnán] had just been forced to humiliate himself and his community by admitting that their use of the traditional Irish eighty-four-year Easter table was in error. It is arguable, therefore, that the composition of [*De Locis Sanctis*] was an implicit defence both of his learning in particular and of that of the Irish church. It proved that he, and the Irish church more generally, were still capable of works of valuable scholarship despite their previous error, as the English would have it ... . It was also an implicit defence of the true catholicism of the Irish church. They were not an inward- or backward-looking church, but were as much concerned with the Holy Land, for example, as anyone else ... [I]t is possible to detect

32 This interpretation does, indeed, raise questions about the published lists of alleged books in the Iona library as was mentioned above, although everything we know about Iona confirms that it must have had a substantial book collection.

33 T. O'Loughlin, 'The *De Locis Sanctis* as a liturgical text', pp 182–3 and references cited therein.

34 But for a recent article favouring the traditional view that this took place during one of Adomnán's journeys to Northumbria in the 680s, see C. Ireland, 'Lutting of Lindisfarne' (forthcoming).

a more positive purpose behind his final selection of material [in the third book of the trio] and the focus on Constantinople in particular. This focus is best explained as a reaction to the English emphasis on Rome. It was a subtle reminder that old Rome had been replaced by New Rome, that the first Christian emperor had founded Constantinople, and that he had done so in response to divine revelation. Old Rome had enjoyed no such favour. In short, it was a reminder of the precariousness of human claims to authority, and, most importantly, that there was more to the world than Rome.[35]

In other words, *De Locis Sanctis* was a kind of gentle manifesto. But Constantinople was not the primary focus of Adomnán's book; there may be an additional purpose behind its emphasis on the sacred city of Jerusalem. For the past few decades there has been a growing appreciation that

> Adomnán ... was a key figure in developing the notion of a monastery as a metaphor for Jerusalem, both as it had been in the past (as the site of incidents in the life of Jesus), the present (the layout, shrines, relics and rituals associated with the Church of the Holy Sepulchre) and the future (salvation in the heavenly Jerusalem).[36]

Campbell and Maldonado go on to highlight Adomnán's role 'in developing ideas of the monastery as an earthly manifestation of the heavenly Jerusalem in his *De Locis Sanctis* and in his *Vita Columbae*' and further argue that for Adomnán 'the layout and structures associated with the Church of the Holy Sepulchre was a more influential model at Iona.'[37] Referring to the traditional pilgrim route leading from the landing place at Martyr's Bay to the cathedral (site of the original monastery) on Iona, which incorporates the ancient Sràid nan Marbh, Campbell and Maldonado say:

> The devotional landscape of Iona can also be interpreted more generally as representing a journey towards salvation, with the monastery being seen as a metaphor for both earthly and heavenly Jerusalem. The route mimics the journey of pilgrims to the Church of the Holy Sepulchre in Jerusalem, with the objective of reaching the holiest places on the island, St Columba's [burial] shrine and the altar of the church.[38]

---

35 D. Woods, 'On the circumstances', pp 203–4
36 Campbell & Maldonado, 'A new Jerusalem', p. 35.
37 Ibid., p. 37.
38 Ibid., p. 57.

Using an idealized plan of the layout of Jerusalem in the vicinity of the Holy Sepulchre as envisaged by Adomnán in *De Locis Sanctis* (both in the text and on the accompanying sketch-plan)[39] Campbell and Maldonado show the almost certainly deliberate parallels in the layout of the monastery on Iona.[40] Although at least some of the elements of the plan would not be realized until long after his death (such as the carving of the major high-crosses) it seems that to add to his other multifaceted enterprises Adomnán was also engaging in a version of town- or (more correctly) monastery-planning.

> What is also becoming apparent is that the layout and internal organization of monastic Iona was both a deliberate act to recreate a mirror of Jerusalem based on biblical exegesis and travellers' accounts, while at the same time allowing the construction of new physical structures for new devotional practices, including bounding enclosures, a paved road, stations of pilgrimage based on impressive stone crosses, stone-built shrine chapels and decorated reliquaries.[41]

It appears that in *De Locis Sanctis* Adomnán was laying out the ground as the 'architect' behind that plan.

Like his earlier work, the *Vita Columbae*, *De Locis Sanctis* would be copied extensively on the Continent throughout the Middle Ages and, indeed, in Thomas O'Loughlin's words 'used [as] a basis for other works'.[42] Within two years of the scenario outlined here, Adomnán would be dead. His afterlife, however, was going to be as interesting as his actual life. The real historical Adomnán was about to be transformed into a somewhat fictionalized St Adamnán.[43]

---

39 D. Meehan, *Adamnan's* De Locis Sanctis, facing p. 47.
40 Campbell & Maldonado, 'A new Jerusalem', p. 75.
41 Campbell & Maldonado, 'A new Jerusalem', p. 77.
42 T. O'Loughlin, 'Adomnán: a man of many parts', p. 48. See also T. O'Loughlin, 'The diffusion of Adomnán's *De Locis Sanctis*'.
43 Most references to him after his death use the form of his name with a middle 'a'. This has given rise to the modern forms Adhamhnán in Irish and Eunan in English.

PART TWO

Adomnán's posthumous life

CHAPTER SEVEN

After Adomnán

Adomnán died in 704, almost certainly on 23 September, the day later celebrated as his feastday as a saint. We have historical evidence that during his life he had been a monk, a priest, an abbot, a comarba of Colum Cille – that is, primate and president of the Columban monastic federation in Ireland and northern Britain. He had also been an administrator, a manager, a sailor, a writer, a historian, a hagiographer, a geographer, a monastery planner, a scholar, a jurist, a poet (?), a visionary, a diplomat and ambassador. He was a politician, a multi-linguist, a proponent of the Irish language, a defender of the Irish against the criticisms of the English of his time, and several other things. He was what I think we can unapologetically describe as a very decent and humane 'Donegal' man. He was obviously well-respected in his lifetime by a huge range of his contemporaries from many walks of life and across a range of nationalities, political, ethnic and linguistic divisions. He was also about to be remembered as a 'saint'. To be blunt: Adomnán would have been, undoubtedly, a hard act to follow!

From shortly after his death the process of turning him into 'St Adamnán' was begun. As was typical of such enterprises in early medieval times a great deal of exaggeration and fictionalization would be employed to extend and expand his reputation, a reputation which, genuinely, didn't actually need any of what we would now call 'spinning'.

According to AU, CS and Tig he was 77 years of age when he died but, as we saw above (chapter 2), that in itself may have been a symbolic fiction. The Fragmentary Annals contrary to all other sources says he was 'in the eighty-third year of his age'. Those annals survive in only one seventeenth-century manuscript, preserved in Brussels. Not much is known about how it came to be composed although its modern editor suggested 'tentatively' that based on an emphasis on Iona and, indeed, also on Adomnán, at least substantial parts of it seem to have been associated with the Columban monastery in Durrow (Co. Offaly).[1] The Fragmentary Annals text is made up of what appear to be genuinely contemporary or near contemporary annalistic entries and long legendary accounts of events that seem to be rooted in 'history' but are otherwise fictionalized if not completely far-fetched. The notice about Adomnán's death follows immediately after one of those long entries. In turn that long entry is preceded by a shorter entry on the death of Adomnán's friend, King Aldfrith

1   J. Radner, *Fragmentary Annals*, p. xxxiii.

of Northumbria, there described by his Irish name Flann Fína and as *dalta Adamnáin*, 'Adomnan's pupil' or 'foster-son'. The long entry has a fictionalized and totally unhistorical account of Adomnán's connection with the Easter controversy. The account compresses time in utter contradiction of what we know from the more reliable historical sources. This is not 'history', but falsified hagiography.

> In this year [704] the men of Ireland accepted a single regulation and rule [*aonsmacht & aoinriagail*] from Adamnán, regarding the celebration of Easter on Sunday, the fourteenth of the moon [*esga*] of April, and regarding the wearing of Peter's tonsure [*coronugh*] by all the clergy of Ireland; for there had been great disturbance in Ireland until then, that is, many of the Irish clergy were celebrating Easter on Sunday, the fourteenth of the moon of April, and were wearing the tonsure of Peter the Apostle, following Patrick [*ar sliocht Phatricc*]. Many others, however, were following [*ag secheamh*] Colum Cille, celebrating Easter on the fourteenth of the moon of April no matter on which day of the week the fourteenth happened to fall, and wearing the tonsure of Simon Magus [*Simoin Druadh*]. A third group was not in accord with either the followers of Patrick or those of Colum Cille. So the clergy of Ireland used to hold many synods [*seanadha*]. And this is how those clerics used to come to the synods: with their people, so that there used to be battle challenges, and many slain among them; and many evils came to Ireland on that account, i.e. the great cattle murrain [*bóár mór*], and the vast famine [*an gorta romhór*], and many plagues [*teadhmanna iomdha*], and foreigners destroying Ireland. It was like that for a long time, that is, until the time of Adamnán. He was the ninth abbot of Iona after Colum Cille.[2]
>
> ... And as Bede tells it in Bede's History [*Stair Bhéid*], most of the bishops of all Europe gathered to condemn Adamnán for celebrating Easter according to [*ar sliocht*] Colum Cille and for wearing the tonsure of Simon Magus (that is, from ear to ear).[3] Bede says that there were many wise men in that synod, and that Adamnán exceeded them all in wisdom and eloquence. Adamnán said that it was not in imitation [of Simon Magus] that he wore that tonsure, but it was rather in imitation of John the Beloved [*Iohannis Bruinne*, (literally) 'John of the Breast'], pupil of the Saviour, and that was the tonsure he had worn; and that though his saviour was beloved [*annsa*] to Peter, John was beloved to the Saviour; and that it

---

2   Actually the eighth. He was the ninth abbot, but that included Columba as the first.

3   The tonsure *ar sliocht Coluim Cille* was triangular or delta-shaped. See D.P. Mc Carthy, 'Representations of tonsure in the Book of Kells'.

was on the fourteenth of the moon of April, whatever day of the week it might be, that the apostles celebrated Easter.

Then an old man, a *seanóir*, persuaded Adomnán to adopt the 'Roman' rule on Easter and the tonsure.

'Let yourself be tonsured, then,' said the bishops.

'It is sufficient,' said Adamnán '[that it be done] at my own monastery.'

'No,' they said, 'but at once.' Adamnán was tonsured then, and no greater honour has been given to a man than that which was accorded to Adamnán then, and that large booty [*an bhrad mór*] was surrendered to him, and he proceeded to his own monastery, Iona.

His congregation [*coimthionól*] was greatly amazed to see him with that tonsure. He was always urging the congregation to adopt the tonsure, and he could not get their consent. But God permitted the community to sin, that is, to expel that Adamnán who had compassion for Ireland. This is what Bede says; for Bede was with Adamnán while he was in England. After that Adamnán came to Ireland [from Iona], and he proclaimed that [rule] in Ireland, and that single regulation for Easter and the tonsure was not accepted from him until this year.

In contradiction of the above, but closer to the historical truth, a few lines down the Fragmentary Annals under the year 718 record that: 'the community [*muintir*] of Iona adopted the tonsure of Peter the Apostle; for until that time they had worn the tonsure of Simon Magus, as Colum Cille had worn it himself' (see below). It is not known when the original of the long account above was written but evidently it dates to later than the completion of Bede's *Historia Ecclesiastica* in 731. The text also exhibits evidence of much of the later confusion about the final years of Adomnán and his alleged dispute with his monks on Iona.

Following Adomnán's death, one of the first major requirements would have been the election of a successor, a new abbot for Iona. The incumbent of that position was, *ex officio*, also *Comarba Coluim Cille* or head of the *Familia Columbae*. But it appears that Adomnán's conversion to the Roman or 'canonical' calculation of the date of Easter may have complicated the matter of his successor and successors. As many authors have pointed out, the record of the appointments of Iona abbots over the next two decades is very confusing and raises many questions about the contemporary state of affairs in that monastery and its wider associations.[4] The record appears to show several overlaps and even

4   M. Herbert, *Iona, Kells and Derry*, pp 57–9.

duplications in the appointment of abbots and other leading officials of the monastery and the *Familia*. Some historians have suggested that this confusion in the record (although almost certainly not only in the record but in actual events also) arises because the monks chosen as abbots etc. were aged or ill and, once in office, only lived a short time after their appointments. Others suggest that the confusion is a reflection of the continuing internal controversies regarding the Easter date issue. That hypothesis suggests that the monks were divided into opposing 'parties' on the matter and that there were probably rival candidates for the offices, some of whom supported the traditional Iona, or so-called 'Celtic', view and others who were more in tune with the 'Roman' canonical position, the position held by Adomnán himself by the time of his death.[5] The implication is that there must have been, in effect, a major split in the *Familia Columbae* on the issue. But so confusing is the partial record and the various attempts at understanding it that one leading expert, Richard Sharpe, was moved to remark: 'Rather than conjecture a schism, we should admit that it is impossible to interpret how the abbacy was occupied during this period.'[6]

It is very difficult to construct a clear narrative about these matters from the Irish annals which, we must remember, for that time derive from the chronicle kept on Iona itself. But part of the modern confusion also derives from the account of the lead up to those events given in his *Historia Ecclesiastica* by Bede. Perhaps however, as we saw above, it is truer to say now that much of the confusion arises more from the incorrect assumptions and misinterpretations by some modern scholars of what Bede actually wrote (see chapter 6 above). In his 2010 article already referred to David Woods seemed to brilliantly resolve many if not all of the chronological problems and contradictions by postulating that Adomnán must have made a third apparently undocumented visit to Northumbria about 702. In that interpretation it would have been on the *c.*702 visit that Adomnán finally changed his own mind on the Easter and tonsure issues. But, having returned to Iona shortly afterwards, he failed to convince the monks there. Instead, he travelled on to Ireland where he had a lot more success and where he 'observed the canonical Easter' in 703 and or 704. Later he returned to Iona, well before the Easter of 705, but died there probably on 23 September 704.

Apart from its general historical importance the Woods interpretation helps us to understand the confusion regarding the office of abbot of Iona following

5   For a discussion of these issues see R. Sharpe, *Adomnán of Iona*, pp 74–5. For a less complicated explanation, see T. Clancy, 'Diarmait *Sapientissimus*', p. 221. More recently James Fraser suggested that work pressure may have resulted in a splitting of responsibilities, e.g., separating the office of abbot of Iona from that of administering the wider *familia*, or parts of it (*From Caledonia*, pp 260–2).

6   R. Sharpe, *Adomnán of Iona*, p. 75.

Adomnán's death. One of the figures who occupied that office – or perhaps the office of bishop on Iona, or perhaps both – was Dorbbéne, seemingly the same man who made the Schaffhausen copy of the *Vita Columbae*. The reason for the confusion about Dorbbéne's role on Iona is because of the words in the obituary for him, the only time the annals actually refer to him. Although much later in date, Tig and AU are understood now to most faithfully copy and represent the actuality of the original entries in the Iona Chronicle (which, itself, does not survive). As it happens (and fairly unusually) both sets of annals have an effectively identical entry about Dorbbéne's death in 713; that is, both seem to reflect a consensus of what the Iona Chronicle actually said originally.

> *Dorbeni kathedram Iae obtenuit & .u. mensibus peractis in primatu, .u. Kl. Nouimbris die Sabbati obiit.*

> Dorbbéne obtained the abbacy[?] of Iona, and after five months in the primacy he died on Saturday, the fifth of the kalends of November [28 October].

Confusion arises because the word *kathedram* although translated above as 'abbot' more realistically suggests the 'see' or office of bishop, while the word *primatu* in the second phrase in the sentence suggests principal authority or 'abbot'.[7] To compound matters, in the previous year the same annals, and again almost identically, had noted the death of Coeddi (one of the 'guarantors' of the *Cáin Adomnáin*) who was unambiguously 'bishop [*episcopus/espoc*] of Iona'. As no other intervening bishop is mentioned, the implication seems to be that Dorbbéne succeeded Coeddi in that office. This is only a small part of the confusion surrounding the leadership of Iona and of the *Familia Columbae* around that time. According to David Woods:

> In so far as the annals depict an unprecedentedly rapid and complicated succession of abbots at Iona between 704 and 724, they seem to indicate that the community went through some sort of crisis of leadership during this period. At best, if one assumes that there was never more than one abbot at a time, and that Dorbbéne was appointed bishop of Iona rather than abbot in 713, then the community had five different abbots in quick succession during this period ... This was hardly due to old age or illness in every case, and so suggests some deeper crisis. The most plausible explanation is that the community was deeply split on the Easter question,

---

7   There has been much debate among scholars in modern times about the respective authority of abbots and bishops in early Irish monasteries. For a detailed discussion of this issue, see, for instance, C. Etchingham, *Church organization in Ireland, AD 650–1000*.

and that a succession of abbots resigned in exasperation as they failed to resolve this issue or, indeed, were forced to resign as the feeling within the community swayed first one way, then the other ... A worse case scenario would see rival factions elect two different abbots for part of the period 704–724 at least, an almost unavoidable conclusion if we accept that Dorbénne was actually abbot rather than bishop in 713. Yet, even if we cannot reconstruct the exact dates and circumstances of the succession, there was clearly a crisis of some sort, and the Easter controversy seems to be the only matter which could have provoked it at this period. The important point here is that this is exactly the sort of evidence for a crisis that one would have expected to find for a much earlier period if Adomnán had indeed converted to the Roman position by the mid-680s. The fact that this evidence occurs so late, suggests that Adomnán's change of heart on this issue was itself late [*c.*702], exactly as implied by Bede's location of it in his narrative.[8]

With all this long-lasting controversy about the Easter and tonsure matters – before, during and after his abbacy of Iona – it might be presumed that Adomnán himself would have written something substantial about it. However, if he did mention it, and that is a big 'if', he certainly didn't overemphasize it. As we saw in the last chapter David Woods suggested that, in a subtle challenge to the English emphasis on the canonical Easter as emanating from Rome, in *De Locis Sanctis* Adomnán chose to highlight the glories of Constantinople as a

> reminder that old Rome had been replaced by New Rome [that is, Constantinople], that the first Christian emperor had founded Constantinople, and that he had done so in response to divine revelation. Old Rome had enjoyed no such favour.[9]

As a further indication that Adomnán was not passionately driven about the Easter issue, one way or the other, in contrast apparently to Bede's obsession with the matter, there is only one reference to the controversy in the *Vita Columbae*, and that is just in passing. As we saw in Chapter 5, Mark Stansbury queries whether even that modest reference was written by Adomnán. According to Stansbury that reference occurs in what he called the additional 'authenticating sentences', that is, material that was 'stitched' into the narrative of the *Vita* at a late stage in its production and, maybe, by someone other than Adomnán himself.[10] So we have no proof that even this brief reference to the Easter controversy was written

8   D. Woods, 'On the circumstances', pp 197–8.
9   Ibid., pp 203–4.
10 M. Stansbury, 'The Schaffhausen manuscript', p. 73, especially n. 18.

by Adomnán. Indeed, somewhat suggestive of external interference in support of an agenda about this matter, Stansbury goes on to say that several of what he has identified as the late 'post-Adomnán changes [to the *Vita*] ... seem designed to position the saint [that is, Columba] (and, by extension, his Iona community) in the political struggles of the late-seventh and early-eighth centuries.'[11]

The Dorbbéne of the annals died on 28 October 713. Although absolute certainty is impossible for those early medieval times he is usually and logically identified with the person who includes his name in a short colophon in Latin at the very end of the Schaffhausen manuscript of Adomnán's *Vita Columbae*, indicating that he was its scribe:

> Whoever may read these books about St Columba's miraculous powers, pray to God for me Dorbbéne [*Dorbbeneo*] that after death I may have life eternal.

Dorbbéne is a very rare name in early Irish contexts.[12] But peculiarly it occurs again in the annals for 716 also in connection with Iona. As AU says:

> Faelchú, son of Dorbbéne, in the 74th[13] year of his age assumed the see [*kathedram*, 'bishopric'?] of Columba on Saturday the fourth of the kalends of September [29 August].

Given the rarity of the name and the closeness of the references to two of them in the annals, it would be natural to assume that Faelchú was the 'son' of the Dorbbéne who died in 713. However, they are given quite different pedigrees in the (apparently tenth-century?) genealogies of abbots of Iona in the Book of Lecan.[14] The pedigrees even have the appropriate number of generations, placing Faelchú correctly in the generation after Dorbbéne. However improbable that there should have been two different men with the extremely rare name of Dorbbéne, both of whom were associated with Iona in a very short space of time, that is exactly what the genealogies indicate, further demonstrating that they both belonged to the same generation (Table 9). Although the second Dorbbéne's connection with Iona is shown only as indirect – that is, as the father

---

11 M. Stansbury, 'The Schaffhausen manuscript', p. 87.

12 It is not to be found for example in such comprehensive lists of medieval Irish names as the indexes to M. O'Brien, *Corpus genealogiarum Hiberniae*, or N. Ó Muraíle, *The Great Book of Irish Genealogies*. The only instance in AFM is the 713 death as above. But see a few related references in DIL, p. 354.

13 The Tig entry is almost identical but says '*lxxx.uii. etatis [sue] anno ...*', i.e. 87 years of age. Either age estimate could be a copying error, so it is not clear which is correct.

14 See M. Herbert, *Iona, Kells and Derry*, pp 36–7. Also P. Ó Riain, *Corpus genealogiarum sanctorum Hiberniae*, p. 54: 342; p. 55: 343.

of the holder of the *kathedra* – it must nevertheless throw some doubt on the exact identity of the scribe of the Schaffhausen manuscript.

Table 9: Alleged genealogical relationships of the two Dorbbénes with Adomnán

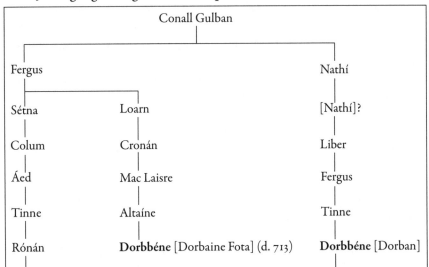

Whichever of those Dorbbénes (or, in the very unlikely event, some other) was actually the scribe of the Schaffhausen copy of Adomnán's *Vita Columbae*, his manuscript left Iona and was transferred to continental Europe where it engendered its own fascinating history.[15] It is still preserved in the town library of Schaffhausen in Switzerland where it had arrived by the end of the eighteenth century. It formerly belonged to the nearby monastery of Reichenau on an island in Lake Constance and, prior to that, to a series of continental monasteries that had various Irish connections. Almost certainly, it had been taken to the Continent in the eighth century, but it took some time to reach Reichenau. From the close examination of details, such as for instance the copying and transmission of errors, peculiar spellings etc., we can say that Dorbbéne's manuscript was also the source of all the other copies and abridgments of the *Vita Columbae* made on the Continent in later medieval times. Jean-Michel Picard has outlined the travels and adventures of that manuscript and of the copies made from it. He thought that it might have been brought from Iona to

---

15 See below, chapter 12. J.M. Picard, 'Schaffhausen, Stadtbibliotek, Generalia 1', gives a full account of the history of the manuscript on the Continent in so far as it is known, from early medieval times right through to the twentieth century.

the Continent very shortly after it was finished, almost definitely at some point in the eighth century.[16] He suggested that it may have been taken originally to one or other of the monasteries associated with the Irish Saint Fursa in northern France and Belgium, such as Peronne or Fosses. It may even have been brought there as a result of a specific request for a copy from one of those monasteries where the cult of Saint Columba was already known. The most likely link between those various institutions might have been the monastery of Louth in Ireland, with which both Iona and Peronne had close associations. Other material relating to Adomnán and Iona seems to have passed to the Continent by way of these monasteries also. A study of the provenance and context of the mid-ninth-century copy of the Dorbbéne manuscript from the monastery of St-Mihiel in Lorraine, France, also suggests that there was a connection with the Peronne or Fosses area, a region in which Irish monks of the period were particularly active. The cult of Saint Columba was also known in the Metz area of Lorraine. However, around Metz there seems to have been some confusion with Saint Columbanus, arising from the fact that the latter had actually visited that area in 610. About 980, or maybe a little later, a new version of Adomnán's *Vita Columbae* was produced in Metz. This is a shortened version which contains only about a sixth of the original text. However, unlike other abbreviated versions where a great deal of the Irish material, especially Irish personal and place-names, is deleted, the Metz version was clearly written by an educated Irish person. Professor Picard has shown, for example, that the person in question was fully familiar with the changes that had taken place in the Irish language between Adomnán's time and his own, particularly the changes that had occurred in the writing of names. It is also clear that instead of the St Mihiel copy of the *Vita* mentioned above, the compiler of the Metz version used as his exemplar a text closer to Dorbbéne's copy, possibly even that manuscript itself. In turn, the Metz version was copied later into manuscripts of the eleventh, twelfth and thirteenth centuries although, again, there was frequent confusion with St Columbanus.

A shortened version of the *Vita Columbae*, dating to the twelfth and thirteenth centuries but also based ultimately on the Dorbbéne copy, circulated in north-eastern France in the Cambrai and St-Omer region. That version was later attributed inaccurately to Cumméne, the seventh abbot of Iona who had died in 669. In fact, as we saw, Cumméne had written a study in Latin which Adomnán refers to as 'the book on the miraculous powers of Saint Columba', but that is not the text that circulated in the Cambrai and St Omer region. As we saw above,

---

16 However, that view has been challenged by T. Clancy ('Diarmait *sapientissimus*', pp 228–9), who argues that it may have been brought in the middle of the ninth century to the monastery of Sankt Gallen or St Gall (in Switzerland) by the then abbot of Iona, Diarmait.

a quotation from Cumméne's book, the only portion that actually does survive, was inserted into Dorbbéne's copy of the *Vita Columbae*, apparently on Iona, after that text had otherwise been effectively completed. An appropriate gap had been left in the original text for the Cumméne quotation to be inserted later. Evidently, it was written by the same scribe as the main text but in much smaller lettering.

A greatly shortened copy of the *Vita Columbae* was also produced at the monastery of Sankt Gallen in Switzerland between 850 and 870, by which stage Dorbbéne's manuscript had reached that region. The Sankt Gallen text was later copied and circulated very widely in Europe throughout the whole of the Middle Ages. But that version had concentrated mainly on the miraculous deeds of the saint and largely ignored details about Iona and Ireland. As Professor Picard pointed out, even proper personal names and place-names were deleted from that text being seen as having little or no interest or relevance for its non-Irish and non-Scottish continental readership. The Dorbbéne manuscript was still at Sankt Gallen in the 890s when it was used by another German monk, Notker Balbulus, in the compilation of his martyrology. Balbulus gives a full entry on Saint Columba or Colum Cille as he also calls him, quoting liberally from Adomnán's *Vita Columbae*. Professor Picard tells us that Dorbbéne's manuscript remained at Sankt Gallen in the mid-to-late tenth century but that sometime between then and the thirteenth century it was acquired by the monastery at Reichenau.[17]

By 716 the Easter issue seems to have been largely settled or at least on its way to being settled on Iona. For that year the annals record that the date of 'Easter is changed in the monastery of Iona'.[18] Bede tells us that:

> the most reverend and holy father, Bishop Egbert, an Englishman, who had spent many years of exile in Ireland for the love of Christ, and was most learned in the scriptures, and renowned for lifelong holiness came [to Iona] and corrected their error.

Bede describes what happened, using the opportunity to praise the Irish for bringing the knowledge of Christ to the (Anglo-Saxon) English and simultaneously condemning the Britons, the ancient Celtic-speaking inhabitants (what we now know as the ancestors of the Welsh), for not being as generous with their knowledge.

17   J.M. Picard, 'Schaffhausen, Stadtbibliotek, Generalia 1', pp 62–3.
18   Incidentally in both AU and Tig that information is immediately followed by the appointment of Faelchú son of Dorbbéne as discussed above. Two years later (in 718) Tig and CS record that the canonical tonsure was accepted on Iona. See E. James, 'Bede and the tonsure question'. For the shape of the rejected tonsure see D.P. Mc Carthy, 'Representations of tonsure in the Book of Kells'.

Being a very persuasive teacher who carefully practiced what he taught, Egbert was listened to by all, and by his continual, pious preachings he drew them [the monks of Iona] away from the obsolete traditions of their forefathers ... This occurred through a wonderful manifestation of God's grace, so that the [Irish] nation which had willingly and generously laboured to pass on its own knowledge of God to the English nation might later, through that very same English nation, come to the correct knowledge [of the Easter issue etc.] which they had not previously possessed. In contrast the Britons, who had not shared their knowledge of Christ's Faith with the English, continue even now [i.e., up to 731], when the English nation does believe, and is fully instructed in the teachings of the Catholic Faith, to be stubborn and crippled with error, going about with their heads incorrectly tonsured, and keeping Christ's [Easter] ceremonies without unity with the Christian church.

Bede goes on to tell us that Egbert remained a further thirteen years on Iona and died there, paradoxically, on Easter Sunday (according to the Roman calculation), 24 April 729. We could be forgiven for being a bit sceptical about Bede, evidently *parti-pris* in this matter, who may have overemphasized the role of the Englishman Egbert in bringing the Irish monks around to the correct practices at issue. Indeed, it seems likely that he may have overemphasized the importance of the Easter and tonsure issues themselves, in the first place. Prof. Picard has shown how Bede's text, especially because it was entitled a *Historia*, has tended to be taken at face value as a superior account of what happened as opposed, for instance, to the ideas conveyed in the openly hagiographical work of Adomnán.[19] The norm among modern historians was to have accepted Bede's account uncritically as if he was one of their own, that is, an objective historian in the contemporary sense instead of a cleric with a very deliberate sectional view and set agenda. While the Easter and tonsure issues had clearly been of importance to Adomnán, evidently he was not obsessed by them as was Bede, who still felt passionately about those matters as late as 731, long after they had been settled for the most part. Unlike the negative language of the latter, Adomnán's approach to the necessary changes seems to have been guided by a sense of respect for tradition and tolerance of difference.

According to AU for 727 'the relics of Adomnán [*Adomnani reliquie*] were brought over to Ireland [from Iona] and the Law [of Adomnán was] promulgated anew [*renovatur*].' Adomnán was dead almost a quarter of a century by then. One explanantion of this event is that even by that early date Adomnán himself was being treated as a saint, with his relics being exhibited as objects of veneration

---

19   J.M. Picard, 'Bede, Adomnán, and the writing of history'.

and devotion. However, the wording of the entry is slightly ambiguous: were the relics in question associated with Adomnán himself, sacred objects specifically connected with him, or were they the relics of other saints as collected together by Adomnán and in that sense 'his'? A note and an accompanying poem in an early sixteenth-century Ó Cléirigh manuscript (and, more briefly earlier, in the mid-twelfth-century Book of Leinster) purports to resolve the matter. The poem, known as *A maccáin na sruith* (see below) but sometimes also referred to as *Scrín Adamnáin*, 'Adamnán's Shrine-box', is attributed, impossibly of course, to Adomnán.

> Illustrious was the man Adamnán; great was his love towards God and towards his neighbour. By him the great relics of the saints were assembled in a single shrine [*mór-martra noeb i n-oen-scrín*], and that was the shrine which Cíllíne Droichtheach mac Díochlocha [the southern Uí Néill abbot of Iona, *c.*726–52] conveyed to Ireland to make intercession of peace [*do dénam sid ocus attaic*] between Cenél Conaill and Cenél nEógain.[20]

Earlier for that same year, 727, before the entry in the annals about the relics, AU had recorded a major battle between Cenél Conaill and Cenél nEogain. This was part of an ongoing war between those two Donegal polities that lasted for about a century and which would be resolved finally in the latter's favour at the battle of Clóitech in 789.[21] Whatever their nature, the relics in question remained away from Iona for about three years because for 730 AU records: 'the return of the relics of Adomnán [*Adomnani*] from Ireland in the month of October'.

We cannot be certain of course that the two things, relics and battle in 727, were connected. There is a gap of over four hundred years between the events and the earliest surviving explanation of a connection between them, but it does seem both possible and probable. At any rate, whenever the process commenced, Adomnán would eventually come to be treated fully as a saint himself, although not without a few cosmetic additions as the 'campaign' for that title progressed.

The note about the relics quoted above continues with the following phrase introducing the related poem: 'This then is the enumeration of the relics as Adamnán said'. The poem is addressed *A maccáin na sruith* which is translated as to the 'Lad of sages' but, as it was composed in the voice of Adomnán, the intention was probably something more along the lines of the 'father' abbot

---

20   L. Gwynn, 'The Reliquary of Adamnan', pp 204 and 208; W. Stokes, *Martyrology of Oengus*, pp 210–11.

21   The issue is complicated and will not be pursued further here, but see Lacey, *CC*, passim but especially pp 258–309; R. Sharpe, *Adomnán of Iona*, p. 77. See also W. Stokes, *Martyrology of Óengus*, p. 211.

speaking to his monastic 'son'. The language of the poem dates to the eleventh or twelfth centuries. Its editor, Lucius Gwynn, thought that its nineteen verses had no great literary merit but, at very least, the organization of the names of the diverse relics into rhyming quatrains is itself a clever literary feat. The *maccáin* is warned to be careful when carrying the bag (*in tíag*) that contains the relics. But the warning was evidently metaphorical, as we will see it would have been something of a miracle itself for a single bag to have held them all. Here the poem has been compressed and only the names of the relics are listed:

> A Gospel book; a piece of the Virgin Mary's clothing stitched by herself; a covering (cloth) that belonged to the King's son (Jesus) with his blood on it; the *sanctum sanctorum*? ('holy of holies'?); a piece of the tree on which St Paul was slain; a faggot of the tree (cross) on which Christ was crucified; the girdle (*saer-criss*) of Paul, the first Christian hermit; St Martin's cloak (*brat*); St Patrick's tooth; a tooth of Declan of Ardmore (Co. Waterford); tresses (*folt*) of the Virgin Mary's hair; St Brigid's hairshirt (*fesléne*); Senach of Clonard's cloak (*casol*); Senán of Scattery Island's cloak (*casol*); a stone (*cloch*) from Molua's island; a rib (*asnao*) from Finán Cam's body (a saint of Kinnity, Co. Offaly); the mantle (*cassal*) of Enda of Árainn; the kneecap (*almu*) of St Donnán of Eigg in Scotland; the shoulder blade (*guala*) of Colmán mac Crimhthainn; St Columba of Iona's tunic (*cnesléne*); St Brendan's lay? (*laidh*); the skull (*mullach*) of Mochuda of Lismore (Co. Waterford); the skull of Mochóe of Antrim; the skull of Mochaemhóc (St Kevin of Glendalough); the cloak (*brat*) of Cainneach (of Kilkenny); the cloth (*in t-éduch*) of Bairre (of Iona?).

It may need to be pointed out that this list derives from a poem composed many centuries after the event to which it purports to refer. It is not at all necessary to accept that this is an accurate list of the actual relics brought to Ireland from Iona in 727, although it probably reflects the general nature of what was believed to have been the origins of the objects in question.

The year after the relics left Ireland, 731, the annals record the death of another Adomnán, the bishop of Ráith Maige Aenaig in Donegal. A number of suggestions have been made as to the location of Ráith Maige Aenaig. Arguments for Raymoghy near the east shore of Lough Swilly are often put forward but almost certainly it was at Rateen, a site in east Donegal above the Swillyburn stream as it neared its junction with the Foyle, about nine kilometers north-east of Raphoe.[22] The later twelfth-century additional scholia or notes attached to the main part of the Martyrology of Óengus claim that: *Adamnan .i.*

---

22 B. Lacey, 'The church of Ráith Maige Oenaig'; Lacey, *CC*, pp 124–6.

diminutiuum a nomine quod est Adam, 'Adamnán i.e. a diminutive of the name Adam'. That may have been partly true of the spelling *Adamnán* but not for *Adomnán*. As we saw above the name Adomnán came from the Old Irish root word *omun/omna*, 'terror' or 'fear'. But wherever the misunderstanding derived from, it came to be accepted, both for the abbot of Iona and bishop Adomnán of Ráith Maige Aenaig, that their names had actually been Adamnán,[23] as we will see in the next chapter. On the surface there appears to be no connection between those two Adomnáns but, as we will see also, the identities of both seem to have been retrospectively combined in the creation of a new saint – Adamnán (*sic*) of Raphoe.

23 The matter was further confused in modern times. The Mac Airt and Mac Niocaill 1983 edition and translation of the Annals of Ulster gives the original Latin text as 'Adomnanus episcopus Ratho Maighe Oinaigh [pausauit]'. But in the translation, Adomnán's name, which clearly has a middle 'o', is rendered as 'Adamnán' (*sic*) with a middle 'a'.

CHAPTER EIGHT

St Adamnán and Raphoe

The ancient church of Raphoe situated amidst the richly fertile agricultural lands of east Donegal is especially associated with Adomnán in his characterization as a saint – Adamnán – although it is not claimed that he was its founder. He continues to be honoured, however, as the patron saint of the diocese of Raphoe, established originally in the early twelfth century, for both the Protestant Church of Ireland and the Roman Catholic Church.[1] How and when did Adomnán become thought of as a saint? Unlike the current process of canonization in the Catholic church, which began to be formalized about the eleventh century, a saint in the early church was 'made' by popular acclamation, urged on no doubt by the individual's close followers, supporters and families. He or she was in essence a local religious hero and champion. By virtue of his extraordinary career and achievements, however, Adomnán was much more than that, he was a national and even an international religious hero.

During his lifetime Adomnán was clearly thought very highly of in both Ireland and northern Britain. This must have been particularly true among the monks of his own *Familia Columbae*, despite the fact that, apparently, the majority of them had disagreed with him in his last years about the Easter controversy. That issue was settled however on Iona and among most of the monks of the *Familia Columbae*, at least officially, in 716.[2] Without any doubt objects associated with Adomnán and writings about him must have been preserved in the monastery on Iona. When those objects would have begun to be thought of formally as relics is not known but it is likely that this happened relatively soon and maybe immediately after his death. Neither do we know when the bits and pieces of biographical information preserved there were turned into a formal

1   The Church of Ireland cathedral is located in the small market town of Raphoe, the original centre of the diocese and from where it takes its name. This relatively small building is in part medieval (especially some of its decorative features) with an attached ecclesiastical court that is the only survivor of its type in Ireland. For a description of the medieval elements see Lacy, *Archaeological survey*, pp 284–6 and P. Harbison, 'The biblical iconography', pp 271–3. It is dedicated to Adomnán although using the modern forms of his name: Adhamhnán in Irish, Eunan in English. The magnificent Catholic cathedral (1890–1900) of the diocese is located in the principal town in Donegal, Letterkenny, and is dedicated to St Eunan and (appropriately) St Columba. However, the addition of the latter dedication is a modern innovation.

2   But see D.P. Mc Carthy for ongoing opposition on the matter as much as a century later: '[The monastery of] Kells [Co. Meath] was rather a new, independent, and reactionary foundation committed to maintaining those doctrinal ideals of Columba [on the Easter and tonsure issues] that had been abandoned in Iona' ('The illustration and text on the Book of Kells, folio 114RV', p. 32). See also D.P. Mc Carthy, 'Representations of tonsure'.

137

hagiographical Life. That would have been composed originally on Iona in Latin and, arguably, parts of it still survive as fossilized elements in what is known as the Breviary of Aberdeen (see below). But, effectively, the only hagiographical Life we have of Adomnán is the problematic mid-tenth-century *Betha Adamnáin* in Irish. That text will be discussed further below (chapter 9), but it is worth saying at this stage that it contains little if anything relating to Adomnán's actual historical life and no mention of his connection, real or otherwise, with Raphoe.

Whenever precisely it happened, Adomnán was eventually recognized as a saint and, as we will see below (chapter 11), many churches were specifically dedicated to him in both Ireland and Scotland (and the Isle of Man), including a number known as *Scrín Adomnáin* or 'Adomnán's Shrine'. Perhaps the oldest formal recognition we have of his being treated as a saint is the quatrain for him under 23 September in the main body of the Martyrology of Óengus.

Do Adamnán Íae	To Adamnán of Iona,
assa tóidlech tóiden,	whose troop [followers?] appears to blaze(?)
ro ír Ísu úasal	noble Jesus has granted
sóerad mbúan mban nGóidel.	full freedom for the women of the Gaels.[3]

The Martyrology of Óengus has been dated by Pádraig Ó Riain to between the years 829 and 833. It may just be a coincidence, but those dates are only a few decades after what will be described below as the real foundation date of the monastery of Raphoe, the main church in Ireland with which Adomnán was associated.

That association is itself problematic and, from a modern point of view, perhaps somewhat puzzling. Raphoe is only twenty-five kilometres south-east of the Gartan area, the undoubted birthplace of Columba or Colum Cille, who normally trumped all other saints in Donegal. But Raphoe is in the centre of an area of much better and richer agricultural land.[4] Very importantly, it was also located on a significant medieval boundary that survives to the present as the border in this area between the diocese of Derry and the diocese of Raphoe (see below). That diocesan boundary reflects a more ancient border, which almost certainly formed part of the line agreed between the Síl Lugdach and Cenél nÉogain following their division of the former Cenél Conaill lands north of Barnesmore in the aftermath of the battle of Clóitech in 789. The same border may have had an even more ancient incarnation as the boundary in the early

---

3 Text in Irish: W. Stokes, *Martyrology of Oengus*, p. 196. Translation by this author after Stokes.
4 The small district known as Gartan is a sort of island of good land, a 'garden', surrounded by poorer land on the edge of the mountainous and rocky bogland area of central Donegal.

sixth century between Cenél Conaill and Cenél nÉnnai,[5] the people to whom Adomnán's father and mother belonged respectively.

By the early and mid-twelfth century when the dioceses were being established and fine-tuned all over Ireland, Derry (which then would have been thought of as very much a part of Donegal) had, as it were, cornered the market on Columba.[6] In the middle of the twelfth century the Middle Irish Life of Columba was composed in Derry as a propaganda statement outlining the claims of that church to have been founded by Columba/Colum Cille as his first and thus best loved church. That claim was almost certainly false, but it was believed and continues to be believed to the present day. Although Derry was not confirmed as a diocesan centre for another hundred years or so, until the middle of the thirteenth century and then under the patronage of St Eoghan of Ardstraw, it managed to hold on to its position as the chief centre of devotion to Columba in Ireland throughout the later Middle Ages.[7] Those complications and twists arose from the influence of contemporary secular politics on medieval ecclesiastical administration and geography, but they leave a number of puzzles for us in the present.

As it happens, the earliest, alleged, narrative description of the foundation of Raphoe also occurs in the Middle Irish Life of Colum Cille. As mentioned above, that was a Derry propaganda document; in fact, it was the text of a sermon for preaching on Columba's feastday, 9 June. The Life has been dated by Máire Herbert to the period 1150–82, and probably before 1169.[8]

> Afterwards Colum Cille founded Raphoe. It was there that he revived the carpenter [*saer*] who had been drowned in the mill-pond [*llind in mulind*]. In Raphoe, also, when his community [*muintirsium*] lacked a ploughshare [*socc*], he blessed the hands of the little lad who was beside him. The latter, who was named Fergna, made the ploughshare, and was an expert smith [*heolach goibnechta*] from that time onwards because of Colum Cille's blessing.[9]

Without adding anything to help explain what they mean, those two episodes – the reference to the carpenter and separately to Fergna – are repeated at slightly greater length in Manus Ó Domnaill's *Betha Colaim Chille* of 1532.

5   Lacey, *CC*, pp 122–3.
6   In the mid-twelfth-century Derry propaganda text, the Middle Irish Life of Colmcille, Kilmacrenan is a notable exception in the saint's alleged tour of Ireland founding churches. Kilmacrenan, close to Gartan, had formerly been a major centre for the promotion of the saint's cult. Its absence from the Life may reflect some hostility or even jealousy about this on the part of the apologists for Derry.
7   B. Lacey, *Medieval and monastic Derry*, p. 106.
8   M. Herbert, *Iona, Kells and Derry*, pp 188–93.
9   Ibid., p. 257.

Colum Cille founded and blessed the monastery of Raphoe after that. And a craftsman who was building a mill in that settlement was drowned in his own mill-pond [*lind an muilinn*]. When this was told to Colum Cille, he went to the body which had been taken from the pond and fell on his knees praying earnestly to God to revive the craftsman for him. When he had finished praying, Colum Cille rose up confidently and made a sign of the cross with his staff on the chest of the craftsman, telling him to rise up alive in the name of Jesus Christ. At Colum Cille's word the craftsman got up straightaway, just as he would from sleep ...

Another time when Colum Cille was in Raphoe a coulter of the plough [*iarand na seisrighe*] was lost by the ploughman. Colum Cille blessed the hand of a lad called Fergna that was with him, who never before had done any blacksmith work, and asked him to make a coulter [*iaraind*] in place of the one that was lost. Fergna did it as well as if he had been always at that sort of work up to then. He became a master smith from then on by virtue of Colum Cille's blessing.[10]

We don't know what the references to the 'carpenter' and the 'little lad' actually meant but they may have figured in background explanatory tales for some relics or monuments in Raphoe that the twelfth-century Derry writer was acquainted with. Below we will see a somewhat earlier reference to a significant 'bath' in Raphoe. The 'bath' could have been what is here referred to as a 'mill-pond', and which may have been believed to have had healing properties as a result of Columba's alleged miracle there. In addition, the area is extremely good farming land and ploughing would have been a significant local activity. Perhaps there was a special coulter that for some reason was recognized as a relic and had rituals associated with it that would 'guarantee' successful ploughing in the area. However, there could be many other explanations for the prominence given to these two 'miracles'.

In the absence of other contemporary or near contemporary evidence, it has to be said that little or no reliance can be placed on these stories about the foundation of the church of Raphoe by Columba. The earliest date for those stories is about six hundred years after the events they purport to describe. The Middle Irish Life, for example, also gives Columba the role of founder of the monastery of Derry although such contemporary evidence as we have does not support that identification.[11] Somewhat more ambiguously the same Life also involves the saint in the establishment of the monastery at Kells (Co. Meath) although we know that this was not founded until between the years 804 and

10 Trans.: B. Lacey, *The Life of Colum Cille*, p. 55; Irish text: A. O'Kelleher & G. Schoepperle, *Betha Colaim Chille: Life of Columcille*, pp 84 and 86.
11 B. Lacey, *Medieval and monastic Derry*, pp 25–37.

807, over two hundred years after Columba's death. It is not inconceivable that Columba (or Adomnán) could have founded a church in the Raphoe area, which was relatively close to where both of them may have grown up but, if they did, no historical or archaeological evidence for it has come to light so far. It will be argued below that the church of Raphoe is unlikely to have existed in any sense for more than two hundred years after Columba's death or about a hundred years after Adomnán's death.

There is no historical evidence that the monastery of Raphoe had been founded as early as the dates of either Colum Cille or Adomnán, although that in itself cannot be taken as proof that it did not exist during the lifetime of either of them. The 'battle of *Both*', which according to Tig was fought in 630 between the victorious Suibne Menn son of Fiachna of the Cenél nÉogain of Inishowen and the defeated Domnall mac Áedo of the Cenél Conaill, may have been fought in the vicinity of Raphoe, Ráith Both.[12] If that was the case then the 630 mention of *Both* seems to be the earliest reference we have to what would become Raphoe. The vicinity of Raphoe would have been an appropriate location for an encounter between those two opposing Donegal kingdoms. Indeed, the 'rath' of Ráith Both (Raphoe) may have been, in origin, a secular hillfort-type monument of some sort, although there is no hard evidence for that.

Raphoe lies in an area of exceptional archaeological, historical, legendary and mythological interest.[13] Although there has hardly been any archaeological study of the layout of the town itself, which is dominated now by the design of the early seventeenth-century Ulster Plantation settlement, the possibility is sometimes suggested that the streetscape and neighbouring field boundaries do preserve some elements of the plan of the ancient monastic enclosure.[14] In addition, the adjacent landscape, extending to the River Finn ten kilometers to the east, is extraordinarily rich in archaeological remains of all periods, from the first arrival of humans in Ireland in the Mesolithic period onwards. The area is extremely fertile and is drained by a network of navigable rivers – the Finn, Foyle and Mourne – that, ultimately, lead out to (or, more importantly in this context, lead in from) the Atlantic Ocean. The economic surplus that would

---

12 Lacey, *CC*, pp 220–1. Raphoe is only about 8kms south-east of Lough Swilly, which would have provided a direct water highway for an assault on Cenél Conaill by Cenél nÉogain coming from Inishowen. Such a scenario would have been similar to Suibne Menn's victory over Domnall's brother Máel Cobo at the battle of Sliab Tuath in 613, which attack, likewise, almost certainly came from the sea (Lacey, *CC*, p. 216).

13 Lacey, *CC*, pp 131–41. See also B. Lacey, 'The "Bend of the Finn": an archaeological landscape in east Donegal'.

14 A. Spears, 'Vestiges of ancient Raphoe'. See also the reference in T. Ó Canann, 'Máel Coba Ua Gallchobair' (p. 41 and pp 67–8, n. 86), for the pre-seventeenth-century ownership by the church stewards of Raphoe of the townland of Muntertinny, 4kms north-west of Raphoe cathedral, the presumed site of the early ecclesiastical enclosure.

have been generated in the area by such abundant natural resources ensured that its inhabitants were always among the richest and thus politically most powerful people in Donegal. Although the seventeenth-century Plantations of English and Scottish colonists caused an immense cultural shift, with consequent damage and destruction of earlier archaeological structures and undoubted loss of cultural memory, the area still has a remarkable collection of major archaeological sites and monuments such as the Beltany Stone Circle and the passage-tomb cemetery and other features on and surrounding Croghan Hill.[15]

In early historic times this area, centred on the lower valley of the River Finn, was known as Mag nItha, 'the plain of Ith'. Ith was a mythical character said to have been one of the earliest humans to arrive in Ireland.[16] The simple translation of *Mag* (Latin, *campus*) is 'plain', but as we saw above it appears normally to have been used to indicate something greater. In place-names it seems that it was applied to well-cultivated areas of farmed land in contrast to the untamed areas of woods, mountains and bogs,[17] and, by extension, to the polities located on such lands. Such a description fits very well with the fertile landscape of Mag nItha.

The area occupied by the town of Raphoe, at a slightly higher altitude than much of the surrounding land, looks out over Mag nItha, although originally it was probably just outside the exact limits of what constituted that *mag*. In the sixth century Mag nItha was the original homeland of Cenél Conaill, the people who gave their name (in the form: Tír Chonaill) to most of Co. Donegal (although the Inishowen peninsula was thought of as a separate territory), and to which both Columba and Adomnán belonged. The early to mid-sixth-century boundary to the north of Cenél Conaill was probably the now relatively insignificant stream known as the Swillyburn, which, originating in a fairly dramatic waterfall,[18] flows to the south and east sides of Raphoe, leaving it outside the original Cenél Conaill territory. The Swillyburn continues in a north-eastern direction eventually widening and flowing into the River Foyle north of Lifford. For some of its route the Swillyburn is still, significantly, the boundary between the diocese of Derry and the diocese of Raphoe. Although those dioceses were not established until the twelfth century, it seems that this boundary may be a lot older going back originally to the sixth century (and earlier?), and continually reused in later times as we saw above. It is not very obvious now but the medieval church at Raphoe was (and, in ecclesiastical terms, still is) located on an important political border.

15 B. Lacy et al., *Archaeological survey of County Donegal*, pp 36–7, 72–3 and 113–15 and references therein to other sites in the area; now online at Archaeology.ie. Also B. Lacey, 'The "Bend of the Finn".

16 E. Gwynn, *The Metrical Dindshenchas*, pp 90–3.

17 T. Charles-Edwards, *Early Christian Ireland*, p. 13.

18 I am grateful to Mary Harte for pointing this out to me.

The land to the northern and western side of the Swillyburn (the area in which Raphoe is located) seems to have been the original territory of the people known as Cenél nÉnnai, the people to whom Adomnán's mother, Ronnat, is said to have belonged. But that small kingdom was over-run and conquered by Cenél Conaill around the middle or last quarter of the sixth century.[19] However, the Cenél nÉnnai seem to have hung on in some sense to re-emerge independently in the tenth and eleventh centuries, perhaps spurred on by the success of the cult of Adomnán and, of course, by the defeat and departure south of Barnesmore of their former overlords, Cenél Conaill.[20] The original Ráith Both (that is whatever physical monument had that name) and the impressive Beltany Stone Circle – respectively on different sides of the Swillyburn, as well as that watercourse itself running between them – seem to have marked and defined the boundary between these two kingdoms up to about 579.[21] In the twelfth century the Beltany Stone Circle, then known as *Carn Glas*, was used as one of the points to demarcate the diocese of the Cenél nEógain (more or less the diocese of Derry) from the diocese of the Cenél Conaill (more or less the diocese of Raphoe), although the line of the stream below it, the Swillyburn, was undoubtedly the actual border.

Across the valley drained by the Swillyburn and the River Deele to the east and south of Raphoe is the Croghan Hill ridge. The ridge runs parallel to the Lower Finn and the present N15 main road coming northwards from Connacht. That road itself follows the line of a very ancient routeway mentioned by Tírechán as early as *c.*690 (see above, chapter 1). Croghan Hill, the Tara of Donegal, is of tremendous archaeological and mythological importance although that significance has been all but lost since Plantation times. From the sixth to the late eighth century it was the *caput* of Cenél Conaill. Almost certainly Adomnán would have been a frequent visitor to his paternal relatives there. Thus the general area around Raphoe encompassing the lands of both Cenél Conaill and Cenél nÉnnai, the people from whom Adomnán's father and mother are said to have come respectively, was extremely important at the time of the latter's birth, as well as previously at the time of the birth of his hero Columba. However, by the time of the foundation of the church of Raphoe, which it will be argued below did not occur until about AD 800, the area had lost that outstanding political significance, although it still retained its border characteristics.

19 Lacey, *CC*, p. 130.
20 See below. The re-emergence of previously conquered small kingdoms was a feature, apparently, of Irish politics in the eleventh and twelfth centuries.
21 Elsewhere I have argued that the battle of Druim Meic Erce in that year was the decisive turning point for overall Cenél Conaill victory in the area with the consequent rearrangement of its political geography and the abolition of Cenél nÉnnai as a separate polity, at least for the next four or five centuries. See Lacey, *CC*, p. 130.

Our understanding of the origins of the church of Ráith Both is clouded in confusion. As we saw above, it is common to attribute its foundation to Colum Cille but to qualify that by claiming that Adomnán was also associated as 'patron' from his time onwards.[22] William Reeves pointed out in 1857 that the matter was further confused by a tradition of a separate, second Adomnán/ Adamnán (known in English as Eunan) who was believed to have been the founding bishop of that church.

> [W]hen Raphoe became an Episcopal see [in the twelfth century] but under its old patronage, after-ages, supposing that a bishop's see must originate with a bishop, took advantage of Adamnan's phonetic name *Eunan*, and created a bishop *Eunan* patron of the diocese, moving his festival a fortnight back in the month, and leaving *Adamnan* to enjoy his old abbatial honours on the 23rd [September]. Pope Clement XII [1730–40] approved of a mass for Bishop Eunan's festival on the 7th of September, which was printed in Paris in 1734. Accordingly the Bollandists [a specialized unit within the Roman Catholic church established to research the history and historicity of saints] place the commemoration of 'S. Eunanus Episcopus, Confessor, Raphoae in Hibernia', at Sept. vii, in a short notice edited by Joannes Stiltingus. Alban Butler [1710–73], following this authority, repeats the error at the same day; and in the Irish Calendar appended to the Dublin edition of his valuable book, the same fictitious patron intrudes on another saint's day.[23]

The latter confusion was clarified somewhat in the 1860s by the removal of this second St Eunan from the calendar of saints.[24] The matter of a second St Eunan (Adomnán/Adamnán) will be returned to below. Surprisingly, however, if the better known Adomnán – the ninth abbot of Iona – did have genuine connections with the church of Raphoe, there is no mention of this in his hagiographical Life, the *Betha Adamnáin* (see below, chapter 9). But the editors of that text have shown that it was composed in the monastery of Kells (Co. Meath) between the years 961 and 964, as a sort of *roman-à-clef*.

> While purporting to be a life of a saint who died in 704, ... [it] in fact deals with the relationship between his successor at Kells and the secular power in Ireland at a very much later period ... the second half of the tenth century.[25]

22 See, for example, Gwynn and Hadcock, p. 94.
23 W. Reeves (ed.), *The Life of St Columba*, pp lxi–lxii; see also pp 256–8.
24 J. Silke, *Two abbots*, p. 63.
25 M. Herbert & P. Ó Riain, *Betha Adamnáin*, p. 41.

Nevertheless, the absence of any mention of Raphoe in the *Betha Adamnáin* is striking; the church of Raphoe had been in existence for at least a century and a half before the *Betha Adamnáin* was composed. Neither is there any mention of Raphoe in any of the sets of annals during the sixth, seventh or eighth centuries. Given the later alleged personal connections of Raphoe with both Columba and Adomnán, and given that the exemplar of the annals was actually being compiled at the centre of the Columban world in Iona for most of that period, the absence of any reference to the Donegal church in them is surely also striking, and telling. By the time that it is mentioned unambiguously for the first time in the annals, at the year 817, the church of Raphoe was definitely associated with the Columban monastic federation:

> Máel Dúin son of Cenn Fáelad, superior [*princeps*] of Ráith Both, a member of Colum Cille's community [*de familia Columbe*], was killed [*iugulatus est*].[26]

The only other entry in the annals explicitly relating to Raphoe prior to the twelfth century is noted in AU for 959 when the death of Aengus ua Lapáin[27] is recorded. Aengus is not further identified there, neither his role nor the place where he died (and lived?). But AFM noticing the same event (inaccurately at the year 957) tells us that he was *epscop Ratha both*, 'bishop of Raphoe'. There is no independent supporting evidence for that, and it may be just a retrospective guess (as we know were made sometimes in the seventeenth-century AFM in other similar circumstances). The Uí Lapáin were clearly connected with the excellent farmland between Raphoe and Derry.[28] The killing of another Aengus ua (or more likely 'Ua') Lapáin, described in a secondary hand as 'king of Cenél nÉnnaí', is recorded in AU at 1011. His death is linked to the simultaneous killing of the Síl Lugdach king in what was evidently a battle involving the latter (and their Cenél nÉnnai allies?) against the Cenél nEógain.[29] The Uí Lapáin family

---

26 AU, 816.7.

27 This is the period when surnames are beginning to appear in Ireland, as distinct from patronymics. The particle 'ua', depending on context, can mean that the person in question was either the 'grandson' of the associated individual or that they used the latter's personal name as a surname beginning with 'Ua' (modern 'Ó'). It is not always easy to decide which, and the editors and translators of the annals are not always clear and decisive about the matter either. See below for a clearly related second Aengus who was almost certainly an 'Ua' rather than an 'ua' Lapáin.

28 Although in early medieval times, there may have been a lot more wetland there than is apparent now.

29 'Máel Ruanaid ua Domnaill, king of Cenél Lugdach, was killed by the Fir Maige Itha [of Cenél nEógain], [and] Aengus Ua Lapáin (i.e., king of Cenél [n]Énnai), [was killed] by the Cenél [n]Eógain of Inis [Eógain]' (AU, 1010.4). See below for a reference to a formal alliance between these two peoples: i.e. Síl Lugdach and Cenél nÉnnai.

must have been connected with Loch Lapáin (now greatly reduced in size and known as 'Port Lough'), fifteen kilometers north-east of Raphoe and ten kilometers south-west of Derry. They possibly had a crannog there which may have been their *caput*.

The notice in the annals for 817 of the killing of Máel Dúin, the *princeps* of Raphoe, has been taken as being linked to the entry which immediately follows it: 'Colum Cille's community (*muinnter*) went to Tara to excommunicate Áed'. The implication is that this Áed was involved in some way with the killing of the abbot of Raphoe. Although not identified further the subject of the excommunication was undoubtedly the Cenél nEogain high-king of Tara, Áed Oirnide, who died himself two years later. Why he should have been involved in the killing of Máel Dúin is not clear.

Although also not identified in any more detail by the annalist, the abbot Máel Dúin almost certainly belonged to the Síl Lugdach (see Table 4).[30] His father, Cenn Fáelad (although it was a relatively common name in Ireland in early medieval times), was probably the person of that name who was the son of Airnelach and grandfather of Dálach the son of Muirchertach, 'killed by his own people (*a gennte sua*)' in 870.[31] From his position in the pedigrees, the floruit of that Cenn Fáelad must have been around the year 800. An earlier Síl Lugdach Cenn Fáelad – the son of Garb and listed in the same pedigree[32] – would have lived at too early a date (around 700) to have been the father of Máel Dúin the superior of Raphoe. It might be noted also in this context that the general area from which the Síl Lugdach originated in north-west Donegal is nowadays known in English as Cloghaneely, that is, Cloch Chinn Fháelaid ('Fhaola'), 'stone of Cenn Faelad'.[33] Except for a few small pockets the land there is marginal from an agricultural point of view. But gradually, beginning in the aftermath of the battle of Allen in 722 (of which they seem to have been indirect beneficiaries),[34] Síl Lugdach began to push eastwards towards the good land of east Donegal. The collapse of Cenél Conaill north of the Barnesmore Gap following their overwhelming defeat by Cenél nEógain at the battle of Clóitech in 789 meant that Síl Lugdach were able to achieve that goal. The surrendered Cenél Conaill land north of Barnesmore was divided out between Cenél nEogain and the

---

30 Lacey, *Lug*, pp 43–4 and 122–3.
31 AU 870.3; M. O'Brien, *Corpus genealogiarum Hiberniae*, p. 164: 144f8.
32 Ibid., 144f11.
33 There is an elaborate local origin legend, first published by John O'Donovan in 1856, about the identity of a fictional character who gives his name to the area. But it is much more likely to have been derived from the real historical Cenn Fáelad whose floruit was about AD 700–25. There is also a monument in this area, near Falcarragh, a block of white stone with dark veins (said to be fossilized 'blood'!), which it is claimed is the actual Cloch Chinn Fháelaid referred to in both the legend and the place-name (see Lacey, *Lug*, pp 39–41 and 70–5).
34 Lacey, *Lug*, pp 16 and 41.

Síl Lugdach. The Swillyburn, an ancient boundary that 350 years later would become the border in this area between the diocese of Derry and the diocese of Raphoe, seems to have been the line agreed at the time between Cenél nEógain and Síl Lugdach for the sharing out of this newly conquered land. Síl Lugdach thus took control of the Gartan, Kilmacrenan and Raphoe districts, including many of the sites said to have been connected with the birth and first years of Columba, as well as, probably, the early life of Adomnán.[35] The political (and, possibly, military) might that the Síl Lugdach used to achieve this was backed up by a propaganda campaign based on the manipulation of the genealogies which was orchestrated, most probably, by the 'historians' of Kilmacrenan.[36]

From then on the Síl Lugdach (almost certainly with the assistance and permission of their overlords, Cenél nÉogain) grew into a formidable polity themselves, taking on many aspects of the former Cenél Conaill rulers of the kingdom, a part of whose forfeited lands they then acquired. As a result, the Síl Lugdach became more Cenél Conaill than the defeated Cenél Conaill themselves, especially in their cultivation of and devotion to the cults of St Columba and St Adamnán. Around 880 it was even claimed that one of them, Flann son of Máel Dúin (Table 4), had been abbot of Iona and comarba of Colum Cille.[37] The Síl Lugdach would go on to play a major role in the preservation of and almost certainly also in the propagandistic distortion of various aspects of the Columban heritage, including some of the traditions about Adomnán. Their descendants of later medieval times, the Uí Domnaill (and to a lesser degree the Uí Dochartaigh), vigorously cultivated and exploited that Columban patrimony. That Uí Domnaill cultivation of Columban lore could be said to have culminated in the composition by one of their descendants, Manus Ó Domnaill,

35 For Columba see Lacey, *Lug*, pp 59–66. For Adomnán see chapter 2 above.
36 Lacey, *Lug*, pp 41–2, 54 and 59. It should be admitted that we have no primary evidence at all for this intervention by officials of the Kilmacrenan monastery. The scenario outlined here has emerged as a thesis from a study of the *realpolitik* and the evident manipulation of the genealogies, which we are told was enshrined in the no-longer surviving 'Book of Kilmacrenan', transmitted to us through two poems, 'Ard na scéla, a mheic na Ccuach', and 'A Eolcha Conaill ceoluig', in the much later Book of Fenagh. Initially, following the disaster for them of the 789 battle of Clóitech, the Columban monks at Kilmacrenan must have been appalled to lose their Cenél Conaill overlords and patrons (the actual real family of Colum Cille) as a result of the triumph of Cenél nÉogain and their allies, the *arriviste* Síl Lugdach. But on the principle that 'if you can't beat them ...' and, no doubt relatively quickly, the Kilmacrenan monks must have accommodated themselves to the new regime under the Síl Lugdach. That regime-change would have been made easier to swallow when, serendipitously (through careful combing and 'embroidering' of the genealogies), the Kilmacrenan 'historians' 'discovered' that their new Síl Lugdach rulers were not just some weird alien tribe from west of the mountains but, actually, just another 'part' of the defeated Cenél Conaill. Better still, it could also be 'shown' (utterly falsely) that the Síl Lugdach were close 'relatives' of the monastery's beloved Colum Cille!
37 M. Herbert, *Iona, Kells and Derry*, pp 74–5. But see below, chapter 11.

of his extraordinary *Betha Colaim Chille*, finished in 1532. The official historians to the Uí Domnaill, most especially the phenomenal early seventeenth-century Mícheál Ó Cléirigh (see below), would continue to rescue and preserve much of the outstanding literary heritage of Donegal, including much that related to both Columba and Adomnán, as well as to Raphoe.[38]

As we saw above there were actually traditions of two Adomnáns (or more properly Adamnáns) connected with Raphoe, the feastday of one (said to have been a bishop) occurred on 7 September. However, despite the alleged connections of the other Adamnán (Adomnán of Iona, who was not a bishop and whose feastday is 23 September) with the church of Raphoe, the only person of that name in that part of Donegal of whom we have any genuine historical evidence is the early eighth-century Adomnán, the bishop of Ráith Maige Aenaig who died in 731 (AU). Ráith Maige Aenaig, as was said above, was almost certainly a site now known as Rateen further downstream on the Swillyburn about eight kilometers north-east of Raphoe. Indeed, its postulated location is similar geographically to that of Raphoe: on an east-facing hillside overlooking a large open landscape below. Ráith Maige Aenaig was associated with the very early saint Brugach mac Dega (see above, chapter 1) and appears to have been an important church that ceased to exist (or at very least ceased to be mentioned in the annals) around the end of the eighth century. There is only one further reference to it in the annals after the death of its bishop Adomnán: in 784 when its abbot Ciarán dies.[39] That is the last contemporary reference to that church, and we hear no more about it except in the later, retrospective Lives of Patrick and Columba. In fact, Ráith Maige Aenaig disappears from the annals more or less at the same time (or close to it) that references to Raphoe, Ráith Both, begin to appear. It looks as if genuine traditions about bishop Adomnán of Ráith Maige Aenaig got transferred somehow to a newly established early ninth-century church at Raphoe, becoming part of a falsified legend of Adomnán of Iona and his (equally false) connection with the latter church. As a corollarary, it seems also probable that it was Adomnán of Ráith Maige Aenaig, who definitely was a bishop according to the annals, whose feastday occurred on 7 September, the 'second' Eunan (Adomnán/Adamnán) as referred to by William Reeves (see above). The coincidence of names was either exploited deliberately to create a new legend for an episcopal see at Raphoe (fictionally linking it with Adomnán of Iona), or else a genuine historical memory had become so corrupted (or partially forgotten) that it facilitated the same end.

38 E. Bhreathnach & B. Cunningham, *Writing Irish history: the Four Masters and their world* (Dublin, 2007), and see below.
39 AU 783.2. He is actually styled 'abbot' of Ráith Maige Aenaig and Tech Mo-Fhinnu. The latter is normally identified as being in Co. Wexford at the opposite end of the country. But for a possible, and more likely, Tech Mo-Fhinnu in Donegal see Lacey, *CC*, pp 141–2.

One of the principal vehicles for the propagation of the fictional legend about Adomnán of Iona's connection with the Síl Lugdach and hence with Raphoe (located in territory which had only been acquired by them about 800) was what used to be called the Middle Irish 'Preface'[40] to the *Cáin Adomnáin*. The whole text of the *Cáin Adomnáin* (*sic*) survives in only two much later manuscripts, which indicate that it derives from an earlier but now lost manuscript called the 'Old Book of Raphoe.' Máirín Ní Dhonnchadha pointed out that Mícheál Ó Cléirigh, who copied the *Cáin Adomnáin* in Donegal on 31 March 1627, also copied there the *Betha Adamnáin* (see chapter 9 below) and the *Fís Adamnáin* (chapter 10 below). She suggested that the church at Raphoe probably 'had a dossier of materials on the saint [Adamnán] in the Middle Ages, and [that] the "Old Book of Raphoe" may well have been just such a dossier.'[41]

Sections 1 to 27 of the *Cáin Adomnáin*[42] of *c.*1000 purport to explain the circumstances of the composition of the original law *c.*697. It is, however, a much later piece of political propaganda composed in Raphoe on behalf of that church and the local ruling dynasty, the Síl Lugdach. It opens with a statement of Adamnán's Síl Lugdach pedigree, which has been shown to be false (see above, chapter 2):

> Women were in servitude and in oppression during that time, until there came Adamnán son of Rónan, son of Tinne, son of Áed, son of Colum, son of **Lugaid**, son of Sétna, son of Fergus, son of Conall, son of Níall.[43]

The insertion of the name Lugaid son of Sétna in this pedigree perpetrated two useful falsehoods: it wrongly connected the real Adomnán with the Síl Lugdach and, separately, wrongly connected the Síl Lugdach with Cenél Conaill. Both these things have been demonstrated to be fictions.[44] The text is

---

40 The title 'Preface' was used to refer to the first 27 (of 53) sections of the text, on the understanding that this was a separate composition from (most of) the remainder. However, as we saw in chapter 4, James Houlihan has now demonstrated that with the exception of the original seventh-century core – section 28 shorn of the identifying titles, and sections 34–49 – all the rest belongs to a single composition put together close to the year 1000 (although some individual short sections incorporated within that main body are probably older reused texts: M. Ní Dhonnchadha, 'The guarantor-list', p. 182, n. 1, and see below). Much, if not all, of that later text is fictional. For ease of reference the term *Cáin Adomnáin* is used here for the 697 document, while *Cáin Adomnáin* (*sic*) refers to the enlarged recension of *c.*1000. In addition, the name Adamnán (*sic*) is used below for the fictional version of the historical Adomnán (*sic*).

41 M. Ní Dhonnchadha, 'Birr and the Law', p. 16.

42 G. Márkus, *Adomnán's Law*, pp 8–14

43 G. Márkus, *Adomnán's 'Law'*, p. 8. All quotations here from sections 1–27 are drawn from this, with a few small alterations by the present author. The emphasis here in bold on **Lugaid** is by this author.

44 Lacey, *CC*, pp 87–9; B. Lacey, 'Adomnán and Donegal', pp 22–3.

also something of a geographical marker. The Síl Lugdach kingdom originated in the Cloghaneely and Gaoth Dobhair areas of west Donegal, but from about 725 they had begun to expand eastward and by *c*.800 they were ensconced on the much richer lands around Raphoe.[45] *Cáin Adamnáin* is a Raphoe document. In addition, as we saw above, traditions about a bishop Adomnán who died in 731 were, as it were, pushed back in time and transferred from his true church of Ráith Maige Aenaig to the relatively nearby site of Ráith Both which had not been mentioned in the annals as an ecclesiastical centre of any kind before 817. Thus, through the fiction of these opening paragraphs (and other appropriately 'doctored' or misinterpreted texts) what was most likely a newly founded Columban (and Síl Lugdach) church at Raphoe was provided with, in effect, an invented antiquity. That fiction also provided a connection with two of the most important local saints: Columba and Adomnán. The Síl Lugdach and their new Raphoe church were undoubtedly the beneficiary of these sleights-of-hand but they, themselves, would not have had the resources or authority to achieve them. The extremely clever mixing of facts and fictions that resulted in this fabricated 'foundation legend' for Raphoe must have been engineered by a monastic school of 'historians' and 'genealogists', one that had a vested interest in that falsification. The nearest and most obvious contenders for that role were the scholars at the Columban monastery of Kilmacrenan, about twenty kilometers to the north-west of Raphoe. Kilmacrenan was part of Síl Lugdach territory from about 800.

After the introductory false pedigree, the text continues with an equally fictional and extravagant outline of the disadvantages suffered by women until Adamnán's time. Their domestic life was atrocious and in times of war a woman's husband would hide behind her, 'flogging her into battle'. The text adds gruesomely that 'it was a woman's head or her two breasts that were carried off [from battle by the enemy] as a trophy at that time'.

> After the coming of Adamnán now, a good woman is not deprived of her testimony on earth, if it is secured by righteous deeds. For a mother is a venerable treasure, a mother is a good treasure, the mother of saints and bishops and just men, one deserving of the kingdom of heaven and a propagation on earth.

Adamnán is shown to have suffered a lot to secure the rights and legal protections for women; as a result, the *Cáin* 'is the first law in heaven and on earth which was arranged for women'.[46]

---

45 Lacey, *Lug*.
46 As demonstrated by James Houlihan (and as mentioned above) the *Cáin Adamnáin* of *c*.1000 has shifted towards women alone from the emphasis given in the *Cáin Adamnáin* of 697 to the protection of other classes of non-combatants also, for example, clerics and young boys.

A (fictional) story of how Adamnán came to make the law is then outlined. Adamnán and his mother Ronnat were travelling by foot near Drogheda. Despite his attempt to be kind to her she remonstrated with him that he had done nothing to free women from their misery. They travel on and pass a battlefield covered with the bodies of slaughtered women.

> Of all they saw on the battlefield, they saw nothing which they found more touching or more wretched than the head of a woman lying in one place and her body in another, and her infant on the breast of her corpse. There was a stream of milk on one of its [the baby's] cheeks and a stream of blood on the other cheek.

Ronnat then expressed the wish that she could feed the baby herself, but she was too old and her breasts were dry. She implored her son to revive the woman, which he dutifully did, re-attaching her head and using his staff to make the sign of the cross over her. The woman who turned out to be a high-ranking aristocrat and a leader of the other slaughtered women then thanked Adamnán and the Virgin Mary[47] for the mercy shown to her. Ronnat saw this as an opportunity to force her son to 'free the women of the western world', commanding him to fast from food and drink until he did so. The action then moves abruptly, and without any explanation, back to Donegal.

> Then Ronnat went to Brugach son of Dega and got a chain from him. She put it around her son's breast under the bridge of the Swilly in Cenél Conaill, the place where the covenant had been made between his mother's kindred and his father's kindred, i.e. between the Cenél nÉnnaí and [Síl] Lugdach, so that whoever of them should break the covenant would be buried alive in the earth, but whoever should fulfill it would dwell with Adamnán in heaven. And she takes a stone which is used for striking fire – it filled her hand. She puts it into one of her son's cheeks, so it was on that he had his satisfaction [his fill] in food and drink.

The covenant mentioned here seems to be referring to political events at the beginning of the eleventh century. By then Cenél nÉnnai and the Síl Lugdach were neighbours in east Donegal. Perhaps the covenant referred to was reflected in the sort of alliance adverted to in 1011, mentioned above, when the Síl Lugdach king, Máel Ruanaid Ua Domnaill, was killed alongside Aengus Ua Lapáin, king of Cenél nÉnnai, by the Cenél nEógain of Inishowen. The place where the covenant in the *Cáin* was made was at a bridge across the 'Swilly', in

---

47 There seems to have been a particular devotion to the Virgin Mary as mother in the churches of the *Familia Columbae*, from, at least, the eighth century onward. See below.

this context a meeting-place on the border between the Síl Lugdach and Cenél nÉnnaí. Indeed the 'covenant' may have been also an agreement by both sides to respect the latter watercourse as the border between them. Almost certainly the place in question was a bridge across what is now called the Swillyburn, not far from Raphoe. As described above, that stream had marked an ancient boundary that continued probably from the sixth century on through the twelfth and seventeenth centuries and, indeed, survives in use as such, in a more limited way, down to the present.

The Brugach mac Dega mentioned here, as has been seen in chapter 1, was a very early cleric honoured as a 'saint'. He was said to have been ordained by St Patrick and, according to the Middle Irish Life of Colum Cille, was said to have met Columba as a child. The latter story suggests in hagiographical terms that Brugach's ecclesiastical 'heirs' (in the twelfth century, when the story was written, probably meaning the clergy of Raphoe) owed some sort of debt to the 'heirs' of Columba in Derry. Brugach was associated originally with the church of Ráith Maige Aenaig, which as shown above seems to have existed from the sixth to the eighth centuries and which, as argued above also, was then sort of re-incarnated in the early ninth-century church of Raphoe. We have no contemporary documentation about Brugach, but he appears several times in the later hagiographical literature associated with both Patrick and Columba. Peculiarly, he will figure in a slightly different guise later in the text of *Cáin Adamnáin*.

Returning to the story in sections 1 to 27 of the *Cáin*, after eighth months Ronnat goes to visit the penance-suffering Adamnán who has still not freed women from their servitude. He asks her to change his penance and she does so, for the worse!

> And not many women would do this to their son: she buried him in a chest of stone in Raphoe of Tír Chonaill, so that maggots ate the root of his tongue, and the slime of his head burst out through his ears.

She left him like that for a while in Raphoe and then brought him to an unidentified place called *Carric in Chulinn* where he stayed another eight months, apparently still trapped inside the stone chest. After four years angels came to him, lifted him out of the chest and brought him to Birr, 'the provincial boundary between the Uí Neill [effectively the northern half of Ireland] and the Men of Munster [the southern half]'. Then, finally, Adamnán and the angels agreed that women should be freed.

There then follows a piece of pure Síl Lugdach political propaganda. The author manages to get in two swipes against what I might call the real Cenél Conaill, introducing the slightly fictionalized character of Loingsech

Bregbán,[48] a misogynist who is opposed to Adamnán's achievement of freedom for women.

> But Loingsech Bregbán said, 'If it [freedom for women] is done, it will not be done during my time.' He was from Fanad of Cenél Conaill. 'It is an evil time when men's sleep is murdered because of women, that women should live and men be slaughtered. Take a sword to the deaf and dumb one [Adamnán] who says anything but that women should be in captivity forever until the very Day of Judgement.'

The Loingsech Bregbán of the story is, in fact, a very thinly disguised version of Loingsech mac Óenguso, a contemporary and Cenél Conaill relative of Adomnán who was king of Tara at the time of the real Synod of Birr. Far from being opposed to the *Cáin Adomnáin*, Loingsech's is actually the first secular name on the list of its 'guarantors'. As king of Tara at the time it is evident that he must have been fully behind such a 'national' event as the synod and the assemblage of lesser kings who supported it, as well as the Law promulgated there. Here the facts of history have been totally and blatantly reversed by the Síl Lugdach propagandist 'historian' as a means of putting Cenél Conaill down. It wasn't sufficient for the Síl Lugdach to have taken the latter's land; in so far as possible their reputation would have to be taken as well. The text then continues with a list of the kings 'who rose up at Loingsech's word to put Adamnán to the sword'. Among those 'kings', surprisingly and clearly utterly incorrectly, is Brugach mac Dega, mentioned above.[49] Apart from anything else, although we have no precise dates for him, his connection in the hagiography with both Saint Patrick and a very young Columba would place his floruit more than a century before that of the historical Adomnán. In the *Cáin Adomnáin* Brugach is represented as a hostile king; but all the earlier and more objective evidence describes him very positively as a cleric, indeed as a saint!

48 The epithet does not make much sense but, in this context, the likelihood is that it was not complimentary! It could indicate something like 'white lie' but Nollaig Ó Muraile points out (pers. comm.) that this is unlikely here: '[I]f attached to a personal name ... one might expect *Bánbhréag*, 'of [the] white lies'. Ó Muraile also points out that DIL (p. 82) cites the word without translation in the entry for Brega, the ancient kingdom encompassing Co. Meath and north Co. Dublin, 'implying that it is a compound of the place-name ... and therefore presumably meaning something like "white/fair/bright like Brega"'. As a Donegal man, Loingsech did not of course come from Brega, but the kingship of Tara, which he did hold, was, at least symbolically, located there.

49 The other names are as follows: (1) Dóelguss m. Óengussa m. Donnfráigh, king of Munster; (2) Élodach, king of Deisi; (3) Cú Cherca, king of Osraige; (4) Cellach the Red, king of Leinster; (5) Írgalach ua Conaing, king of Brega; (6) Fingen Éoganach. At least four of these – 2, 3, 4 and 5 – appear on the seventh-century list of 'guarantors' of the 697 *Cáin Adomnáin*, in contradiction of their alleged role here. Some of these names had also appeared in a negative guise in the *Betha Adamnáin* (see chapter 9 below), which is older – maybe by about forty years or so – than the *Cáin Adomnáin*.

Brugach seems to have belonged to the Cenél nÉnnai to which Ronnat, Adomnán's mother, also allegedly belonged.[50] Cenél nÉnnai was a small kingdom that had been overrun by Cenél Conaill in the late sixth century. Originally it would have included the land in which Raphoe was located. In the centuries after the collapse of Cenél Conaill power north of the Barnesmore Gap in 789, however, there seems to be some evidence that Cenél nÉnnai were making a bit of a comeback in their own right. That seems to be at least part of the import of the reference c.1000 in the Preface to 'the covenant ... made between his mother's kindred and his father's kindred'. As we saw above the annalistic evidence would also suggest that Cenél nÉnnai were attempting a comeback around the early eleventh century.

In this section of the *Cáin Adamnáin* its Síl Lugdach-supporting author was trying deliberately, and almost certainly knowingly, to turn history on its head. The author manages to foment hostility or at least opposition towards two of the Síl Lugdach's opponents and sometime enemies: Cenél Conaill proper, parts of whose lands they had occupied only within the previous two centuries,[51] and their immediate neighbours, Cenél nÉnnai, whose lands they would occupy and take over within the next century.[52]

In the fictional world of the c.1000 *Cáin*, Adamnán counters the opposition to him by striking his bell and uttering curses against his opponents, predicting failure for themselves and their descendants. The subcode is plain: oppose Adamnán, and most especially his Law, at your peril. Adamnán's bell, 'the bell of Adamnán's anger', is repeatedly mentioned as the instrument he uses to effect his punishments.

> The bell of truly miraculous Adamnán
> has laid waste many kings.
> Each one against whom it gives battle, one thing awaits,
> it has laid them waste.

50 Two alleged pedigrees for Brugach survive showing his descent from (i) the Airgialla or (ii) the Dál nAraide. However, in both of these, his father's name is given as Énna. The latter may have been the actual eponym of Cenél nÉnnai (see B. Lacey, 'The church of Ráith Maige Oenaig and the Donegal Cenél nÉnnai').

51 Some of that hostility seems to have been directed specifically at Fanad, the alleged home-place of Loingsech Bregbán. There is no definite evidence that the real Loingsech mac Óenguso was connected with Fanad. The only references to him in the annals, as with his father, connect him to the south of Donegal and further south (AU 672.1, Tig and Frag; and AU 703.2, CS, Frag). His uncle Fergus and first cousin Congal were connected with Fanad and adjacent areas (Lacey, *CC*, p. 103). Whether Loingsech did or did not come from Fanad the latter place is introduced here as an additional negative. We will see later other manifestations by the Síl Lugdach of hostility towards Fanad (chapter 10).

52 See B. Lacey, 'The origins of the Uí Dochartaigh', p. 63.

The references almost certainly confirm that a treasured relic, the Bell of Adamnán, was kept in Raphoe at the time.[53]

The text continues with a list of 'sureties and bonds' for the implementation of the *Cáin*. This is quite separate and different to the list of royal and ecclesiastical 'guarantors' that seems to have been attached to the original seventh-century *Cáin Adomnáin*. This later list includes the 'sun and moon, and all the elements of God' followed by the names of apostles, saints, bishops and abbots. Perhaps surprisingly Columba's name is not on the list but Gregory the Great's is. The opening, or *exordium*, of the *Betha Adamnáin* (to be considered in the next chapter) is a passage from Gregory's *Moralia in Iob*. As Máire Herbert pointed out there is no real connection between that passage and the text of the Life that follows it.[54] However the reference to Gregory in both the *Cáin Adamnáin* and in his hagiographical Life might suggest some sort of connection between them. There are one or two other probable connections as well, as will be seen.

We are told that all the people named in this late list shouted out a malediction on any man who would kill a woman. Then the same gathering gave a blessing to 'every woman who would do something for the community of Adamnán [*muntir nAdamnán*], though his relics were to come [be taken on a visit to them] often'. This is the heart of the matter; a quite mercenary list of suggested tolls to be paid to Adamnán (or his agents) in return for his protection of women:[55]

---

53 I am not aware of the survival of an object known as the Bell of Adamnán although a possibly related so-called Gartan Bell is preserved in the National Museum of Ireland. Interestingly bells from Iona also figure in Raphoe's history at the beginning of the seventeenth century. The Protestant bishop John Leslie, like his predecessor, had previously been bishop of the Isles, the Scottish diocese that included the island of Iona. In 1635, King Charles I wrote to Bishop Leslie at Raphoe concerning a matter which, originally, had been the business of his predecessor.

Reverend Father in God: Whereas we are informed that Andrew late Bishop of Raphoe at his transportation from the Bishopric of the Isles did without just cause or any warrant from our late royal father [James I of England and Ireland, VI of Scotland] or us, carry with him two of the principal bells that were in Icolmkill [Iona] and place them in some of the churches of Raphoe; To which purpose we do remember that at the time of your being Bishop of the Isles you were a suitor to us for effectuating that thing at your predecessor the Bishop of Raphoe's hands which we now require of you: Therefore and in regard we have given order to the present Bishop of the Isles for repairing the cathedral church of that bishopric [on Iona], and that it is fit for such things as do properly belong thereunto be restored; it is our pleasure that you cause deliver unto the said bishop these two bells for use of the said cathedral church with such timely convenience as may be; Which we will acknowledge as acceptable service done unto us. Whitehall, 14 March 1635.

It is not clear if the bells in question were ever returned to Iona.

54 M. Herbert, *Iona, Kells and Derry*, pp 151–2.

55 It might need to be stressed here that this is not the historical Adomnán's seventh-century list of tolls. Instead it dates from about three hundred years after his death when the Irish church, not just Raphoe, had become quite secularized and mercenary.

a horse every quarter-year to his relics, to his heir [abbot of Raphoe] to be brought to the bath in Raphoe, but that [the 'horse' etc.] is only from queens. Other women give according to their ability.

Women said and promised that they would give half of their household to Adamnán for delivering them from the bondage and oppression in which they had been. Adamnán would take only a little from them, i.e., a white tunic with a black border from each penitent spouse, a scruple of gold from each ruler's wife [*bantósigi*], a linen cloth from each sub-chieftain's wife [*mná ócthigern*], seven loaves from each unfree woman, a wether from every small flock, and the first lamb that is born in every house, whether it be black or white, for God and for Adamnán.

The reference to the bath (*in fothracud*) in Raphoe as the collection spot for the donations is interesting although it is not clear what sort of feature it could have been. But, as we saw above, in the fictional origin legend for the foundation of Raphoe contained in the Middle Irish Life of Colum Cille a miracle is wrought by Columba in the mill-pond (*llind in mulind*) there. Could it be that that pool of water was venerated as a possible source of cures in the same way that various holy wells and other water features were so respected throughout Ireland and in other parts of the Christian world such as, for instance but much later, the baths at Lourdes? The bath would then have been a pilgrimage destination and a source of income for the church of Raphoe.[56] Alternatively the 'bath' in question could have been something similar to the carved stone basin outside the west door of the late medieval abbey church on Iona and another close to the south-west corner of Templemolaise on Inishmurray. The Iona (and, possibly, the Inishmurray) basin seems to have been used by pilgrims to wash before entering the church.[57] A somewhat comparable 'basin' or 'trough' is located with other displaced stone features at St John's Altar on Tory Island,[58] and similar objects are known at other early Christian sites in Ireland also.

At any rate, the *Cáin Adamnáin* text continues with a blatant marketing message on behalf of the graveyard attached to the church of Raphoe. In return for the tribute to Adamnán:

two [buried] women would go with him to heaven every Monday; three women every Tuesday, four women every Wednesday, five women every Thursday, six women every Friday, twelve women every Saturday and fifty

56 Along the lines of St Mullins in Co. Carlow and Struell Wells in Co. Down. See, for instance, L. Nugent, *Journeys of faith*, pp 137–42 and 263–77.
57 Campbell & Maldonado, 'A new Jerusalem', p. 74; O'Sullivan & Ó Carragáin, *Inishmurray*, pp 90–1.
58 B. Lacy, *Archaeological survey*, p. 296.

women on Sunday. In addition, any name-sake of his mother, any woman on earth who is called Ronnat, and every woman who chooses to be buried in his cemetery [in Raphoe], it is decided that they should be carried into Heaven without judgement.

Adomnán's Law of the Innocents of 697, almost certainly promulgated originally for truly humanitarian purposes, had been by *c*.1000 corrupted into an instrument for the gathering of wealth by the grasping and presumably secularized, but certainly not unique in this regard, authorities of the church of Raphoe. This section of the *Cáin Adamnáin* then concludes with instructions for the collection of any bad debts that arise and is signed off with an admonition allegedly from Adamnán himself.

If you do not do good to my community [*muintir*] on behalf of the women of this world, the children you beget will fail, or they will perish in their sins. Scarcity shall fill your larder and the kingdom of heaven will not be yours. You will not flee Adamnán of Iona by your meanness or falsehood.
Adamnán of Iona
will help you, O women.
Give to your lord
every good thing that is yours.

Adamnán of Iona, loved by all ...

In the composite Raphoe *Cáin Adamnáin* of *c*.1000, there next follows a short paragraph referring to the Synod of Birr and the list of the so-called 'guarantors'. As said before, the list of names seems to be contemporary to 697 but titles and other identifications have been added later. The list is followed by prayers for those who implement the Law and maledictions for those who don't. Even with the prayers the mercenary tone continues:

Then all the holy churches of Ireland, around Adamnán, begged the divine Unity, Father and Son and Holy Spirit, and the community of heaven and the saints of earth, that everyone who fulfills this law in claiming and levying and fulfillment and payment should have long life and wealth and that he may be honoured by God and man, and that he be exalted in heaven and earth.

The section referring to those who 'shall violate the *Cáin Adamnán* ... [and] shall not enforce it' is followed by a brief outline of a procedure, a liturgy of malediction, for those defaulters. The liturgy could be spread over a period of up to twenty days, perhaps to give the defaulters time to reconsider their position. The text then lists specific psalms to be chanted each day and a particular apostle or saint to be 'invoked' respectively.

One occasion when a comparable liturgy may have been 'performed' was in 817, following the death of Máel Dúin son of Cenn Fáelad, the *princeps* (principal cleric) of Raphoe mentioned above, when the community (*muinnter*) of Colum Cille went to Tara to 'curse' the high-king Áed Oirdnide. The word used in the annals for Máel Dúin's death was *iugulatus*, implying a violent death, possibly a murder or assassination. It must be remembered that this was not just the killing of somebody somewhere, but the killing of a senior cleric from Raphoe. It was a direct challenge to the letter and spirit of Adomnán's Law as originally promulgated in 697, and to those who continued to administer it. By 817 Raphoe was probably a major shrine to Adomnán/Adamnán (or on its way to becoming such) and also a hub for enforcing his Law. The implication in the journey to Tara is that, for whatever reason, Áed who had been the Cenél nEógain king of Tara since 797 was, at minimum, responsible in some way for Máel Dúin's death. Patrick O'Neill drew attention to the fictional description in the Irish Life of St Ruadán of a similar event when the latter cursed the high-king Diarmait at Tara.[59]

> Ro triallsat a cclucca & a cceolana do bein for Diarmait, go ros gortaighset aga mbein. Co ngabhsat fós a psalma esccaine & innighte fair ...
>
> They [Ruadán and his monks] proceeded to ring their bells, both large and small, against Diarmait (so violently) that they damaged the bells in ringing them. They also sang psalms of cursing and vengeance against him ...[60]

We have seen above the evidence that *c.*1000 (whatever about 817) the clergy of Raphoe were equipped with just such a bell, 'the bell of Adamnán's anger'! As Dr O'Neill pointed out the cursing ceremony described in St Ruadán's Life involved three elements: the assembly of the clergy; the vigorous ringing of bells; and the chanting of appropriate psalms. Is this fictional description similar to what actually did occur in Tara in 817? As has been pointed out, such events would have been formal, solemn, ceremonial liturgies, certainly not personal outbursts of anger.

Although the translation of the AU entry for 817 tells us that the high-king Áed was 'excommunicated', the original word in Irish is *escuine*, which might be better translated as 'cursed'. The same word, *escuine*, is used in the Ruadán

59   P. O'Neill, 'A Middle Irish poem on the maledictory Psalms', p. 40.
60   C. Plummer, *Lives of Irish saints,* Irish text, vol. I, p. 323:36. Trans., vol. II, pp 314–15:36.

quotation above and, more relevantly, in the *Cáin Adamnáin* description of the cursing liturgy that Adamnán himself is said to have established. Although that document is generally dated to about AD 1000, it has been suggested that this section may go back to the ninth century.[61]

> Adamnán moreover has established an order of malediction [*ordd n-escoine*] for them [the holy churches of Ireland], to wit, [the recital of] a psalm each day until the end of twenty days and an apostle or a noble saint besides to be invoked each day ...[62]

This is followed by a list of the psalms to be recited together with the names of the apostles and saints to be invoked.

The same word (*escaini*) is used in the relatively contemporary (that is, with the *Cáin Adamnáin*) early eleventh-century poem 'Sreth a salmaib suad slán', which also purports to describe a 'cursing' ceremony arranged by Adamnán.[63]

> Sreth a salmaib suad slān
> feib ro-hordaigg Adamnān
> do escaini – mod cen cleith –
> ōnd eclais for cach m-bidbaid.
>
> Drem do nōebaib – mod cen tāir –
> do attach la sālmgabāil
> salm cech lathi-lāthar sōer –
> ardapstal nō uasanōeb.
>
> A selection from the psalms of the noble scholars –
> As Adamnán arranged them –
> Measure without concealment –
> To curse every excommunicate from the Church.
>
> A band of holy men should be invoked – an achievement without reproach –
> Together with chanting of psalms:
> A psalm for each day – a noble design –
> And a chief apostle or a venerable saint.

These first two verses are followed by eight quatrains listing nineteen psalms to be chanted, with a concluding reading of the Canticle of Moses from the

61 P. O'Neill, 'A Middle Irish poem', p. 42, n. 13; p. 45, n. 22 and refs cited therein.
62 M. Ní Dhonnchadha, 'The Law of Adomnán', pp 60–1.
63 For text, translation and commentary see P. O'Neill, 'A Middle Irish poem'. Verses 3–10 (not copied here) list the psalms. The additional verses 11–13 (again not copied here) list the apostles, saints etc. to be invoked. Much of what follows here is based on P. O'Neill's article.

Book of Deuteronomy. Three further verses list the apostles and (only non-Irish) saints to be invoked, respectively. These individuals seem to have been chosen as representatives of different categories of ecclesiastics, and the choice of them follows practices peculiar to the Irish church. All the psalms listed contain denunciations or cursings of those who go against God's will and commandments. But some psalms that might have been chosen because of their stronger language are excluded. The order of chanting them follows their numerical order in the psalter.

The two cursing texts discussed here – the section from the *Cáin Adamnáin* and the poem 'Sreth a salmaib' – although clearly related, are not dependent on each other. The prose text in the *Cáin* appears to be the earlier of the two and seemingly the closest to an original text from which both ultimately derive. A cursing poem and, worse, a formal cursing liturgy, might seem to us now an odd thing for the church to have been associated with, even in medieval times. But as Patrick O'Neill pointed out there were lots of Scriptural parallels for such a thing, most especially in the psalms. It seems that both of these texts must ultimately derive from Raphoe and are probably to be connected in some way to the events of 817. Perhaps they are even a ghost description, or at least an echo, of the journey to Tara that year by the clergy of that church (probably supported by other Columban clergy), and the sombre ceremonies that must have been enacted there on that occasion, with elements of high ceremonial and ecclesiastical theatricality.

In the *Cáin Adamnáin*, the 'cursing order' is followed by a distinct passage (section 33) written in Latin that purports to give other information about the background to the 697 law. Throughout, Adomnán is referred to by his correct name, that is, with the 'o' spelling, perhaps indicating a relatively early date for this section. This portion of the *Cáin* is sometimes referred to as the 'angel's directive' or the 'angel's speech' from its opening and closing phrases.[64]

> Here begins the Angel's directive to Adomnán.
> After fourteen years[65] [*as abbot of Iona*] Adomnán obtained this Law from God and this is the cause. On Pentecost eve a holy angel of the Lord came to him, and again at Pentecost after a year, and took a staff and struck

---

64 The translation here is that of M. Ní Dhonnchadha, 'The Law of Adomnán', pp 61–2, reprinted in J. Houlihan, *Adomnán's* Lex Innocentium, pp 201–2, with some additional comments from the translation by G. Márkus, *Adomnán's 'Law of the Innocents'*, pp 17–18. The inserted editorial interventions in italics are by the present author to distinguish them from those by M. Ní Dhonnchadha.

65 This is incorrect. The correct number would have been about 18. The figure 14 seems to be derived from a misreading of an annalistic reference to Adomnán travelling to Ireland for other business in 692 (AU, CS) 'in the 14th year after the repose of Failbe [his predecessor as abbot of Iona].'

his side[66] and said to him: 'Go forth into Ireland and make a law in that women be not killed in any manner by man, whether through slaughter or any other death, either by poison or in water or in fire or by any beast in a pit or by dogs, except [they die in childbirth] in lawful [*the marriage ?*] bed.[67] You shall establish a law in Ireland and Britain for the sake of the mother of each one, because a mother has borne each one, and for the sake of Mary, the mother of Jesus Christ through whom the whole [human race] is.' Mary along with Adomnán besought her Son about this Law.[68]

And whoever kills a woman shall be condemned to a twofold punishment, that is, before death, his right hand and his left foot shall be cut off and after that he shall die and his kin shall pay seven full *cumals* [*that is, the equivalent of seven 'female slaves'*] and the [the price of] seven years penance. If a payment has been imposed instead of life and amputation, [the payment for] fourteen years of penance and fourteen *cumals* shall be paid. If, however, a multitude have done it, every fifth man up to three hundred shall be condemned to that retribution. If [*they are*] few, they shall be divided into three parts. The first part of them[69] shall be put to death by lot, hand and foot having been cut off. The second [*part*] shall pay fourteen full *cumals*. The third [*part*] shall be cast out into alienage beyond the sea, under the rule of hard regimen. For great is the sin when anyone kills the one who is mother and sister to Christ's mother, and mother of Christ, she who labours in carrying the distaff [*weaves cloth*] and in clothing everyone. But from this day forward, he that shall put a woman to death, and not do penance in accordance with this Law, shall not only perish in eternity and be cursed by God and Adomnán, but all that have heard and do not curse him, and do not censure him according to the judgement of this Law, shall be cursed.

This is the angel's directive to Adomnán.

Apart from being written in Latin instead of Old (or Middle) Irish there are other hints that this section is separate from and later than the *Cáin Adomnáin* of 697. Máirín Ní Dhonnchada has suggested that it was composed, instead, on Iona at a date around 727 when, as AU tells us, Adomán's Law was 'renewed' (*renouator*).[70] James Houlihan, citing the assistance of Dr Anthony Harvey,

---

66 This may be an allusion to a similar episode in Adomnán's *Vita Columbae*, where an angel strikes Columba with a whip while giving him an order. See Sharpe, *Adomnán of Iona*, pp 208–9.

67 Gilbert Márkus translated this last phrase as: 'except shall die in their own lawful bed'.

68 See below for the *Familia Columbae* particularly honouring Mary as mother.

69 Gilbert Márkus translated this phrase as: 'The first group of them, decided by casting lots …'.

70 'The Law of Adomnán', p. 56.

points out that it is not 'possible to date the Latin one way or the other'.[71] Ní Dhonnchada had also pointed to the special recognition in the 'angel's directive' of Mary as the Mother of Christ as well as the mother of humanity in general and, indeed, that all women 'share in Mary's motherhood of Christ'. Ní Dhonnchadha noted the relatively rare (for the time) emphasis on Mary as mother in early Irish, especially in Iona and Columban-related, literature and art.[72] Examples of this include the Mother and Child motifs on St Martin's and St Oran's Crosses on Iona which seem to date to the second half of the eighth century,[73] and on folio 7v of the early ninth-century Book of Kells of undoubted Columban provenance. In addition, there is a beautiful Marian hymn composed by Cú Chuimne of Iona for a two-part choir that also reflects those themes of motherhood. Cú Chuimne, who was a younger contemporary of Adomnán and who died in 747, is credited with being one of the compilers of the immensely influential *Collectio canonum Hibernensis*. The latter quotes from, among other things, the writings of Adomnán. Cú Chuimne appears to have entered monastic life only as a mature adult. As Dáibhí Ó Cróinín says, his hymn in praise of Mary 'is a tour-de-force, with rich rhymes, half-rhymes and alliterations ... the whole is a triumph of technique and artistry'.[74]

Cantemus in omni die	Let us sing every day,
concinentes varie	harmonizing in turns,
conclamantes deo dignum	together proclaiming to God
ymnum sanctae Mariae	a hymn worthy of holy Mary
Per mulierem et lignum	By a woman and a tree
mundus prius periit	the world first perished;
per mulieris virtutem	by the power of a woman
ad salute rediit	it has returned to salvation.

71 J. Houlihan, *Adomnán's* Lex Innocentium, p. 122. Dr Harvey is editor of the Royal Irish Academy's Dictionary of Medieval Latin from Celtic Sources (DMLCS).
72 M. Ní Dhonnchadha, 'Birr and the Law', pp 22–6.
73 I. Fisher, *Early medieval sculpture*, p. 15. Incidentally, the only early medieval sculptural depiction of the Mother and Child motif in Ireland is on a probably early eleventh-century cross at Drumcliff, Co. Sligo. Drumcliff had totally different origins but by the time the cross was sculpted it was a Cenél Conaill church, dedicated to St Colum Cille. Although the cross has been dated variously, and was erected in a polity quite separate from that in which Raphoe was located, good arguments can be made that it was probably carved close to the time of the composition of the *Cáin Adamnáin*. See B. Lacey, 'Cúl Dreimne, Drumcliff and other Sligo associations with Colum Cille'.
74 D. Ó Cróinín, *Early medieval Ireland*, p. 217.

Amen Amen adiuramus	Truly, truly, we implore,
merita puerperae	by the merits of the Child-bearer,
ut non possit flamma pirae	that the flame of the dread fire
nos dirae decepere	be not able to ensnare us.[75]

The much-later preface to the hymn in the early eleventh-century Irish *Liber hymnorum* says that Cú Chuimne composed it:

> to praise the Virgin Mary in the time of Loingsech son of Óengus [Adomnán's relative who died as king of Tara in 703] and of Adamnán ... The cause of its composition was to free [Cú Chuimne] from the evil life in which he had lived, for he had a wife and lived a bad life with her.

The somewhat-misogynistic tone of the eleventh-century preface contrasts with the much more positive feminist message of the eighth-century hymn!

Thus, there seems to be ample evidence in the art and literature that emanated from Iona and the *Familia Columbae* of a particular interest in the condition of women, most especially women as mothers. Adomnán's original *Lex Innocentium* had been concerned with three categories of non-combatants: women, male youths and clerics. But James Houlihan noted that the 'angel's directive' section is 'concerned with women only, making no reference to the other classes of persons who are included in the term "innocents"'.[76] He also notes that women are the main focus of the other added sections of the reworked Raphoe *Cáin Adamnáin* of *c.*1000, such as the stories (as outlined above) in sections 1 to 27. In addition, the four final paragraphs of the *Cáin Adamnáin* (sections 50 to 53), which follow on immediately from the quotation of the original 697 text, are again concerned only with women. Section 50[77] lists particular individual fines for: (i) the forcible rape of a girl; (ii) unwanted sexual touching of a female; (iii) the knocking down of a woman with intention to injure her; (iv) putting a hand under a female's clothing to dishonor her; (v) injury to the head, eye, face, ear, nose, tooth, tongue, foot or hand of a female; (vi) injury to other parts of a female's body. Section 51 lists fines for 'insulting a woman by [accusing her of] lust or by denying her child', with variations for women of different grades 'down to a castaway'. Section 52 outlines fines for making a woman participate in a violent attack (a battle etc.) and for making a woman pregnant 'through

---

75 T. Clancy & G. Márkus (eds), *Iona: the earliest poetry*, pp 182–5. Only three of the thirteen quatrains have been copied here.

76 J. Houlihan, *Adomnán's Lex Innocentium*, p. 122.

77 Translation here and below from M. Ní Dhonnchadha, 'The Law of Adomnán', pp 67–8, reprinted in J. Houlihan, *Adomnán's* Lex Innocentium, pp 205–6. See also G. Márkus, *Adomnán's 'Law of the Innocents'*, pp 21–2.

fornication, without contract, without property, without bride-price without betrothal', that is, outside of formal marriage arrangements. A last ambiguous sentence in this section seems to deal with the theft of items that are the 'hand-produce' of a woman, referencing clothing and dyed cloth. The final section 53 deals with the appointment of 'hostage-sureties for every principal church' for the implementation of the Law 'if there be the [collective] evidence of women'.

It would seem that like various other hagiographical works of the period the *Cáin Adamnáin* (or much of it) is actually the text of (or material for) a sermon, for preaching probably on Adomnán's feastday, 23 September. It was certainly designed to hold the attention of and even to entertain an audience. It contains a variety of narrative styles and genres: drama, pathos, bawdiness, humour, 'history' and parables.

The Iona *Cáin Adamnáin* of 697 dealt with three categories of non-combatants – women, male youths and clerics – but the Raphoe *Cáin Adamnáin* of *c.*1000 seems to be primarily, if not solely, concerned with women, as is made clear in the twelfth-century notes to the Martyrology of Óengus, quoted above. James Houlihan argues that this narrowing of the concerns of Adomnán's Law came about from Armagh's promulgation of the *Cáin Phátraic*, Law of Patrick, in imitation of, and perhaps with some injured pride if not outright jealousy of, Iona's *Cáin Adamnáin*. As the Martyrology of Óengus notes also make clear, Patrick's Law existed *gan [n]a cleirchiu do marbad*, 'not to kill clerics'.[78] As Houlihan says:

> First mention of *Cáin Phátraic* appears in the annals in 734 and we learn that it was in force throughout Ireland in 737. It would appear that Iona, willingly or, more likely, unwillingly, lost possession of the clerical ball to Armagh, who took it [responsibility for the protection of clerics] for themselves.[79]

The Latin section known as the 'Angel's Directive' in the *Cáin Adamnáin*, with its emphasis on women only but its use of the 'o' formulation of Adomnán's name, would, therefore, seem to date to around this mid-eighth-century period also.

By the time that the *Cáin Adamnáin* was formulated in Raphoe *c.*1000 it was concerned principally with the protection of women and, most importantly, with the collection of fines due as a result of breaches of the Law. This would have been understood as a legitimate aspect of the income-raising resources of that church. Just as at other churches and 'monasteries' of the time around

78 W. Stokes, *The Martyrology of Oengus*, pp 210–11.
79 J. Houlihan, *Adomnán's* Lex Innocentium, p. 128.

Ireland (and further afield), a range of objects and features characterized as relics and religious monuments seem to have been important as additional income-raising opportunities at Raphoe. Those would have been resorted to by pilgrims for their own personal purposes and for the wealth-generating benefits of the church. They seem to have included, at least: Adomnán's Bell, a possible relic plough-coulter, the 'bath' and, most importantly, the cemetery.[80] A manuscript of the *Cáin Adamnáin* (and perhaps a separate one of the *Cáin Adomnáin*) and other written material relating to the patron may have also been preserved there as relics.

To return to the very first reference to the existence of a church of some sort in Raphoe: why was the *princeps* of what was almost certainly a relatively new church killed in 817; and why in its aftermath did the Columban monks travel to Tara to curse the high king; and were those events connected as they almost certainly seem to have been? And were the two events connected with any other contemporary conflicts in the church more widely or in the secular realm or, indeed, between those two authorities? The answer to all these questions is that we simply don't know. But Raphoe seems to have been founded around the same time (or a little earlier) as another major Columban church which was established most likely also in controversial circumstances. We know that the church of Kells (Co. Meath) was founded between 807 and 814. Until recently historians tended to characterize it as a 'daughter house' of the mother church in Iona. Without any real evidence, it had often been suggested that it was founded as a kind of refuge from Iona which, recently then, had come under attack from the Vikings. However, in two fascinating articles[81] Dr Daniel Mc Carthy has shown that the extraordinarily detailed and subtle iconography of the Book of Kells provides evidence of the vigorous survival down to that time of opposition to the triumph of the so-called Roman or Petrine party on the questions of the Easter and tonsure controversies, apparently resolved on Iona almost a hundred years earlier *c.*716 (see above, chapter 7).

According to Dr Mc Carthy, the combination of the annalistic entries on the subject[82] and the inferences to be drawn from the pictorial evidence in the Book of Kells indicates that 'Kells was rather a new, independent, and reactionary [that is, critical of the 'final' agreement on the Easter etc. issues] foundation committed to maintaining those doctrinal ideals of Columba that had been abandoned in

---

80 A miraculous cross or crucifix at Raphoe is mentioned in AFM in the later Middle Ages. In 1397, Hugh Mac Mahon recovered his sight by fasting 'in honour of the Holy Cross of Raphoe'. In 1411, the Holy Cross of Raphoe 'poured out blood from its wounds. Many distempers and diseases were healed by that blood.'

81 D. Mc Carthy, 'The illustration and text on the Book of Kells, folio 114RV' and 'Representations of tonsure in the Book of Kells'.

82 M. Herbert, *Iona, Kells and Derry*, pp 68–70.

Iona.' In other words, Kells was an early ninth-century protesting, if not exactly 'protestant', foundation. Could its contemporary, Raphoe, have been something similar and could that have been behind the reason why its *princeps* was killed? There is no evidence to answer the question but, as we will see below (chapter 9), in the tenth century there seem to have been some connections between Raphoe and Kells in the persons of a number of abbots of the latter who were also, unusually, styled comarbas of Colum Cille and Adomnán. In addition, it was the Síl Lugdach aristocrat Cathbarr mac Gilla Críst Ó Domnaill (see table 4), who died in 1106, who commissioned the *cumhdach* or shrine-box for the Cathach of Colum Cille. The *cumhdach* was made in Kells! Cathbarr was described in the annals as Síl Lugdach king at the time, a position that would have made him *ex officio* lay patron of the church at Raphoe;[83] he certainly lived somewhere in Síl Lugdach territory in east Donegal. There is very little evidence but what there is shows us that there were indeed some particular connections between the churches at Kells and Raphoe, in the tenth and eleventh centuries at least.

One totally separate issue could also have lain behind the killing of the *princeps* of Raphoe. As we have seen, the *Cáin Adamnáin* of c.1000 clearly identifies the church of Raphoe as the appropriate recipient of any dues or fines that arose from a breach of that Law. We do not know when that perquisite was asserted; it certainly couldn't have originated with the Law itself in 697. But if it had been proclaimed unilaterally by the Síl Lugdach from the foundation of the church (around 800 or so) then it may have been the cause of whatever tension resulted in the killing of its abbot in 817.

To sum up: as a member of Cenél Conaill with a mother who almost certainly belonged to the Cenél nÉnnai, there is a strong possibility that Adomnán of Iona was born and grew up in the area of east Donegal close to Raphoe. However, there is absolutely no evidence of his connection with a church there which, as outlined above, was probably not founded until about a century after his death. By 817 a church at Raphoe existed and was in the hands of the rising Síl Lugdach dynasty who were most likely its real founders. Whatever its previous history, that Raphoe church was associated with the Columban federation in some way. The Adomnán allegedly associated with that church was not in origin Adomnán of Iona. But the coincidence of names with another Adomnán from the nearby church of Ráith Maige Aenaig was either exploited deliberately to create a new legend for Raphoe (linking it fictionally with the ninth abbot of Iona who, in turn, was fictionally linked with the Síl Lugdach), or else a genuine historical memory had become so corrupted that it gave rise to the same conclusion. There is a strong possibility that Adomnán of Iona was born and grew up in the

---

83   For a discussion about the confusion between this individual and a namesake, see T. Ó Canann, 'Notes on medieval Donegal II', pp 73–7.

neighbourhood of Raphoe, but there is absolutely no evidence of his personal connection with a church there.

During the twelfth and on into the early thirteenth century there was a general reform of the church in Ireland, triggered well before the arrival of the Anglo-Normans but also hastened by that momentous occurrence. A complete transformation of the ecclesiastical geo-politics on the island began to take shape. Among the several changes was the reorganization of many of the ancient monastic institutions into Augustinian houses. Some of those centres, not without later changes, were also chosen as the sees of the bishoprics for the newly formed dioceses that were being carved out at a series of synods held specifically for that purpose. It is evident that the arrangements made at that time owed as much to the demands of secular politics and diplomacy as to anything particularly required by the church. Donegal would be divided, for the most part, between two dioceses that reflected the secular *realpolitik* of the time: the diocese of the Cenél Conaill, later the diocese of Raphoe, based ultimately on the rising importance of the Síl Lugdach Uí Domnaill family; and the diocese of the Cenél nEógain, later the diocese of Derry, based on the patrimony of the, at that time, immensely powerful Mac Lochlainn family. The ancient monastic settlement of Derry on its island-like site, a kind of hub at the centre of the vast territory over which those two dioceses spread, was the subject of dispute and even a kind of tug-of-war between them. The solution eventually arrived at by the early fourteenth century was the partition of that 'island' itself into two zones, one of which went to the diocese of the Cenél nEógain, the other to the diocese of the Cenél Conaill.[84] However, despite all those changes, the Síl Lugdach church at Raphoe, dedicated to St Adamnán, remained the seat of the bishopric after which it and its diocese was named.

---

84 B. Lacey, *Medieval and monastic Derry*, pp 108–9.

CHAPTER NINE

Betha Adamnáin: The 'Lives' of Adomnán

Thomas Clancy has an interesting observation on the later literature allegedly describing Adomnán's life and work. He says: 'He [Adomnán] is a curious example of a saint who, in an indirect way, wrote his own hagiography.' He explains this remark as follows:

> More than a few items of Adomnán's hagiographical dossier [the collection of texts portraying him as a 'saint'] derive directly or in inspiration from themes, plots, details and even wording found in Adomnán's own *Vita Columbae*. In this sense, Adomnán's words lie behind not only our appreciation for and understanding of Adomnán, but also the early medieval Gaelic traditions about him.[1]

Elsewhere in the same article Clancy says: 'the prompt for so many of the [later] texts about Adomnán seems to be, not his life, but his writings'.

Adomnán was treated by the medieval Irish and Scots as a saint. He had the three essential co-ordinates of a saint: a place of resurrection (death) – Iona (and, by extension, Raphoe); a feastday – 23 September; and a *Vita* – a hagiographical Life. In Adomnán's case, and as it has survived to us, the latter is not exactly a *Vita*; it is a *Betha* as it was written mainly in Irish. Almost certainly there had been a Latin *Vita* (or at least a collection of biographical anecdotes) in the monastery on Iona, parts of which may be preserved in the early sixteenth-century *Breviary of Aberdeen* to be discussed below.

The survival of the *Betha Adamnáin* is itself a sort of miracle. Only one copy of the original survives from medieval times. It is written on paper and is now in the Bibliothèque Royale in Brussels (Belgium). That library had inherited some of the collections of the Irish Franciscan College of St Anthony in Leuven/Louvain, about 30kms east of Brussels. The transcript was made by Mícheál Ó Cléirigh[2] who finished copying it in Donegal on 6 May 1628.[3] The manuscript containing the text has its own remarkable story to tell![4]

---

1 Both quotations are from T. Clancy, 'Adomnán in medieval Gaelic literary tradition', p. 122.
2 Known also as *An Bráthair Bocht* ('The Poor Friar') and as *Tadhg an tSléibhe* ('Tadhg of the mountain'), he was the leader of the team of researchers, transcribers and copyists, and 'historians', known to us as the Four Masters; see E. Bhreathnach & B. Cunningham, *Writing Irish history: the Four Masters and their world* (Dublin, 2007).
3 I just can't help pointing out the remarkable (to me) and totally accidental coincidence that I am writing this in Donegal on 6 May 2020.
4 M. Herbert & P. Ó Riain, *Betha Adamnáin*, p. vii.

The *Betha Adamnáin* was composed originally in the middle of the tenth century, 250 years or so after its subject's death and about 650 years before the only surviving copy of it was made. In some ways it is a disappointment, as it gives us virtually no real biographical information about Adomnán. The modern editors of the Life have shown that the work was composed at the monastery of Kells between the years 956 and 964, although other commentators have extended those dates into the 970s.[5] Pádraig Ó Riain pointed out that although comparatively-speaking a lot of knowledge about Adomnán and his various projects was available, 'most of this information was ignored, however, by the saint's panegyrist [author of the *Betha*] whose purpose was manifestly other than the presentation of a true account of his subject.'[6] The *Betha Adamnáin*, as it were, is not really about what it is about! That is to say, its real subject matter is not the ostensible surface story it tells. Like so much writing of the Middle Irish period, especially texts about the saints, it is a code in which a not-so-secret political message for its own time is delivered as a tale set in a more remote past. While it may contain some basic material that relates to its seventh-century subject, the *Betha* is in effect a *roman-à-clef* in which its author as Ó Riain says, 'was presenting the events of his own time in terms of that of Adomnán'. In barely concealed historical fiction the activities of Congalach mac Maíle Mithig, who became king of Tara in 944 and was assassinated in 956, are discussed and criticized. The stories told about the seventh century are structured, not without a lot of twisting of the real historical facts, to parallel the events of the author's own lifetime in the tenth century. The hidden agenda of the Life appears to be the retribution that will be suffered by any king who does not support the community of Colum Cille and Adomnán.

[The] king of Tara [named as Finnachta, son of Dúnchad, elsewhere called Finnechta Fledach] ordered that the lands of Colum Cille should be on the same footing as the lands of [Saints] Patrick, Finnian and Ciarán as regards freedom from imposition. This, in effect, meant the [Columban] lands were declared subject to tribute. The matter was related to Adamnán who thought it unjust, for the men of Ireland had granted freedom of his lands to Colum Cille because he was of more noble descent than any other saint in Ireland. Adamnán said: 'Short will be the life of the king who gave the order. He will be killed by his own kin, none of his race will ever be ruler, and no one of his name will ever [again] be king of Tara.' And all of this came to pass.[7]

5   Herbert & Ó Riain, *Betha Adamnáin*, pp 4–8. See also reviews by C. Breatnach, and M. Ó Briain.
6   M. Herbert & P. Ó Riain, *Betha Adamnáin*, p. 1.
7   M. Herbert & P. Ó Riain, *Betha Adamnáin*, p. 51 (all quotations below from the *Betha* are

The anonymous author of the *Betha* was familiar with both secular and religious sources including the annals and the genealogies. He (the reasonable assumption is that it was a he) also makes use as a model of the *Vita Martini* by Sulpicius Severus, just as Adomnán himself had done when writing his *Vita Columbae*. The *Betha* opens with a short litany of praise for Adamnán 'whose feast and commemoration fall at this particular time and period'. It is evidently, therefore, a homily for preaching on Adomnán's feastday, 23 September. It may be that visiting kings and their supporters were obliged to listen to it and, most importantly, its message, which was specifically addressed to them, sitting or standing captive in a church congregation at the solemn liturgies for the saint's feastday. The underlying message of the Life is that kings would disregard protecting the saint and his community at their peril. And, equally, that the alleged family connections of their founder Colum Cille entitled his community to unquestioning support from the Uí Néill dynasty, whose incumbents north and south shared the kingship of Tara between them, at that time (but not for much longer) the most important kingship in the land.

Sometime earlier than the composition of the *Betha*, the genealogies of fourteen so-called Uí Néill successors of Colum Cille were compiled in Kells using sources that seem mainly to have derived from Iona.[8] The purpose of that compilation was probably to claim historical continuity for the successorship (*comarbacht*) of the saint despite the change of its geographical location from Iona to Kells. It is also possible that some other historical sources relating to Adomnán were transferred to Kells from Iona around this time as well, material that could be used later as sources for the *Betha Adamnáin*. Among them may have been a little verse in which Adomnán is said to speak about his own death on Iona, where it was almost certainly composed (see below).

Although composed mainly in Irish, and as was the norm, the *Betha Adamnáin* opens with an *exordium*, a quotation in Latin from one of the important texts of earlier Christian literature: the *Moralia in Iob* by the sixth-century pope, Gregory the Great. The relevance of the quotation is questionable; it is mainly about 'girding your loins' and restraining lust and includes an insulting phrase about women. As Ó Riain noted, the passage does not seem particularly apposite for a work about Adomnán who, in terms of his own time at least, championed the rights of women. Perhaps mercifully, once stated the theme of the quotation is subsequently ignored in the rest of the *Betha*. But the main text contains another insulting allusion to women, particularly women as mothers. In the relevant episode Adomnán is going around the burial ground (*relec*) on Tory

---

from this source). Adomnán seems to have had genuine connections with Finnechta; see M. Herbert, *Iona, Kells and Derry*, pp 158–9, and chapter 3 above.

8   M. Herbert, *Iona, Kells and Derry*, pp 79–80.

island, examining and blessing it when he says: 'The corpse of a pregnant woman is in the graveyard, a thing which is offensive to the saints.' He points to her grave and says: 'Open it and take her with you to the sea-shore.' No doubt in monastic graveyards women were buried separately from men, especially from monks, but the choice of language used here is certainly not as we would have expected from the historical Adomnán.

The Life is set out in a series of non-chronologically-arranged narrative episodes. No attempt is made to set the scene or to reveal the real Adomnán's origins: his birth, homeland, family, education, vocation etc. The first episode has Adamnán in an assembly (*airecht*) where the devil, mischievously sent by the Munstermen, tries but fails to outwit him. The next episode sees Adamnán at Assaroe (one of only two episodes set in Donegal) where he is presented with a moral dilemma about whether or not a woman who killed another woman should herself be killed. The story 'jumbles' names taken from Donegal's real history and misses an opportunity to point out that the historical Adomnán would have been related genuinely to the individuals so-named; that is, to both the jumbled names and the correct ones on which the former were based. Incidentally, in the other story set in Donegal, the one about the woman's grave on Tory described above, that episode is followed by an interesting pronouncement by Adamnán.

> 'There are', said Adamnán, 'four people buried in the graveyard whose will would be done were they even to ask God to make dry land of the sea between Tory and the mainland,[9] or to raise heaven up from the earth if it fell on it.'

Each episode in the *Betha* will not be analysed here; that has been done very ably by Professors Herbert and Ó Riain.[10] They have pointed out the contemporary political significance of the detail of the stories for the time of the *Betha*'s composition. Most of the stories show Adamnán dealing with individuals and

---

9   Tory is 14.5kms (perhaps more proverbially 9 miles) out from the Donegal mainland, isolated in the Atlantic Ocean. But interestingly nearby Inis Bó Finne is attached to the mainland coast by an underwater sandbar (a tombolo formation) that can sometimes be used to walk to the island at low tide. There are several other such formations along the west coast of Donegal, such as at the monastic island of Inishkeel to the south. Perhaps as a result of being aware of these there was an impossible local aspiration that Tory should be so connected also. The anecdote may hint that the author, despite being associated with Kells (Co. Meath), had some acquaintance with Donegal, even with Tory, which by the tenth century (despite totally different origins, see above, chapter 1) would have been recognized as a Columban foundation. The latter claim would be set out formally in the mid-twelfth-century Middle Irish Life of Colum Cille (Herbert, *Iona, Kells and Derry*, pp 236 and 260).

10   See P. Ó Riain, 'Introduction' in Herbert & Ó Riain, *Betha Adamnáin*, pp 8–36 and M. Herbert, *Iona, Kells and Derry*, pp 158–79.

dynasties from various parts of Ireland, depriving them or their descendants of their kingships, often because of some slight to Adamnán himself or his community, or because they were on the 'wrong' political side.

Such a story is told about a real historical figure from Donegal, Congal Cinn Magair, who reigned as king of Tara between about 704 and 710. A king of Leinster called Cellach was exiled by his people and sought the assistance of Congal to regain his position. Adamnán arrived and warned Congal not to support Cellach. Congal gave what to us now, but not usually to people in medieval times, was a valid response, separating secular and 'ecclesiastical matters':

> Congal said that while they would settle ecclesiastical matters in accordance with the will of Adamnán, the disposition of the affairs of the king and of his kingdom was (entirely) his own prerogative.
>
> Adamnán declared 'Cellach will not be king, nor will there ever be a ruler of his race over the [Leinstermen]. Furthermore, each of his descendants will be worse than the one before.' Then he said to Congal son of Fergus: 'You will not be king from today onwards, and you will not reach your own land [in Donegal] alive, as sudden death will overtake you. Furthermore, no ruler will ever descend from you.' And all of these things happened as Adamnán said.

The real Congal (table 7) died in 710; according to AU 'of a fit' (*do bhidhg*). The odd thing about this story, however, is that despite the enmity shown between them here, the historical Adamnán and Congal were distant relatives and almost certainly friends, as Congal is listed as one of the 'guarantors' of the *Cáin Adomnáin*. The latter's father was known as Fergus of Fanad; Fergus had conquered that territory in the mid-seventh century (during Adamnán's lifetime) as part of the expansion northward of Cenél Conaill. Congal seems to have continued that expansion as his own soubriquet, Cinn Magair, derives from the place-name Cenn Magair on the next peninsula to the west of Fanad. His *caput* seems to have been the lost monument known as Doongonigle, Dún gCongail, now hidden somewhere under Woodquarter Forest to the west of Mulroy Bay.[11] The interesting thing is that by the time the *Betha Adamnáin* was composed Cenél Conaill had lost ownership of that area completely. Instead, it had been taken over by the Síl Lugdach who also controlled Adamnán's church in Raphoe to the south of Fanad. This negative impression of Congal seems to be in line with a similar impression of his Cenél Conaill predecessor, Loingsech mac Óengusa, who again, despite being listed as the first lay 'guarantor' of the

---

11   Lacey, *CC*, p. 271.

697 *Cáin Adamnáin*, is shown in the later *Cáin Adamnáin* quite negatively also, and as being 'from Fanad'. Congal is not mentioned in the *Cáin Adamnáin* but the king of Leinster, Cellach, whom Adamnán urged Congal not to support, is listed negatively, again despite having been in reality a 'guarantor' of the Iona *Cáin*. As we saw above, the *Cáin Adamnáin* is a Raphoe text usually said to date to about 1000, while the *Betha Adomnáin* derives from Kells a little over one generation earlier. But around that time there seems to have been a mutual policy in both Raphoe and Kells of playing down the Cenél Conaill kings of Tara from the time of the historical Adomnán, especially those associated with, or said to have been associated with, Fanad and its environs. That policy must derive from the Síl Lugdach and their appointees in Raphoe. Together with some other written material that will be examined below (see chapter 10) it seems to indicate some hostility on the part of the Síl Lugdach towards Fanad from about 950 (at least) until well into the eleventh century.

One episode in the *Betha* does come reasonably close to what we know from other sources about the real Adomnán: his expedition to Northumbria to secure the release of the Brega hostages in 687 (chapter 3 above). The description here dwells on the miraculous aspects of the story but, as a piece of medieval fiction, it is worth quoting.

The Northumbrians (*Saxain Tuaiscirt*) came to Ireland, plundered Mag Breg as far as Belach Dúin (old name for Castlekieran, near Kells, Co. Meath), and carried off a large number of captives, both men and women. The men of Ireland urged Adamnán to go in search of the captives to the Saxons. Thus Adamnán went to seek the prisoners. He reached the shore of a tidal estuary where the ebb was long, and the flow swift. Its swiftness was such that the best horse among the Saxons, with a good rider, and with the flooding tide, could scarcely carry its rider ashore, [even] by swimming, because of the length of the ebb and the swiftness of the flood. The Saxons moreover, did not allow Adamnán to land on the shore. 'Heave your boats up on to the beach', said Adamnán to his companions, 'for both sea and land obey God, and nothing can be done without Him'. The clerics did as they were told. Adamnán drew a circle with his staff round about the boats. Then God made the beach underneath them become firm, and he also made a high wall of the sea around them. Thus it was as if they were on an island, past which the sea flowed to its limits, and left them unharmed. When the Saxons saw that great miracle they trembled for fear of Adamnán and thereupon granted his entire demand. What Adamnán had demanded was that all the captives should be returned to him, and that the Saxons should never again plunder in Ireland. And Adamnán took back all of the captives.

As we saw in chapter 3, it was of course Adomnán's diplomacy and friendship with the new king of the Northumbrians, Aldfrith, that really secured the release of the captives, not the miracle of the sea.

One other story in the *Betha* connects with the apparent hostility we saw above towards the Fanad area of Donegal. It also links with two other separate texts associated with Adomnán: the traditions of the *Scuab as Fanaid* and the *Fís Adamnáin* (see chapter 10 below). In the *Betha Adamnáin* the saint 'proclaimed that an affliction would come upon the men of Ireland and of Britain around the feast of John'. A young man was visiting an anchorite at Croagh Patrick in Connacht and enquired if Adomnán's prophesy was true. The anchorite confirmed it saying that 'the tribulation consists of Adomnán's departure for heaven [his death?] around this feast of John' (see chapter 10 below). The anchorite sent a message to Adomnán to tell him. '"It is likely that it may prove true", Adomnán said. "In the name of God and Colum Cille, let us make for home [*diar taigh*, i.e. Iona]." *And afterwards he sang*: [the following verses]'.[12]

Má ro-m-thoiccthi écc i n(dh)Í,	If on Iona death should come,
ba gabál di thrócari.	That merciful end would be welcome.
Nícon fettar fo nimh glas	No place under all the sky,
fóttan bad fherr fri ti[u]gbás.	Would be better than there to die.[13]

Following this verse there is a long conventional list of Adomnán's virtues, a standard hagiographical account of his death and transfer to heaven and, to conclude the *Betha*, a description of his alleged continuing influence in this world.

A later Scottish work, the *Breviary of Aberdeen*, contains much material connected with the *Familia Columbae* and the traditions of the early medieval Irish and Columban clergy in Scotland and the north of England. Some of the material in the section on Adomnán seems to be related to similar material in the *Betha Adamnáin*.[14]

The *Breviary of Aberdeen* was one of the first books to have been printed in Scotland. It was compiled for William Elphinstone who was bishop of Aberdeen from 1483 to 1514. Elphinstone was a fascinating man. He was born in

12 This last phrase is in Latin.
13 This rhyming version in English (following the original rhyming version in Irish) is by the present author but based on the literal Herbert & Ó Riain text and translation (*Betha Adamnáin*, pp 60–1).
14 A. Macquarrie, *Legends of the Scottish saints*, pp 232–3. See also P. Ó Riain, 'Introduction' in Herbert & Ó Riain, *Betha Adamnáin*, pp 36–44 and M. Herbert, *Iona, Kells and Derry*, pp 171–3. All the quotations below from the *Breviary* are taken from Macquarrie with some minor modifications.

Glasgow in 1431 but his mother died when he was a child, and he is said to have been brought up to a large extent by the clergy of the city's cathedral. He later studied at universities in Glasgow (where he was ordained a priest) and in Paris. He had many connections with France serving as a Scottish ambassador there as well as in England, Germany and the Netherlands. He was a member of the Scottish parliament and held several senior public offices and was, effectively, the founder of Aberdeen University, which he modelled on his *alma mater* in Paris. As bishop in Aberdeen he was actively involved in rebuilding parts of the ancient cathedral dedicated to Saint Machar, a name that might conceal that of Colum Cille,[15] as well as a bridge over the River Dee. He is credited with being at least partly responsible for the introduction of printing to Scotland about 1507.

The *Breviary* was printed in Edinburgh about 1510. It contains an 'office' for the feastday of Saint Adamnán (*Sanctus Adampnanus*), 23 September. Two of its six particular Adamnán 'lessons' or short paragraphs bear a similarity to parts of the *Betha Adamnáin*. There is still debate among scholars about the degree of that similarity. Máire Herbert has argued that both of those works are based on an original Iona composition that is now lost but Padraig Ó Riain has argued that the Aberdeen text was based on the *Betha Adamnáin*.[16] However, the latter text is in the Irish language whereas the *Breviary* is in Latin.

The 'office' opens with a dedication strangely identifying 'Adampnanus' only as 'patron at Forvie in the Diocese of Aberdeen'. There follows a standard prayer thanking God for the feastday of 'blessed Adamnán, Thy confessor and abbot'. This is followed by six lessons about Adamnán, plus instructions for readings from other material relating more generically to abbots, confessors and virgins. Unlike the *Betha Adamnáin* which ignores the subject, the first lesson talks about Adamnán's birth and descent from 'the very noble race of King Conall [i.e., Cenél Conaill]'. It states that his birth was prophesied by St Columba from whom also, anachronistically, 'he received the monastic habit' and, again incorrectly, claims that he became abbot of the monastery on Lismore island in Loch Linnhe off the Scottish mainland coast near Oban. Of course, the real Adomnán was born a generation after Columba had died so he couldn't have received the 'habit' from the latter. In the debate about where the source material for the 'office' came from it is argued that this unchronological statement plus the untrue reference to Lismore could not have derived from Iona where the basic facts about the historical Adomnán would have been well known.

The next lesson purports to describe Adomnán's election as abbot of Iona, something not found anywhere else in the medieval sources.

15   B. Lacey, *Saint Columba*, p. 121
16   For these contrasting opinions see M. Herbert, *Iona, Kells and Derry*, pp 171–3 and P. Ó Riain, 'Introduction' in Herbert & Ó Riain, *Betha Adamnáin*, pp 36–44.

Later, when Failbe, abbot of the monastery of Iona of blessed memory, had died, St Adomnán was chosen and ordained abbot both by divine revelation and by the common consent of the brothers [*communi fratrum consensu*]; in that (office) he shone forth by many powers and signs of miracles.

Lesson number 7 outlines a visit by God to Adomnán when he was an old man. God takes the form of a beautiful male youth:

> After his vigorous years were past, he [Adomnán] built a cell out of wood so that he could devote himself more privately to contemplation. One day he did not come into the church for the celebration of the Hours while he devoted himself to God alone by prayer there. The elders [*seniores*] then came to the cell, and saw a youth of wonderful beauty settled in his bosom, consoling the old man and discoursing with him sweetly.

This little story is very like a description in the *Betha Adamnáin* of a similar miracle.

> At another time when Adomnán was in Iona, he fasted in his closed house [*thigh fhordúnta*] for three days and nights and did not come into the monastery. A few of the faithful went to the house to see how the cleric was. They looked through the keyhole and saw a very beautiful little boy [*mac mbecc roálainn*] in Adomnán's lap in a manner which convinced them that it was Jesus who had come in the form of a child in order to bring solace to Adomnán.[17]

The devil figures a lot, relatively, in these short lessons. The second part of number 2 reads:

> The people came to the blessed man to hear the word of God; while he was preaching to them the devil transformed himself into the shape of a fox, and made everyone laugh with his antics. When the saint saw this, when he made the sign of the cross the enemy [the devil] vanished.

Lesson number 3 features the devil in the disguise of a baby and child.

> While swine were turning over the earth, in their fashion, a live child was also found under an overturned sod. When St Adomnán found him he

---

17 Herbert & Ó Riain, *Betha Adamnáin*, pp 58–9. The same story is told at the entry for Adomnán's feastday in the Martyrology of Donegal (see chapter 12 below).

brought him up like a son, and worked hard to instruct him in liberal studies. Later when he was brought before the man of God [that is, Adamnán] he [the grown-up child] put many questions to him. The saint put the devil to flight, who sought to tempt the man of God in the form of a child, when he made the sign of the cross.

But the devil wasn't finished with Adamnán yet! Lesson number 8 is about a dead man who is brought for burial but rises up 'alive'. Adamnán arrives 'and protected the bystanders with the sign of the cross' and at once the 'demon' departed. Again, this account is close to but much briefer than a similar miracle story told in the *Betha Adamnáin*. Both the story of the beautiful youth and the story of the dead man who rises up follow one another in the same order in both the Aberdeen 'office' and in the *Betha Adamnáin*. The final lesson in the Breviary is a short account of Adamnán's death ending with the sentence: 'His body was buried in the Isle of Iona with due reverence.'

We can be fairly certain that biographical and hagiographical material about the real Adomnán written in Latin would have been preserved in the monastery on Iona. Adomnán was treated as a saint and a major step in the recognition of sainthood in medieval times was the composition of a hagiographical Life of the subject. There continues to be debate about whether or not parts of that original Iona text are preserved in the Aberdeen 'office', and the relationship of that text to the *Betha Adamnáin*.

CHAPTER TEN

Other writings

Other than the handful of sentences about him recorded in the contemporary annals (see Prologue above), which added together would hardly make a decent paragraph, there is no description of Adomnán from his own lifetime. This of course is not unusual; the fact that anything at all was written down about someone in the seventh century and survived to our time is an indication of how tremendously significant that person was in their own lifetime. On the other hand, there is a lot of material about Adomnán in literature that survives from after his death. Some of this material was attributed to him fictionally, and some of it may have been actually written by him; but a lot of it just tells stories about him, both factual, fictional and somewhere in-between.

Perhaps the best place to start is with the earliest separate description that has survived, written by the Venerable Bede. Bede was a Northumbrian Benedictine monk who was born in 672 and died in 735. He is recognized as an important early English saint. He is also acclaimed as one of the great teachers and writers of the early medieval church, particularly for his *Historia ecclesiastica gentis Anglorum*, the *Ecclesiastical history of the English people*. As was pointed out above, however, the fact that this book was entitled a *Historia* sometimes means that it is given a degree of alleged objectivity that it may not actually warrant, for instance in its treatment of the controversy about the calculation of the date of Easter and related matters. Bede's monastery was at Wearmouth/Jarrow, near modern Newcastle-upon-Tyne. As we saw above, Adomnán is known to have visited that monastery but the date of the visit is disputed (see chapters 3 and 6 above). Although he does not say so expressly it seems at least possible that the young Bede may have actually seen or even met the much older Adomnán on that occasion. He definitely praises Adomnán in the *Historia* for the latter's openness to persuasion on the Easter matter, even though the majority of monks on Iona were still maintaining the older controversial practices. And, if imitation is the highest form of flattery, then Bede certainly flattered the Donegal abbot. He made two versions of Adomnán's book about the Holy Land: one a short synopsis in the *Ecclesiastical history* and, sometime before he wrote that, his own separate abridgment of *De Locis Sanctis* (with the same title) which he fully credits to Adomnán's original. As we saw above also, he quotes the letter from Ceolfrith abbot of Wearmouth/Jarrow to King Nechtan of the Picts in which Adomnán was described as a 'renowned priest'.

Various other literary works besides the *Vita Columbae, De Locis Sanctis* and the *Lex Innocentium* are attributed to Adomnán.[1] While it is probable that he did write more than those three well-known works, it is also likely that several of those that are now associated with his name were written by other authors at much later dates.

One thing that Adomnán may have composed is the poem *Adiutor laborantium* ('Helper of workers'). It was thought to have been lost but was identified and published in the 1980s from an eleventh-century Anglo-Saxon manuscript associated with Winchester.[2] This litany-like poem in Latin had been attributed traditionally to Columba and, until recently, that claim was supported by its modern editors.[3] However, in 2010, Gilbert Márkus who had previously championed the latter attribution changed his opinion and argued instead that the poem had been composed by Adomnán.[4] In a fascinating essay Márkus analysed Adomnán's name and its variations (see chapter 2), drawing attention to the cleric as a frequent user of the word *homunculus*, which appears in the poem. Márkus argued that this word may be another (latinized) variation of the name Adomnán (a play on its derivation, real or imagined, from 'Adam'), a sort of pun signifying 'little man'. Márkus further suggests that by including the word in the poem Adomnán had, in effect, covertly signed it.

This short poem has twenty-five lines all ending in the syllable 'um'. It is abecedarian in form, that is, each following line of the poem begins with the next letter of the alphabet.[5] Whoever the author was – Columba, Adomnán or someone else – he identifies himself in the poem as 'a little man trembling and most wretched, rowing through the infinite storm of this age', and appeals to Christ to protect him.[6]

Adiutor laborantium,	O helper of workers,
Bonorum rector omnium,	ruler of all the good,
Custos ad propugnaculum,	guard on the ramparts
Defensorque credentium,	and defender of the faithful,
Exaltator humilium,	who lift[s] up the lowly
Fractor superbientium	and crush[es] the proud,

1   See, for instance, Kenney, *The sources for the early history of Ireland*, especially pp 283–7 and pp 444–5.

2   T. Clancy & G. Márkus, *Iona: the earliest poetry*, p. 69.

3   Ibid., pp 69–82.

4   G. Márkus, *'Adiutor Laborantium'*.

5   *Altus Prosator*, 'The High Creator', is a much longer, abecedarian Latin poem also from a Columban milieu, in fact often attributed to Columba himself (T. Clancy & G. Márkus, *Iona: the earliest poetry*, pp 39–68).

6   Text and translation from Clancy & Márkus, *Iona: the earliest poetry*, pp 72–3; reprinted in G. Márkus, *'Adiutor Laborantium'*, pp 145–7.

Gubernator fidelium	ruler of the faithful,
Hostis inpoenitentium,	enemy of the impenitent
Iudex cunctorum iudicum,	judge of all judges,
Castigator errantium,	who punish[es] those who err,
Casta vita viventium	pure life of the living,
Lumen et pater luminum,	light and father of lights,
Magna luce lucentium,	shining with great light,
Nulli negans sperantium	denying to none of the hopeful
Opem atque auxilium,	your strength and help,
Precor ut me homunculum	I beg that me, a little man
Quassatum ac miserrimum	trembling and most wretched,
Remingantem per tumultum	rowing through the infinite storm
Saeculi istius infinitum	of this age,
Trahat post se ad supernum	Christ may draw after Him to the lofty
Vitae portum pulcherrimum	most beautiful haven of life
Xristus; ... infinitum	... an unending
Ymnum sanctum in seculum	holy hymn forever.
Zelo subtrahas hostium	From the envy of enemies you lead me
Paradisi in gaudium	into the joy of paradise.
Per te, Christe Ihesu	Through you, Christ Jesus,
Qui vivis et regnas	who live[s] and reign[s].

Also attributed to Adomnán is a text in Latin relating to the Roman poet Virgil.[7] A number of manuscripts of about the ninth or tenth centuries preserved in continental libraries – in Berne, Florence and Paris – contain sections of commentaries on Virgil's Bucolics (or Eclogues) and Georgics which were written originally in the first half of the first century BC. One of those manuscripts has an endnote apparently written by the original compiler that says: 'I have collected all this from the commentaries of the Romans, namely Titus Gallus and Gaudentius and especially Junius Philargyrius of Milan'.[8] However, the complete commentaries themselves, from which the extracts were made and copied in the manuscripts referred to here, have been missing since ancient times. The surviving quotations, therefore, preserve material which otherwise would have been lost. The manuscripts differ but it is evident that they were drawn from earlier compilations that were almost certainly Irish in origin. Although the main part of these texts is naturally in Latin, all of them contain glosses in

7   The following remarks are based largely on J.F. Kenney, *The sources for the early history of Ireland*, pp 286–7, with additional material from D. Ó Cróinín, *Early medieval Ireland*, p. 213.
8   Titus Gallus seems to have lived in the fifth or sixth century; Gaudentius may have been the bishop of Brescia who died in 410; the dates for Junius Philargyrius of Milan are not known but are estimated as anywhere between about 425 and the seventh century.

Old Irish dating, it would seem, to around the end of the seventh century. The manuscripts, which are later in date again, are clearly copies of copies etc.; and it is also clear that the latest scribes, and perhaps some of the intervening copyists, did not understand the Irish language, as the glosses have been corrupted and garbled in the course of transmission. As J.F. Kenney said:

> The most plausible explanation of these facts is that some Irish scholar towards the end of the seventh century edited a collection of scholia [explanatory comments] on the Bucolics and Georgics, that more or less modified transcripts of his book were made by his disciples or others, and that several copies derived from these passed to the Continent at the time of the great migration of Irish scholars in the ninth century, and thereafter into the hands of continental scribes.

In the Paris manuscripts the name of the author of the original work from which the extracts have been preserved is represented in the Latinized form as Adananus or Adannanus. Given the suggested date of the text, based on the date of the Old Irish language glosses, most commentators have suggested that Adananus should be equated with Adomnán.[9] But it should be stressed that the Irishman Adananus, whoever he was, was not just a copier of other people's studies. As J.F. Kenney said of him:

> Adananus, or Ad[o]mnán, added considerable matter of his own – illustrations from Latin, Irish and occasionally Greek; references to at least Plautus and Suetonius; grammatical, historical and archaeological information of that half childish, semi-encyclopaedic type so dear to the early Middle Ages. In especial, he expanded his sources continually with Christian allegory.

Denis Meehan argued about these texts that 'the vocabulary, however, shows little similarity with the Latinity of Adomnán as exhibited in the *Vita Columbae*' or *De Locis Sanctis*.[10] Whether or not Adomnán of Iona was the author of these texts remains an open question.

Evidently Adomnán was an accomplished writer in Latin. But did he write also in Irish? There does not seem to be any particular reason why this could not have been so, although the evidence is not so clear that he did. Certainly, at very least as it has come down to us in the surviving manuscripts, the *Lex Innocentium* or *Cáin Adomnáin* is written in Old Irish (see chapter 4 above). Quite a number

9   See Anderson & Anderson, *Adomnan's Life of Columba*, pp 23 and 96.
10 D. Meehan, *De Locis Sanctis*, p. 3, n.2.

of other texts, prose as well as poetry, in Irish are also tentatively attributed to him. A hymn, poem or prayer in the eleventh-century Irish *Liber hymnorum*, although written in Irish, is called the *Oratio S. Adamnan*, 'The prayer of St Adamnán'. The text is headed by the phrase *Adomnan dorigne in n-orthain-se*, 'Adomnán made this prayer'.[11] Several commentators have suggested that it relates in some ways to the famous poem *Amrae Coluimb Chille* and therefore must postdate the latter.[12] The *Amrae* used to be thought of as having been composed shortly after the death of its subject, Columba, that is, around the final decade of the sixth century. But, recently, Jacopo Bisagni has shown that at least as we have it now the *Amrae* is a composition of the ninth century.[13] By extension, that would certainly weaken the case for an attribution of the *Oratio* to Adomnán.

Columb Cille	Colum Cille,
co Día domm eráil	to God, please commend me.
hi tías – ní mos-tías –	when the time comes to die,
	may I not die too soon –
(tucud íar-már,	(after great good fortune
muí mo chélmaine)	it is mine, my prophecy)
buidne co aingel airm	to the place of the angel army
(ainminm huí násadaig Néil,	(the name of Niall's famous offspring,
ní suáil snádud)	not small that protection)
Sïone co harchangliu hÉil,	to God's archangels in Sion,
i ndingnaib Dé Athar,	in God the Father's refuge,
etir comslectaib cethri	in the company of the twenty-four
sen find fichet fírién,	just, wise, and faithful elders
fo-chanat ríched ríg rúinig	who praise the realm of the great,
ruithnigthi;	mysterious King;
núal nád ránic, nád rocma –	sadness does not reach or touch them –
rect muí, mo Chríst	make right, my Christ
cumachtach col.	my enormous sins.[14]

The poem known as *Féilire Adamnáin*, 'Adamnán's Calendar', is a prayer addressed to the saints of the four seasons; that is, the saints whose festivals were celebrated throughout the whole year.[15] The heading identifies Adamnán as the

---

11 J. Bernard & R. Atkinson, *The Irish Liber hymnorum*, vol. I, p. 184; vol. II, p. 81.
12 E.g., Clancy & Márkus, *Iona: the earliest poetry*, pp 164–5.
13 J. Bisagni, Amrae Coluimb Chille: *a critical edition*. See especially pp 250–7.
14 This, to say the least, is a loose translation by the present author based on the more literal translation by Clancy & Márkus (*Iona: the earliest poetry*, p. 171).
15 J.F. Kenney, *The sources for the early history of Ireland*, p. 444; also M. Byrne, 'Féilire Adamnáin', pp 225–8, from which the text and translation here (with some slight modifications) are taken.

author and claims that the poem was dedicated to his mother. Such a dedication is not surprising: Adomnán's mother figures in many of the later texts about him, and the protection of motherhood seems to have been a genuine concern of his. The date of the poem is not clear but its editor, M. Byrne, identified a reference in it to the Martyrology of Óengus (829–33). That reference is certainly not definite (see below) but if true would make the poem, or at least the surviving 'revision' of it, over a century later than Adomnán's life, at least.

Incipit feleire Adamnain dia mathair hic	Here begins Adamnán's Saints' Calendar to his mother
Noimh nac ceithre Ráithe dutracht lim a nguidhe romsaerat ar phiana noimh na bliadhna huile.	The saints of the four seasons, to them I long to pray, may they save me from pain, the saints of the whole year.
Naoimh ind erraigh errdairc lim do deoin Dé daltait	The saints of the glorious spring-time, may they be with me by the will of God's fosterling
im Brighit noigh niodhain im Grighair im Pattraic.	together with Brigid, a maiden pure with Gregory and Patrick.
Naoimh int samraidh tirim impa ata mo baile Ón tírsa co tíssa Co hÍssa mac Maire.	The saints of the dry summer, about them is my poetic frenzy that I may come from this land to Jesus, son of Mary.
Naimh ind foghmair álainn ailim drong na dichéol Co tísat im gaire im Mairie is im Michéol	To the saints of the beautiful autumn, I call, not an inharmonious company, that they may come near me together with Mary and Micheal.
Naimh in geimridh guidim lium fri drogue demhna Im Íosa na nionat in spirat naemh nemhdha.	To the saints of winter I pray, To be with me against the demon throngs, Around Jesus of the mansions In the holy, heavenly spirit.
In feilire naemhsa Bias ag sruithibh saeraibh Cipas lia do randaibh	The saints' calendar[16] That noble sages do have, though more numerous its verses,[17]

16 This line has been interpreted as a reference to the Martyrology of Óengus (829–33).
17 The Martyrology of Óengus is, indeed, written in verse.

Nocha lia do naemaibh	it is not more numerous in saints.
Aitcim naoim in talman	I beseech the saints of earth,
Aithcim aingle ile	I beseech all of the angels,
Aitchim Dia fodeine	I beseech God himself,
Fo eirge is fo lighe	Both at rising and lying down,
Cia denar cia therar	Whatever I do, whatever I say
Co trebhar tir nimhe.	That I may dwell in the land of heaven.

There is a clever but slightly mocking poem in Old Irish about the early eighth-century cleric Cú Chuimne of Iona (mentioned above) and the moral dilemma he had in needing to choose between the monastic and the married life. The poem was sometimes attributed (unfortunately without any proof) to Adomnán, such as in the Preface in the Irish *Liber hymnorum* to another poem, *Cantemus in omni die*, which is attributed to Cú Chuimne himself.[18] The witty translation by John V. Kelleher echoes the reputation that Cú Chuimne did not always practice the highest ideals of monastic celibacy.

Cú Chuimne	Cú Chuimne in youth
Ro legh suithi co druimne,	Read his way through half the Truth.
A lleth n-aill hiaratha	He let the other half lie –
Ro leici ar chaillecha.	While he gave women the try.
Ando Coin Cuimne ro-mboi,	Well for him in old age.
im-rualaid de conid soi,	He became a holy sage.
ro-lec caillecha ha faill	He gave women the laugh.
ro leig al-aill arith-mboi.	He read the other half.[19]

Two short verses in Irish – in total three quatrains – incorporated in the tenth-century *Betha Adamnáin* are also attributed to Adomnán;[20] they may have belonged originally to a longer poem or poems. The first quotation consists of two quatrains that refer to Adomnán's friend Bruide mac Bili, the king of the Picts who died in 693 and was allegedly buried on Iona (see chapter 3 above).[21]

18 Bernard & Atkinson, *The Irish Liber hymnorum*, vol. I, p. 32; vol. II, p. 17. At its appearance in the margins of Cú Chuimne's death notice for 747 (746.5) in AU, which refers to him as *sapiens*, 'the learned', the poem is attributed to his *muime*, 'fostermother', which seems even less likely!

19 Quoted by D. Ó Cróinín, *Early medieval Ireland*, p. 216, from J. Kelleher, *Too small for stove wood*, p. 12.

20 T. Clancy & G. Márkus, *Iona: the earliest poetry*, pp 166–7; A. Smyth, *Warlords and holy men*, p. 136.

21 The text in Irish used here is the reconstruction by Clancy & Márkus (*Iona: the earliest poetry*, p. 167), which incorporates a few small changes from that as printed in Herbert & Ó Riain (*Betha Adamnáin*, p. 58), most notably the switching of lines 3 and 4 in the first quatrain. The loose translation here is my own.

Mór do ingantu do-[g]ní,	Great wonders are worked
in Rí génair ó M[a]ir[i];	By the king born of Mary,
écc do Bruide mac Bili	Death to Bruide mac Bile
betha scuabán i mM[a]ili.	But life to Scuabán[22] on Mull.

Is annam,	It must be, at least, unexpected,
íar mbeith í rríge thuaithe:	For he who was king of a *tuath* ['kingdom']
ceppán cauë crín dara	That an old, hollow trunk of an oak-tree[23]
im mac ríg Ala Cluaith[e]	Should enclose him, the prince of Ail Cluaith.

Short as they are, these verses present a number of problems. Ail Cluaith mentioned in the second verse was the Rock of the Clyde or Dumbarton, where the king of the Strathclyde Britons lived. But here, for whatever reason, it seems to be connected with the king of the Picts. However, both these kingdoms used P Celtic languages, which were probably very close, and the poet might have thought of the polities as somehow interchangeable. It is not clear either what the reference to 'Scuabán on Mull' means. It seems as if Scuabán was 'at death's door' but was subsequently reprieved 'by the king born of Mary'. Most authors have taken Scuabán as a personal name but, if it was, then the trail runs cold at this point. Clancy and Márkus, however, read it as a diminutive of the Gaelic word *scuab* in this context meaning 'little sheaves (of grain)'. If that was its intended meaning then the verse seems to be contrasting the death of the king with 'the burgeoning harvest on Mull'.[24]

That theme of death, and burial on Iona is picked up in the second verse quotation in the *Betha*, which is also attributed to Adomnán.

Má ro-m-thoiccthi écc i n(dh)Í	If on Iona death should come,
ba gabál di thrócari.	That merciful end would be welcome.
Nícon fettar fo nimh glas	No place under all the sky,
fóttan bad fherr fri ti[u]gbás	Would be better than, for there, to die.[25]

There is also a clever little quatrain about the universal experience of death which, together with the basic concept behind it, pops up occasionally in various items of Gaelic literature and folklore. Manus Ó Domnaill put it into the mouth of Colum Cille, but its composition is sometimes attributed to Adomnán.[26]

---

22 Or 'scuabán'. See below.

23 Early medieval burials inside logs, 'log burials', have indeed been found during archaeological excavations on Iona (Campell & Maldonado, 'A new Jerusalem', pp 63 and 65, and references cited therein).

24 Clancy & Márkus, *Iona: the earliest poetry*, p. 167.

25 Loose translation by this author.

26 For instance in Clancy & Márkus, *Iona: the earliest poetry*, p. 168, citing in support Adomnán's use in the *Vita Columbae* of the Latin *terrulam* as an equivalent to the Irish word *fód* etc.

Trí fodain nach sechantar,	They speak in a proverb of three little sods,
mar aderid a mór-fhocuil:	Impossible from which anyone to save:
fód a gene, fód a bais	The sod of his birth, the sod of his death,
& fód a adhnacuil	And lastly, of course, the sod of his grave.[27]

There are two 'vision' texts in Irish named after Adamnán. To distinguish them they are usually referred to as *Fís Adamnáin*, the Vision of Adamnán, and the Second Vision of Adamnán. The earlier of them, *Fís Adamnáin*, is dated to the tenth or eleventh century. Thomas Clancy referred to it as 'the most famous Adomnán text'[28] but others might challenge that characterization. It purports to be a description of a vision that Adamnán is said to have seen sometime before the Synod of Birr in 697. In fact, it is a later imaginative literary description of heaven and hell. It is an example of a *genre* of similar texts from various cultures both Christian and non-Christian, among them several Irish examples, the best-known of which to us now is Dante's *Divine Comedy*.[29] The *Fís* survives variously in four manuscripts, the earliest of which is the early twelfth-century Lebor na hUidre. Like so many contemporary texts the *Fís* is cast in the form of a homily for preaching. As we have it now it is a written text but it must be remembered that it was designed to be spoken, with all the additional nuances of tone and gesture that speech can convey.[30]

The *Fís* opens with two short quotations from Psalm 147 (verses 5 and 6) together with an exposition of the wisdom and power of the Lord, who 'raises up the meek [to heaven] but casts sinners down to earth [and hell]'. It reminds us that the 'mysteries and secrets' of heaven and hell had often been revealed to many of the apostles and the saints. It continues:

> [W]hat is preached here was revealed to Adamnán grandson of Tinne, the chief scholar of the west of the world, when his soul departed from his body on the feast of John the Baptist,[31] and was borne to heaven with the

27 Text from A. Kelleher & G. Schoepperle, *Betha Colaim Chille*, p. 102; loose translation from B. Lacey, *The Life of Colum Cille*, p. 62.
28 'Adomnán in medieval Gaelic literary tradition', p. 119.
29 See C.S. Boswell, *An Irish precursor of Dante*.
30 The translations quoted below have been taken from J. Carey, '*Fís Adamnáin*', but I have changed 'Adomnán' to 'Adamnán' (see Kenney, *Sources for the early history of Ireland*, p. 444) to emphasize that this text is not about the historical ninth abbot of Iona but his fictionalized, post-mortem alter ego.
31 There are three feastdays for St John the Baptist (see below): 24 June, 29 August and 23 September. The latter was also Adomnán's feastday and might, therefore, be the day referred to here; but that is not certain. In the *Fís*, Adamnán visits heaven etc. but returns to 'life' afterwards. See also the reference to 'the feast of John' in the *Betha Adamnáin* referred to in the last chapter.

angels of heaven, and to hell with its rebel army. When Adamnán's soul parted from his body, he immediately saw the [guardian] angel which had attended him for as long as he was in the flesh ...

Adamnán's soul and his guardian angel are then conveyed to heaven. They first come to the land of the saints. The saints are divided into four quarters: those from the east, west, north and south respectively. The saints are dressed in white and are all within the sound of heavenly music and within sight of the next highest enclosure containing 'the nine orders of heaven'. There are various other divisions of heaven, and the twelve apostles and Virgin Mary are kept slightly apart, close to the Lord. The patriarchs, prophets and disciples are near by and everyone is 'served' by 'companies of angels'. This is the way everyone will remain until the Day of Judgement when they'll be assigned to the place they'll remain in for the rest of eternity. The narrative continues with ever-more fantastic descriptions of God's throne, God himself (*sic*) and the fabulous glories surrounding him.

> Vast and strange to tell of is the ordering of that stronghold [heaven]; all that we have related of its varied ranks and its wonders is only a small part of its greatness.

The next section of the *Fís* describes the difficult path that ordinary human souls must take to reach 'the throne of the Creator'. There are very many hardships 'on the ladder of the seven heavens'. The soul must proceed up through the six heavens, each of them guarded and supervised by angels and archangels. Fiery streams, walls, furnaces and a whirlpool test the individual souls; the righteous pass on with little difficulty, sinners are held back, sometimes for years, to suffer the torments and trials before proceeding to the next heaven. All of heaven rejoices at the ultimate arrival of an 'innocent and righteous' soul, but the 'unrighteous and imperfect' having seen what they are going to miss for eternity are handed over to be passed down to hell.

> Then twelve fiery dragons swallow it [the 'unrighteous and imperfect' soul], one after the other, until the lowest dragon releases it into the Devil's mouth. There it finds fulfillment of evil and lack of every good thing, in the presence of the household of hell forever.

Having seen heaven, Adamnán is then brought by his guardian angel to visit hell. They come to a black, scorched country and beyond it a valley of fire. A bridge traverses the valley which, incrementally, gets more difficult to cross for the various grades of sinners. Beyond that is an area of torment which seems to correspond (although without so naming it) to the concept of purgatory,[32] as for its occupants on the Day of judgement 'their good will consume their evil … [and] they will be borne thereafter to the haven of life, to be before God's face forever.'

Beyond all these are those who are burned ferociously by fire and cold. The worst of this punishment is reserved for those who 'killed their kin and devastated God's church'. Among the latter are:

> Pitiless superiors of religious communities who have been given charge of the relics of the saints so as to collect gifts and tithes for God, but they take that wealth as their own possession rather than bestowing it upon the Lord's guests and the poor.

Further terrible torments are reserved for other corrupt members of the clergy:

> Priests who have violated their vows, and those whose faith is cold, and [religious] liars who mislead and deceive the multitudes and take it upon themselves to perform for them feats and miracles which they cannot accomplish.

Some of the damned have nails driven through their tongues or even their heads. Those so punished are:

> The folk given to grasping and refusal, lacking charity and the love of God; thieves and perjurers and traitors and slanderers and ravagers and raiders, unjust judges and troublemakers, witches and satirists, relapsed brigands and [maybe worst of all? – we can take the hint!] scholars who teach heresy.

The composer of the text was obviously put to the pin of his collar trying to find variations of torments for the different categories of the damned that had to be accommodated in his schema. Showers of 'red-flaming arrows' shot at them by demons constitute the punishment for:

> [D]ishonest artisans and comb-makers and merchants, the unjust judges of the Jews, and faithless kings, crooked sinful superiors of [religious?] communities, adulterous women and the go-betweens who seduce them into wickedness, and satirists.

Another crowd is packed onto islands in the middle of a sea of fire but are somewhat protected by a silver wall made of the alms they had given. This is another kind of purgatory as these are people who had led relatively good lives

---

32 Although there was a long history of the concept of a third realm alongside heaven and hell, it appears that it was not so named until the late twelfth century, and not officially defined as doctrine until the Second Council of Lyon in 1274.

in terms of giving charity and things like that, 'but in other respects lead lax lives, concerned with fleshly [sexual] things'. They will be reprieved on the Day of Judgment and conveyed to heaven.

The text continues with a litany-like description of virtually every nasty thing that could be said about hell. This seems to be really a list of all the negative things that could be experienced in or said about Ireland itself, all of them exaggerated to fantastic dimensions. Included among many other things are: great brambly bogs, filthy ever-dark pathways, slippery sharp cutting stones, rough wintry winds, putrid monster-filled lakes, terrible storms, and four kinds of fire!

At the end of all this, a presumably relieved Adamnán was brought back to the land of the saints in heaven. But when his soul seemed to want to linger there it was returned to his body on earth where he 'related in assemblies and gatherings of laity and clergy the rewards of the household of heaven and the punishments of hell'.

The *Fís* goes on to say that Adamnán continued to preach about these things for the rest of his life including: 'at the great assembly of the men of Ireland, when he imposed the Law of Adomnán upon the Gaels [the Synod of Birr in 697] ...' The conclusion of the text rehearses how the same themes were preached by St Patrick, the apostles and the prophets, and how 'the folk of the world' should fear Doomsday, finally beseeching 'God's mercy through the prayers of Adamnán ...'

There is not very much evidence in the text itself to indicate where or in what context it was composed. Its suggested date (tenth–eleventh centuries) is derived from the form of the language in which it was written. It has also been suggested, based on the central role given to Adamnán, that it may have been composed by a cleric who belonged to one of the monasteries of the Columban community. If so, the cleric in question may be exhibiting some anger at (and 'blowing the whistle' on) his seniors in the section (quoted above) about the 'pitiless superiors of religious communities ... given charge of the relics of the saints so as to collect gifts and tithes for God' but who take those offerings 'as their own possession rather than bestowing it upon the Lord's guests and the poor'. The lists of occupations referred to, both clerical and lay, might suggest that it emanated from a highly urbanized setting such as we know the Columban ecclesiastical settlement at Kells (Co. Meath) was at the time of its composition. But at this stage we really have no definite ideas about its provenance, other than through speculation.

The Second Vision of Adamnán also survives in four manuscript copies, dating from the fourteenth to the seventeenth centuries. The text itself dates from close to the fateful year of 1096 and is described by its latest editor as 'a homily containing an exhortation to fasting and prayer'.[33] Those penances should

33   Nicole Volmering, 'The rhetoric of catastrophe ... the Second Vision of Adomnán', p. 11.

be embraced because in that year Ireland was threatened with a disaster of an unclear nature but probably including plague, famine and fire from the heavens. According to the text, the people of Ireland had been forewarned about this by a revelation made by an angel to Adamnán, which is rehearsed at the beginning.[34] Further on the text tells us that it was the (dead) saints of Ireland themselves who besought the Lord to send the disaster to the country. They were driven to do so in order to cleanse their former churches because of the wickedness of the people who were currently in them, that is, the incumbent monks and other clergy.

The *Fís* text and the legend behind it are associated with the year 1096 because a number of coincidences that were believed to be significant would occur then: (i) the conjunction of a leap year with (ii) an embolismal year,[35] and (iii) a year when the Feast of the Decollation (beheading) of John the Baptist (29 August) would fall on a Friday.[36] It is not clear where this apocalyptic prophecy originated but it is thought that the widespread fear and panic generated in Europe by the millennial year of 1000, or the impending end of the century in 1100 (although few ordinary people then would have been aware of either of those dates), may have contributed to it. In the run up to 1096 there were a number of genuine disasters: bad weather and scarcity in 1094; very heavy snow in January 1095 and then pestilence from August 1095 through to May 1096.[37]

Apart from his role at the outset in receiving the prophecy from the angel and transmitting the message onward, Adamnán, otherwise, has no part to play in the text or its scenario. It is St Patrick or, more to the point, his successor (comarba) in Armagh, who will deliver the Irish from the doom, provided they fulfill the requirements of penance, some of them highly detailed and legal in nature, set out in the rest of the Vision. Effectively any saint could have functioned in the role given to Adamnán in the text, but there is at least one good reason why Adamnán's involvement was apposite if not strictly required by the narrative. John the Baptist has three feastdays: 24 June his birth date but, at least in Ireland, starting the previous 'eve', the evening of 23; 29 August the date of his decollation or beheading (his death) and 23 September the date of his conception.[38] He shares the last-mentioned date with Adamnán's feastday, marking the day the Donegal saint was believed to have died.

34 The historical Adomnán had, of course, died almost 400 years before these events were to come to pass.
35 A year with a thirteenth moon.
36 A fourth condition, the completion of a lunar cycle, did not occur in 1096 but that condition seems to have been ignored. Such a matter would have been known to very few people at the time, anyway.
37 These are recorded in the Irish annals.
38 This feastday was not widely acknowledged in the Latin church but, somehow, knowledge of it was available in early medieval Ireland.

Ireland was to suffer the impending disaster in 1096 because in contemporary folk belief it was an Irish druid, Mogh Ruith – in the legend an apprentice of the detested New Testament figure Simon Magus – who was understood to have actually beheaded John the Baptist. All the Irish would suffer because of that terrible crime. Thus, several issues contributed to these legends and the rumours that must have been circulating widely at the time: (i) the millennial fear at the year 1000, and/or the impending end of the eleventh century in 1100; (ii) the conjunction of a number of significant dates and events in 1096; (iii) the belief that an Irish druid had been responsible for the death of John the Baptist and that punishment would come to the whole Irish people eventually as a result; and (iv) a number of genuine natural disasters that had already occurred in the run up to and at the beginning of that year.

The punishment was predicted to be of various kinds, and it was given various names. For the most part it was believed that it would come from the south (south-west or south-east) of the country; actually, from the sea beyond. However, one version called it the *Scuab as Fánait*, 'the broom/besom[?] from Fanad'.

One variation of these ideas can be found in the twelfth-century notes added to the early ninth-century Martyrology of Óengus.

> In vengeance for the killing of John the Baptist [*Eoin Bautist*] comes the Besom out of Fanad [*scuab as Fánait*] to expurgate Ireland at the end of the world, as [St] Ailerán the wise[39] and Colum Cille foretold, i.e., at terce [9 a.m.] precisely will come the Besom out of Fanad, as Colum Cille said: 'Like the grazing of two horses in a yoke will be the diligence with which it will cleanse Ireland.'
>
> Of the Besom Ailerán said: 'two alehouses [*coirmtech*] will be in the one enclosure [*lis*] side by side. He who will go out of one house into the other will find no one before him alive in the house he will enter, and [when he returns] no one alive in the house from which he will go. Such will be the swiftness with which the Besom shall go out of Fanad.'
>
> [St] Riagail[40] said: 'Three days and three nights and a year will this plague [*in plaighsi*] be in Ireland. When a boat on Loch Rudraige [Dundrum Bay, Co. Down] shall be clearly seen from the door of the refectory, then comes the Besom out of Fanad.'
>
> A Tuesday in spring after Easter, now, is the day of the week on which the Besom will come in vengeance for John's passion [*i ndighail cesta Eoin*].[41]

39 Appropriately, he is believed to have died during the plague known as the *Buidhe Chonaill* of 665–8.
40 Associated with the Co. Down parish of Tyrella, i.e., *Teach Riaghla*.
41 W. Stokes, *Martyrology of Oengus*, pp 191–2, with slight modifications.

Whitley Stokes who edited the Martyrology of Óengus (and its later notes) drew attention to a possible link with the reference to a broom in the Old Testament, Book of Isaiah 14. 22 and 23:

> 'I will rise up against them,' says the Lord of hosts, 'and will cut off from Babylon name and remnant, offspring and posterity, says the Lord.
>   And I will make it a possession of the hedgehog, and pools of water, and I will sweep it [Babylon] with the broom of destruction, says the Lord of hosts.'

It is not at all clear why Fanad would have been thought of as the source of this destructive agent. As we have seen in various texts of the tenth and eleventh century, however, writers dealing with Adamnán, and mainly connected with Raphoe, portrayed Fanad and its occupants in a fairly negative way. The *Scuab as Fánait* may have been a reflex of a local common perception, even if only in joke form, that everything bad came 'out of Fanad'. The Fanad Peninsula[42] is in the northern part of the area taken over from Cenél Conaill *c.*800 by the Síl Lugdach who championed the cult of Adamnán at Raphoe. The Fanad area may well have harboured some remnants of the defeated and recalcitrant Cenél Conaill (or those loyal to them) who might have felt themselves to be 'enemies' of the new rulers, generating real opposition to the successful Síl Lugdach. An anti-Fanad prejudice would have arisen naturally in that situation.[43] However, as Arthur

---

42 Elsewhere, when discussing the birthplace of Columba and the origins of his mother Eithne, I have argued that what appears to have been the petty kingdom of Fanad seems to have decreased in size over time. I suspect that in the sixth and seventh centuries, at least, Fanad may have been understood to have included the Gartan area. But as time passed, right down to modern times, the idea of what constituted Fanad as it were retreated onto and up what is now called the Fanad Peninsula (Lacey, *CC*, pp 190–1; B. Lacey, *Saint Columba*, pp 25–6).

43 Breandán Mac Suibhne and David Dickson have noted that in the nineteenth and early twentieth centuries Fanad's reputation, even within – maybe especially within – Donegal, was less than positive. The area, allegedly, had 'a well-established reputation for violence'. The neighbouring parishes tended to blame 'the "men of Fánaid" for riots and brawls at their fairs and markets.'

> For all that Fánaid changed, outsiders continued to regard the district as separate and distinct, its inhabitants hidebound in tradition or backwardness, clannish, rough and ready, or simply rough. Even today [2000], people from Rathmullan still protest too much when it is suggested they are 'really from Fánaid'; 'put a coat on a brush and send it to Fánaid', they say, 'and it will come back with a woman'. Around Milford a person who has gone 'out of this world and into Fánaid' is in a very remote place indeed, and in the few Irish-speaking homes left in the western and always more genteel peninsula of Ros Goill, '*Ordógaí Fhánada*' (clumsy Fánaid oaf) remains the choice rebuke to the awkward and the ungainly (B. Mac Suibhne & D. Dickson, *The outer edge of Ulster*, pp 2 and 5).

I am grateful to Prof. Lillis Ó Laoire for drawing these passages to my attention and to Prof. Breandán Mac Suibhne for discussion about them.

Spears pointed out, there was a significant comet sighting all over the world in 1097, which the Chinese called the 'broom' comet, presumably on the basis of its shape as seen by them.[44] It is hard to believe that there could have been any direct transmission of this idea from China to Ireland but if the comet was named from its shape then the same name could have been applied coincidentally in Ireland. The phrase 'broom out of Fanad' of course related to where the speaker/ viewer was standing. The kingdom of the Síl Lugdach, which may have been an enemy or at least hostile to the contemporary people of Fanad, was by the late eleventh century stretched out across the southern edge of the latter territory, from Gartan Lough and Kilmacrenan to Raphoe. Any apparition in the sky to the north of them could easily have been described as 'out of Fanad'.[45]

The Second Vision of Adamnán doesn't mention the *Scuab as Fánait*, but the background to it evidently arose from the same general context. The following is the opening section of the text, the only part that actually refers to Adamnán:

> The vision which Adamnán, a man full of the Holy Spirit, saw, that is, the angel of the Lord said these words of his to him:
> 'Woe! Woe! Woe to the men of the island of Ireland transgressing the Lord's commandments! Woe to the kings and princes who do not love truth and love injustice and plunder! Woe to the teachers who do not teach truth and consent to the folly of the imperfect! Woe to the harlots and sinners who will be burned up like hay and stubble by a fire kindled in an embolismic leap year and at the end of a cycle and on the [Feast of] the Decollation of John the Baptist! On a Friday in this year a plague will come, unless devout penance will have prevented it, just as the Ninevites did!'
> This, then, is the principle and law of spiritual direction of the men of Ireland, for the benefit of their bodies and souls, for the banishing of plagues and heathens and mortality from them, as was revealed to Adamnán ua Tinne through the counsel of God and Patrick, with a warning and a message to them, that the men of Ireland should beware and fear zealously the mortality which will come to them unless God's mercy and Patrick's prayer to the Creator turn it back. One mortality after the other, then, will come to them up to the mortality of the Feast of John [the Baptist]. It is Patrick, then, who bears the chief responsibility for sorrowful pleading for

44 A. Spears, 'An Scuab as Fánaid', p. 12.
45 Another of the several coincidences that have occurred as I write these words is that at this time, 14 July 2020, the comet Neowise, which comes close to earth only once in every 7000 years or so, is providing a spectacle in the northern skies as seen from Donegal. The last time it could be seen there was before farming, pottery or megalithic tombs were known on the island of Ireland; all of those things then still a long way in the future.

mercy for the men of Ireland, because it is he whom the Lord has entrusted with saving them from paganism, idolatry and unfaith. It is he who will be their judge and advocate on Doomsday.

The saints of Ireland [*noim Erenn*], however, are beseeching the Lord that the plague might come to cleanse their churches on account of the amount of guilts and treacheries and contentions of the people who are in them.[46]

The rest of the text places the avoidance of the awaited dangers in the hands of St Patrick – actually, his successor at Armagh – assuming that the people of Ireland co-operate by observing the fasts and prayers set out by Patrick. The Annals of the Four Masters records the situation in 1096 in the following way.

The festival of John fell on Friday this year; the men of Ireland were seized with great fear in consequence, and the resolution adopted by the clergy of Ireland, with the successor of Patrick [at their head], to protect them against the pestilence which had been predicted to them at a remote period, was to command all in general to observe abstinence, from Wednesday till Sunday, every month, and to fast [on one meal] every day till the end of the year, except on Sundays, solemnities, and great festivals; and they also made alms and many offerings to God; and many lands were granted to churches and clergymen by kings and chieftains; and the people of Ireland were saved for that time from the fire of vengeance [*ar téine na díoghla*].

As it happened, no particularly bad disaster was experienced in Ireland in 1096; but the 'visions' of Adamnán went on to have a literary life of their own.

Adamnán appears quite frequently in the fictional material in both the prose sections and poems in the Book of Fenagh, as indeed do other figures from the early history of Donegal such as Colum Cille and the Conall from whom the Cenél Conaill dynasty was named. The Book of Fenagh is dated to 1516 but is an augmented copy of an older manuscript compiled between 1258 and 1281, which no longer survives.[47] The early church site of Fenagh is in Co. Leitrim. Leitrim borders the extreme south of Donegal but Fenagh is a further sixty kilometers south-east of where the two counties actually meet. Ostensibly, Fenagh should have had no connection with Donegal history or, indeed, with Adomnán. But

46 Nicole Volmering, 'The Second Vision of Adamnán', pp 657 and 659.
47 The Book of Fenagh (and its antecedents) has a complex history which is outlined fully in R.A.S. Macalister, *Book of Fenagh: supplementary volume*, pp 3–32. See also R. Gillespie, S. Ryan & B. Scott (eds), *Making the Book of Fenagh*. I have not dealt here with every mention or appearance of Adamnán in the Book. For the date of the earlier manuscript see T. Ó Canann, 'Trí Saorthuatha Mhuintire Chanannáin', p. 34 and n. 122.

a local legend dating back to medieval times points to a Neolithic portal-tomb there as the burial place of the Conall who gave rise to the Cenél Conaill, he having been killed according to the legend in an encounter nearby. That fiction underlies many if not all of the appearances of Adamnán, and the other Donegal connections, in the Book of Fenagh.

In the book, for various reasons, Caillín (the Fenagh saint) makes many grasping demands for dues from Cenél Conaill, from Colum Cille and from Adamnán, and claims (impossibly, of course) to have been the tutor of the two latter clerics.[48] In turn the two Donegal saints are shown as issuing strict orders under the threat of various punishments that Caillín's church at Fenagh must be supported by the laity.

In the final long poem in the book[49] – the second of two with the opening line *Caillín cáid cumachtach*, 'The Holy, powerful Caillín' – the Fenagh cleric is requested by Cenél Conaill to resuscitate their dead eponymous ancestor, Conall. He does as they ask and, as a result, they owe further tribute to Caillín and his church. Later Adamnán came to Caillín and the latter bestowed various benefits on Cenél Conaill, including 'the strength of a hundred in every nine [fighting men], the strength of nine in each man [i.e. in battle]'. Then Caillín goes on a circuit of Ireland, leaving Adamnán behind in Fenagh, apparently in charge there according to a misplaced verse in the poem. Caillín eventually arrived at the River Moy (Co. Mayo). The local Uí Fiachrach and Uí Amhalghaidh (the chief families of Tireragh and Tirawley) gave Caillín permission to bring there the *Leac Adamnáin* ('Adomnán's slab', see chapter 11 below), which he had found. For this, Adamnán has to pay him even more tribute. The following is just a small selection of verses from the poem which, as it were, progress the story.[50]

Iar cuairt Erend ardmoire,	After visiting very great Ireland,
Co Fidnacha ar cúl;	[Caillín] returns back to Fenagh;
Gur chuir uada Adamnán,	Then he sent Adamnán away,
Co na scrinn chaid chumdaighhi,	With his holy, covered shrine,
I tir Fiachrach is Amalgaid,	To Tír Fiachrach and [Tír] Amhalghaidh,
No gur gab in mur.	Till he reached the sea [at Skreen].
...	...

48 Adomnán's life was roughly a hundred years later than Colum Cille's. Interestingly, Pádraig Ó Riain points out that Caillín 'is a diminutive of Caille, a hypocoristic [endearing] form of Colum ... [Caillín] may thus have originated as [a] localization of Colum Cille of Iona.' *Dictionary*, pp 135–6.

49 The date of the poem is not clear but presumably it belongs to the Middle Irish period (*c.*900–1200).

50 The translation by this author is based on an augmentation of the version published by W.M. Hennessy & D.H. Kelly, *The Book of Fenagh*, pp 406–15. See also corrections etc. in R.A.S. Macalister, *Book of Fenagh: supplementary volume*, especially p. 51.

Mo dub diglach degfertach,	'My miracle-working, good *dub diglach*[51]
Bid agat a Adamnain,	You can have, O Adamnán,
Bind a guth ra bein.	Its tone sounds sweet.'
Bidh e in *clagan Adamnain*	'Let it be the *Clogán Adamnáin*,[52]
D'Uibh Fiacrach, d'Uib Amalgaid,	For Uí Fiachrach and Uí Amhalghaidh,
'S do shil Chonuill choscraig,	And for victorious Conall's offspring,
Mairg airech gus ricfasan	Woe to him to whom [its sound] will reach
Mana beth da réir.	Unless he obey it.'
Gabais tnúth is mor formatt,	Then jealousy and great envy seized
Popal Caillin cumachtaig,	Mighty Caillín's people [monks?],
Ri hAdamnan adamru,	Against illustrious Adamnán,
Gura chlaechlo a li.	So that their esteem[?] for him changed.
Gurro cuirset Adamnan,	And they sent Adamnán away,
O a manchaib, o a manchesaib,	From his monks, from his privileges,
Andiaid Choluim chumahtaigh,	After powerful Colum [Cille]
No go riachd co hI.	Till he reached Iona.

While it is difficult and maybe impossible to explain why Adomnán of Iona becomes involved with the stories about Caillín, one explanation may be found in the genealogies of the Conmaicne that are found in the Book of Fenagh; Caillín is said to have belonged to the Conmaicne. The latter certainly did have a presence in south Leitrim, where they were known as the Conmaicne Maige Réin, but they were present also in other parts of Connacht.[53] In 'the genealogy of the Conmaicni of Cúil Tola' (Kilmaine in south Mayo) there occurs an instance of the very rare name Adamnán. He is depicted as belonging to the tenth generation after 'Cairid (who bent the knee to Patrick at Tara).'[54] Assuming that we can date Patrick's alleged 'visit' to Tara to *c.*460, and that each generation can be assessed as lasting about 30 years, then Adamnán of Cúil Tola may have been alive about the middle of the eighth century, not very long after the death of Adomnán of Iona. In addition, also in the Book of Fenagh, Caillín is addressed in a poem as 'a descendant' of Cairid although, as the editors pointed out, Cairid is not found in the (patently false) pedigree of Caillín near the beginning of the book. Attempting to rationalize this anomaly, the editors suggested that Cairid

---

51 'Black revenge', the name of a bell.
52 'Adamnán's little bell', the new name for the *dub diglach*.
53 They give their name for instance to Connemara, Co. Galway, Conmhaicne Mara.
54 *Book of Fenagh*, pp 384–5. The same pedigree but using the form 'Adomnán' is found in the earlier twelfth-century sources, Rawlinson B 502 and the Book of Leinster, as well as in other later medieval texts (M. O'Brien, *Corpus genealogiarum Hiberniae*, p. 319: 161b15).

may indeed have been an ancestor of the Fenagh saint but 'in the female line'.[55] Adomnán of Iona's alleged connection with St Caillín could have come about as a distortion of a real tradition about an Adomnán/Adamnán belonging to the Conmaicne, But then the name Caillín itself may be some sort of distortion of the name Colum Cille!

Adomnán, in his various characterizations, appears in a wide range of other pieces of medieval Irish literature. But the selection discussed here is, hopefully, enough to give an impression of his popularity as a fictionalized character in addition to his achievements as a real historical person.

55 *Book of Fenagh*, pp 157, 384.

CHAPTER ELEVEN

Comarbas, *maors* and churches

The ecclesiastical settlement at Raphoe was almost certainly a new foundation created by the Síl Lugdach around 800.[1] The Síl Lugdach dynasty came originally – in the sixth and seventh centuries – from a relatively impoverished, small, coastal petty kingdom in the Cloghaneely area of north-west Donegal. Throughout the eighth and ninth centuries they expanded their territory inland. After the seismic battle of Clóitech in 789, when the political construction of Donegal was totally reorganized, the Síl Lugdach acquired some of the former territory of Cenél Conaill in the good agricultural lands of east Donegal. This included the area around Raphoe and also, most importantly, the territory around Kilmacrenan and Gartan where the churches and sites connected with the birth and young life of Colum Cille were located. They also took over some of the principal attributes of the former rulers of the area, Cenél Conaill, among which was lay support for the cult of Colum Cille as propagated principally by the clergy of Kilmacrenan. Up until then, Kilmacrenan had been among the chief churches, if not *the* chief church, in north-west Donegal. In effect, Síl Lugdach became the main guardians of the patrimony of the young Colum Cille. In that role, and no doubt under the tutelage of the monks of Kilmacrenan, they had also falsely incorporated aspects of the Columban narrative into their own origin legends, including the false retrospective recruitment of Adomnán (and Columba) into their own family ranks. They achieved that by manipulating the genealogical record and by claiming, inaccurately, that they were descended from a sixth-century figure called Lugaid. In actual fact there was a sixth-century Donegal Lugaid who was a first cousin of Columba, but he was not the eponymous ancestor of the Síl Lugdach. We don't have proper dates for the Lugaid who was Columba's cousin but, based on his position in the pedigrees, he must have died about the middle of the sixth century.

According to the dates of 'his descendants' for whom we have absolute death years and based on his position in their pedigrees, the alleged Síl Lugdach Lugaid would have had to have died about 630 (see table 4 above), that is at least two generations after the Cenél Conaill individual of the same name. That

1 The Síl Lugdach were assisted in their rise to prominence almost certainly by their military collaboration with the powerful Cenél nEógain and the backing of the propagandists ('historians') of the monastery at Kilmacrenan (see above). The greatly important families of Uí Domnaill and Uí Dochartaigh emerged from the Síl Lugdach in the course of the ninth and tenth centuries (see table 4 above) around the same time as the foundation and early growth of the church at Raphoe.

Table 10: Cenél Conaill III: relationship between Columba and Lugaid

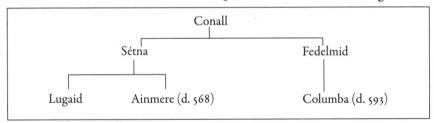

Cenél Conaill Lugaid was not the Síl Lugdach ancestor; instead, they derived their dynastic name from some totemic connection with the pre-Christian god Lug.[2] However, so successful were Síl Lugdach at adapting to their new role as guardians of Colum Cille's heritage in north-west Donegal that about 880, following the death of his predecessor, one of their members, Flann mac Maíle Dúin, became (or claimed to have become, see below) *Comarba Coluim Cille*, head of the Columban confederation of monasteries. Wherever Flann located himself in that role we can assume that his previous home church was either at Kilmacrenan or Raphoe, or possibly at both.

After its establishment, Adomnán of Iona (characterized as Adamnán) was credited as being the presiding saint of the church at Raphoe, although not its founder. Around the same time his status as a saint was confirmed, and as it were ratified, by his inclusion in the Martyrology of Óengus. It is extremely unlikely that there was any real historical connection between the genuine Adomnán and the church at Raphoe. He may have been born and raised close by, but that was just a coincidence that may have been exploited by the real founders of Raphoe c.800. It seems doubtful that the new Síl Lugdach rulers of the area would have been previously aware of that link of two hundred years earlier, but the 'historians' at Kilmacrenan, who almost certainly were orchestrating the situation, may have been conscious of Adomnán's alleged birthplace and maternal family associations. Somewhat serendipitously, as we have seen above, a similarly named bishop, Adomnán, had died in 731 at the nearby (and by the early ninth century, apparently, abandoned) church of Ráith Maige Aenaig. That factor seems to have been distorted and exploited to assist in the creation of a new origin legend for Raphoe. So strongly did this false identification of the real Adomnán with Raphoe become that the latter came to be recognized as 'his' most important church. In addition, whether by natural evolution or, as is more likely, through deliberate propagandistic manouevring by the heads of Raphoe (and/or their lay supporters), Adomnán began to be recognized as the near equivalent of – if not precisely on the same par as – his predecessor

2   Lacey, *Lug*.

and relative, Saint Columba.[3] However, by the time of the composition of the Middle Irish Life of Colum Cille in the middle of the twelfth century, the almost certainly equally-fictional legend of Raphoe's foundation by Colum Cille had been established firmly enough for it to be narrated unambiguously and unapologetically in that text. That legend, for which there was no historical basis, must have been in circulation for some time before it was so brazenly stated by the Derry author of the Life.

The word comarba (literally 'heir') is usually understood as the original formal designation of the head of a federation of churches associated with a saint in whatever form that existed at the time. However, as the early Middle Ages came to an end, it increasingly came to mean the head of a specific, single church only, especially an important church in that saint's patrimony. AU records the death in 938 of Dubthach, 'successor (comarba) of Colum Cille and Adómnán (sic)'. There was not a separate Familia Adomnani but evidently Adomnán was by then considered important enough to have his name joined with that of his predecessor, at least in some quarters. In the absence of specific evidence, Dubthach's precise title, as also that of his successor Robartach who died in 954 (AU; similarly named comarba Coluim Cille & Adomnáin [sic]), has often been taken by commentators such as William Reeves to mean that he must have had some particular connection with the church at Raphoe beforehand, and that he may have been the abbot there. However, we cannot be certain about that because we have virtually no records, specifically, about the abbots or heads of the church at Raphoe for the first few centuries of its existence after c.800. An 'Old Book of Raphoe' certainly did exist and probably contained such a chronicle but it has not survived except in the portions quoted in other sources. It seems likely also that there was some overlap or even institutional relationship between Raphoe and the more ancient church of Kilmacrenan about twenty kilometers to the north-west. As with Raphoe, a Book of Kilmacrenan certainly did exist and we know something about its contents. It definitely seems to have contained a chronicle, annals (?), of some kind.[4]

---

3   Adomnán certainly deserved that honour. In many ways he appears to have been an even more important historical figure than Columba. Apart from the foundation of Iona and its daughter houses, the only reputation that Columba really achieved was what was attributed to him, rightly or wrongly, by Adomnán, in the Vita Columbae.

4   Lacey, Lug, pp 41–2, 54, 66–7. See also T. Ó Canann, 'Máel Coba', p. 34 and p. 61, n. 17 where he refers to John Colgan's reference to the Codex de Killmhicnenan.
   The poem 'A eolcha Conaill ceoluig' in the Book of Fenagh has the following quatrain:
   'Gid cia ro shired gan crad / Lebar chilli mic nEnan, / Ro geabtha ar a lor co lom / Fis gacha dala i Conoll.' [But if without much pain you searched / The Book of Kilmacrenan, / There in its pages you'd plainly find / The knowledge of each event in [Tír] Chonaill.]

Dubthach probably took up his position as comarba of Colum Cille (at minimum) in 927 on the death of his relative Máel Brigte son of Tornán.[5] As Máire Herbert pointed out 'there is no evidence of his [Máel Brigte's] residence in Iona as its abbot ... All that is recorded of his career indicates that he was based in Ireland throughout.'[6] Whatever had happened at an institutional level, it is clear that the titles of comarba of Colum Cille and abbot of Iona were no longer considered to be synonymous; nor was it necessary for the comarba to be based any longer on Iona.[7] Máel Brigte, who belonged to the Cenél mBogaine of south-west Donegal, was also comarba of Patrick, possibly since 883. In an unprecedented and revolutionary manner he became comarba of Colum Cille in 891, apparently on the death of the Síl Lugdach incumbent Flann mac Maíle Dúin.[8] In fact, at his death on 22 February 927, *felici senectute*, 'in happy old age', the Annals of the Four Masters refers to Máel Brigte as comarba of Patrick, Colum Cille and Adomnán,[9] as well as 'head of the piety of all Ireland, and the greater part of Europe'. Máire Herbert has written: 'Whatever the circumstances of his appointment, Máel Brigte's tenure of office as comarba of Colum Cille may be seen to mark an important departure in the history of the saint's community'.[10] As mentioned, Máel Brigte's predecessor as comarba of Colum Cille appears to have been Flann mac Maíle Dúin. Flann's people, the Síl Lugdach, and presumably Flann himself, would by that stage have come from the area of Donegal that contained all the sites associated with the birth and young life of Columba, as well as the important Columban churches at Kilmacrenan and Raphoe. They must have thought of themselves as the primary guardians of the memory of both Columba and Adomnán.

Although on his death in 891, AU describes Flann as *abbas I*, 'abbot of Iona', the question must naturally arise as to whether, like Máel Brigte, he had ever been based in Iona.[11] There is some confusion regarding Flann's genealogy and

5   According to the genealogies Dubthach's great-great-grandfather was Máel Brigte's great-grandfather. See chart opposite p. 342 in W. Reeves, *The Life of St Columba*.
6   M. Herbert, *Iona, Kells and Derry*, pp 74–5.
7   Something similar seems to have occurred in relation to the kingship of Tara, that is, the incumbent did not need to be resident at Tara.
8   For Flann see T. Ó Canann, 'Clann Fhiangusa'.
9   Adomnán's name occurs in Máel Brigte's title only in AFM, under the year 925; it is not listed in AU. It seems as if the Four Masters have gilded the lily a little bit in this instance. However, both in his own personal name and in his ecclesiastical titles, Máel Brigte was a living memorial to the three patron saints of medieval Ireland: Brigid, Colum Cille and Patrick.
10 M. Herbert, *Iona, Kells and Derry*, p. 75
11 A slab on Iona decorated with a ringed cross has two almost identical inscriptions asking [o]*roit ar anm*[*ain*] *Flainn*, 'A prayer for the soul of Flann'. It has been suggested sometimes that this commemorates Flann mac Maíle Dúin. But 'on epigraphical grounds' that attribution has been dismissed in favour of an eighth-century date (*Argyll 4*, p. 187, no. 46, with illustration on p. 186). Flann was, of course, a relatively common Gaelic name.

identity.[12] His ancestry is set out in a collection of the pedigrees of fourteen comarbas of Colum Cille. This is preserved in the late fourteenth-century Great Book of Lecan but was compiled in Kells in the tenth century.[13] Flann's pedigree (or someone with a similar though slightly different lineage) is also preserved in the seventeenth-century Mac Fhirbhisigh secular genealogies (155.3) where the individual concerned appears to be a significant lay leader. As a resolution of these problems Tomás Ó Canann presciently suggested that:

> the dual placement of Flann's genealogy in Lecan and [the Mac Fhirbhisigh genealogies] implicitly casts him in the familiar mould of a warrior cleric, an archetype frequently encountered in early medieval sources. These twin [genealogical] settings would seem to reinforce a putative joint-role as a secular head of Clann Fhiangusa [sub-branch of Síl Lugdach in the Kilmacrenan/Raphoe area of Donegal] and the comharba of Colum Cille/abbot of Iona.[14]

Perhaps the latter claim was not much more than that, just a claim!

Whatever positions they had held previously, Máire Herbert has shown that Dubthach and his successor Robartach (mentioned above, and each described as *comarba* of Colum Cille and Adomnán) were both abbots of the monastery at Kells (Co. Meath). She also accepted that 'the possibility cannot be discounted that Dubthach, first holder of the title ... held the abbacy of Raphoe, or of another church associated with Adomnán, at some time previous to his appointment as *comarba*'.[15] This may well be the case. Dubthach definitely did have an association with the north-west of the country. He belonged to Cenél mBogaine whose territory lay in the south-west part of Co. Donegal, the area where Gleann Coluim Chille is located.

As we saw above, Dubthach was a relative of Máel Brigte mac Tornáin. Another relative of Dubthach, his uncle, Caencomhrac son of Maeluidir, died about 929. Caencomhrac was described as abbot and bishop (*abb & epscop*) of the monastery of Derry (*Daire Calcchaich*) and steward of the Law of Adomnán (*maor cána Adhamnáin*). The account occurs, however, only in the seventeenth-century Annals of the Four Masters[16] and there is little further information about Caencomhrac. His feastday was commemorated on 6 September,[17] perhaps with some added significance as that was the day before the feastday of one of the

12 T. Ó Canann, 'Clann Fhiangusa and the pedigree of Flann mac Maíle Dúin'.
13 M. Herbert, *Iona, Kells and Derry*, p. 79.
14 'Clann Fhiangusa', p. 22.
15 M. Herbert, *Iona, Kells and Derry*, p. 80.
16 At the year 927.
17 W. Reeves, *The Life of St Columba*, p. 393.

two Raphoe Adamnáns (see chapter 8 above). If Caencomhrac was genuinely associated with Derry, by the tenth century almost certainly he would have had to have belonged to, or at least been associated with, Cenél nEógain. However, his office as steward of Adamnán's Law suggests a different association and William Reeves showed his descent from Cenél mBogaine.[18] But it looks as if the Four Masters, who were of course writing seven hundred years later (as well as other writers), occasionally misread references to Daire [Eithne] or Kilmacrenan as referring instead to Daire [Calgaich] or Derry. Several other entries in the annals, especially in AFM, seem to confuse Derry and Kilmacrenan.[19] It is therefore not certain at all that Caencomhrac had any connection with Derry. It is much more likely that his church was Daire Eithne/ Kilmacrenan. That would make his alleged role as steward of the Law of Adomnán, effectively collector or receiver of the relevant fines and dues arising from the *Cáin Adomnáin*, far more understandable. In this scenario I would suggest that, although he was probably abbot of Kilmacrenan, his episcopal 'see' – that is, if he actually had one – may have been located at Raphoe.

Under the year 950, but properly corrected to 952, the Annals of the Four Masters records the death of Adhlann son of Éichneach son of Dálach, who is described there as the *comharba* of 'Daire Colaim Chille'.[20] Adhlann belonged to the Síl Lugdach. His grandfather Dálach was given the somewhat restrained title of 'chief (*dux*) of Cenél Conaill' by the chroniclers when he died in 870 (AU).[21] Whatever about any connections on his maternal side and despite a long-standing propagandistic tradition, it is extremely unlikely that Dálach, or his ancestors and successors, was genealogically part of the Cenél Conaill, as is strongly argued in much of the later medieval literature. His son, usually known by the endearing form of his name as Éichecán, was unambiguously claimed as king (*rex*) of the Cenél Conaill when his death is recorded in 906 (AU). That Éichnecán was Adhlann's father. John Colgan lists Adhlann as one of his Derry

18 W. Reeves, *The Life of St Columba*, table facing p. 342.
19 B. Lacey, *Medieval and monastic Derry*, pp 46–9. Another example of this is the reference to 'Doire donn' in the poem 'Ard na scéla, a mheic na, ccuach'. The modern editor of the poem, Margaret Dobbs, took it, almost certainly mistakenly, that this was a reference to Derry ('A poem ascribed to Flann mac Lonáin', p. 33), whereas it is much more likely that Doire Eithne, Kilmacrenan, was the place in question (B. Lacey, *Medieval and monastic Derry*, p. 48).
20 Adhlann was a brother of the Domnall from whom the famous Uí Domnaill family took its name.
21 Despite the fact that the contemporary annals state that he was 'killed by his own people', Dálach was remembered fondly as a significant ancestor (the 'father') of several of Donegal's most important medieval families, most notably the Uí Domnaill (O'Donnells). In fact, the label in Irish 'Dálaigh', referring back to this Dálach, is still used locally to signify someone from a Donegal background. Such a contradiction could be explained if the people who killed him had been the real Cenél Conaill, angered by his theft of their dynastic title (see B. Lacey, *Medieval and monastic Derry*, p. 47).

'saints', but it is unlikely that he had any connection with Derry. It is much more likely that he was comarba of Daire Eithne, the church of Kilmacrenan, rather than of Daire Calgaich or Daire Coluim Chille, Derry.

This is not the only instance in which AFM may have expanded a title without good reason. Recording his death in 989 AFM gives Dúnchad ua Robocáin the title of comarba of Colum Cille and Adamnán but, in its entry, AU does not include the latter saint. The same applies to: Muiredach mac Críchán in 1011 (who was definitely associated with Armagh); Máel Muire ua hUchtáin in 1040; and Robartach mac Ferdomnaigh in 1057. Unlike AU, AFM accords all these men the title of comarba of Colum Cille and Adamnán. It is not at all definite that this was justified. It seems that AFM may have accorded them the title of the combined comarbships retrospectively and, at least to some extent, gratuitously.

In the later Middle Ages AFM conferred the title of comarba of Adamnán on Gilla-Adhamhnáin Ó Firghil who died in 1328 and Donnchadh Ó Gallchubhair who died in 1450. Both of these seem to have been associated with Raphoe and, therefore, their titles appear to have been justified, although carrying a somewhat more limited meaning than would have been the case before the reforms of the twelfth century.

Adomnán was certainly not the founder of a separate monastic *familia* but in his characterization as a saint a number of churches in both Ireland and Scotland began to be dedicated particularly to him, led by 'his' chief church at Raphoe. A number of these churches came to be known as Scrín Adomnáin or 'Adomnán's Shrine' or had similar titles or associations – perhaps originally because they housed either permanently or temporarily a *scrín* or shrine-box which held relics of the saint. In 832 the 'heathens' (Vikings?) had captured Tuathal son of Feradach and *scrín Adomnáin* (*sic*), 'Adomnán's shrine', at a place called *Domnach Maigen*. The latter has often been identified as Donaghmoyne in Co. Monaghan but a site near the east coast close to Lambay Island might have been the real location. Tuathal survived his capture and, when he died in 850, he is described in AU *abbas Rechrand & Dermaighe*, 'abbot of Lambay and Durrow', both of which were Columban churches in Leinster.[22] CS for 978 records that: '*Scrín Adomnáin* was plundered by Domnall ua Neill', but nothing more is said in explanation about the incident. Although Nollaig Ó Muraíle opted for the site of that name in Co. Sligo,[23] in fact, neither the location of this place nor the circumstances of its plundering by the high-king are clear.

Adomnán had definitely died and been buried on Iona. But a later tradition claimed that his relics (bones?) were kept at *Scrín Adamnáin* 'the shrine of

22 B. Lacey, *Saint Columba*, pp 150 and 180. However, Edel Bhreathnach, 'The political context' p. 65, provides some tentative back-up evidence in support of Donaghmoyne.
23 N. Ó Muraíle, 'The Columban onomastic legacy', p. 216.

Adamnán', now Skreen in the barony of Tireragh, Co. Sligo.[24] Nollaig Ó Muraile notes that a former name for that place had been *Tulach na Maoile*,[25] so it could be that the dedicatory name was derived subsequently from a portable collection of relics housed there. The belief about Adomnán's relics being located there is difficult to explain although AFM, for 1022, records the death of Máel Coba Ua Gallchóir, *comhorba Scríne Adhamhnáin*.[26] John O'Donovan identified this as the Co. Sligo Skreen but Tomás Ó Canann suggested a much more logical location for an Ua Gallchóir connection, that is, Skreen townland in the parish of Drumhome in south Donegal.[27] Máel Coba belonged to the Cenél Conaill to which Adomnán had also belonged. In fact, the Uí Gallchobhair claimed descent from a common Cenél Conaill ancestor of Adomnán, Sétna son of Fergus. For some time prior to Máel Coba's death the (real) Cenél Conaill under their powerful king Máel Ruanaid ua Maíl Doraid had been making inroads into what is now Co. Sligo. If O'Donovan's identification was correct, then *Scrín Adamnáin* may have fitted-in somehow as a religio-cultural counterpart of Máel Ruanaid's military advance. But Tomás Ó Canann's identification of a site in south Donegal seems much more likely. However, eight years later, in 1030, AFM records that:

> Donnchadh, tighearna Cairpre, do mharbhadh la hUibh Fiachrach Muirisc i ndoras tighe Scríne Adhamhnáin.

> Donnchadh, lord of Cairbre, was killed by the Uí Fiachrach Muirisc, in the doorway of the house of *Scrín Adhamhnáin*.

The political/dynastic identifications for the people involved in this incident confirms that Skreen in Co. Sligo was definitely the place in question. In 1395 the death of the vicar of *Sccrín Adamnáin*, Ó Flannghaile, is noted in AFM. John O'Donovan identified that place also as Skreen, Co. Sligo.

One possibility for this unusual dedication to Adomnán of Iona in Co. Sligo may have arisen from confusion with a similarly named individual. As we saw

---

24 There is a holy well dedicated to Adamnán near the church remains at Skreen that gives its name *Tobar Adhamhnáin* (anglicized as Toberawnaun) to an adjacent townland. In addition, *Drehid Awnaun*, *Droichead Adhamhnáin*, 'Adamnán's Bridge', across a small stream was also venerated there as a memorial of the saint (W. Reeves, *The Life of St Columba*, pp lxii–lxiii). But see below also for an alternative *Droichead Adhamhnáin*. A poem in the Book of Fenagh mentions a *leic Adhamhnáin* 'Adamnán's flagstone'. The modern editors of the Book of Fenagh suggested that this might refer to the stone slab that formed the 'bridge' at Skreen (W. Hennessy & D. Kelly, *Book of Fenagh*, p. 410, n. 3).

25 'The Columban onomastic legacy', p. 216.

26 See also T. Ó Canann, 'Máel Coba' where (pp 36–7) it is suggested that the information on Máel Coba's death may have been derived from a lost and otherwise unknown *Lebar Droma Thuama*, 'Book of Drumhome'.

27 T. Ó Canann, 'Máel Coba', pp 41–2.

in the last chapter, in the genealogy of the Conmaicni of Cúil Tola cited in the Book of Fenagh there is a person with the name Adomnán/Adamnán. Although we have no precise dates for him, a rough calculation based on a generation length of *c.*30 years would seem to place him in the early eighth century; that is, that he overlapped with the lifespan of Adomnán of Iona. There is no evidence that Adamnán of the Conmaicne was a cleric. But the link with St Caillín who is also linked, as we saw, with Skreen may have contributed to the evolution of the legend of *Scrín Adhamhnáin* in Co. Sligo.

In 1857 William Reeves, following a number of earlier writers including the seventeenth-century Donegal cleric John Colgan, provided a list of churches and other religious sites dedicated to Adomnán.[28] He listed ten such sites in Ireland and eight in Scotland. Some of Reeves's sites might be discounted now while others could be added in. For instance, Reeves includes Drumhome in Donegal for which there is no evidence of a dedication to Adomnán beyond a brief reference to it as a border-marking church in the *Vita Columbae* (see above, chapter 1).[29] Reeves included another church, the vicinity of which (but not the site itself) was mentioned by Adomnán in the *Vita*. That church was Dunbo in both the county and the diocese of Derry. This was near to the site of the significant battle of *Dún Ceithirn* in 632.[30] There seems to be no valid reason for including Dunbo as a church dedicated to Adomnán. Reeves also listed Bovevagh in the same county and diocese on the mistaken assumption that the reported dedication to 'S. Eugenius the patron ... may be regarded as a Latin form of Eunan [i.e. Adhamhnán].' But Eugenius is the Latin form of Eógan of *Ard Srátha*, the patron saint of the diocese of Derry.

A church site, again in both the county and diocese of Derry, that does seem to have been dedicated to Adamnán for whatever reason was at what is now known as Ballintemple (*Baile an tempuill*, 'townland of the church') in Errigal parish in the barony of Coleraine. The anglicized parish name is derived from *Airecal Adhamhnáin* indicating something like 'Adomnán's habitation' or 'praying place'. Located there also was *Carraig Adhamhnáin*, 'Adomnán's Rock'; known in English as 'Onan's Cap'.

Reeves also listed a dedication to Adomnán at Templemoyle, Greallach, in the parish of Cloncha in Inishowen, Co. Donegal (but in the diocese of Derry). There is still a graveyard there with a hint of a ruined rectangular (12m E–W,

28 *The Life of St Columba*, pp lxi–lxviii
29 However, T. Ó Canann, 'Máel Coba', pp 40–1 noted (as had Reeves in the mid-nineteenth century) that the great Donegal, early seventeenth-century scholar based in Leuven, Fr Hugh Ward, had referred to *Dabhach Adamnáin* as a Holy Well in Drumhome parish. This well has not been identified in recent times.
30 R. Sharpe, *Adomnán of Iona*, p. 315. But the date has been corrected here in accordance with the Mc Carthy synchronisms. See also Lacey, *CC*, pp 223–7.

10.4m N–S) stone building, a 'church'? The site includes a number of other enigmatic stone and earthen features including a small stone cross. Older reports claim that a now destroyed Holy Well and *dallán* or 'pillar stone' nearby were also dedicated to St Adhamhnán.[31]

Also, in Co. Donegal and only about six kilometers south-east of Raphoe is the village of Ballindrait, *Baile an Droichid*, 'the townland of the bridge', formerly known as *Droichead Adhamhnáin*, 'Adomnán's Bridge'. The bridge in question crossed the River Deele (*Daol*). Reeves, following earlier suggestions, noted this as a church site dedicated to Adamnán but there is no real evidence for that. Another bridge connected with Adamnán and close to Raphoe, but this time crossing the more minor, but more important, Swillyburn stream, is referred to in the Raphoe *Cáin Adamnáin* of *c*.1000 (see chapter 10 above). There is a Swilly Bridge there to this day, about eight kilometers due east of Raphoe.

Reeves also noted two Adamnán-related sites away from what might be described as the saint's natural hinterland in the north-west of Ireland. The first was Syonan, *Suidhe Adhamhnáin*, 'Adamnán's Seat' in Ardnurcher parish, in the diocese of Meath but the county of Westmeath. Reeves reported a local tradition that Adamnán had preached there on one occasion, hence the name. Reeves also listed Killonan in Derrygalvin parish, Co. Limerick, as possibly derived from *Cill Adhamhnáin*. But Nollaig Ó Muraile, citing a reference in AI for 1252 to the death of Mór, wife of Cormac Mac Carthaig in that place, named there as Cill Lonin, dismissed that suggestion.[32]

Ó Muraíle noted that a separate *Suidhe Adhamhnáin*, 'Adamnán's Seat', along with two other Adamnán-related monuments had been recorded in the *dinnshenchus* ('place-lore') for the royal site at the Hill of Tara (Co. Meath). These had been described in the Middle Irish prose text *Dindgnai Temrach* ('Tara's remarkable places').[33] No trace of the Tara *Suidhe Adhamhnáin* survives, at least above ground. One of the other two sites listed for Tara (both by Ó Muraíle and in the *Dindgnai Temrach*) is the *Cros Adhamhnáin*, Cross of Adamnán, to the north of the *Suidhe*.[34] Although reservations have been expressed about it, the 'cross' is usually identified with a limestone monument inside the graveyard beside the church near the summit of the hill. The monument, however, is not a cross at all (at least since it has been identified by that name in modern times), but a rectangular-sectioned standing stone 1.8m high. Peculiarly, near the base of the stone on its east face there is a carving of an 'overtly sexual' sheela-na-gig,

31 B. Lacy, *Archaeological survey*, pp 294–5.
32 Pers. comm.
33 N. Ó Muraíle, 'The Columban onomastic legacy', p. 216; E. Bhreathnach, 'The topography of Tara: the documentary evidence'.
34 See especially the schematic plan of Tara with the sites marked, in E. Bhreathnach, 'The topography of Tara', p. 71, fig. 37.

a female grotesque figure.[35] Perhaps as a result of that image Adomnán's various association with women led to the attribution of his name to this stone.

The third Adamnán-related monument at Tara was described as *Lathrach pupaill Adomnáin*,[36] 'the place of Adomnán's tent'. Its location according to the *Dindgnai Temrach* was west of the Cross and the *Suidhe*, and close to, if not actually on, the monument known as Ráith na Senad, 'the enclosure of the Synods'. Adomnán was of course famous for his participation in and probable organization of the major Synod in 697, but that was at Birr (Co. Offaly), not at Tara. However, it is quite possible, indeed more than likely, that he may have participated in other synods (and certainly meetings with kings), some of which could have taken place at Tara. Another site, named *Dumha Adhamhnáin*, the 'mound of Adamnán, is shown on a plan of Tara by George Petrie (dated 1839). Its location is shown as being just south of the *Cros Adhamhnáin*.[37]

It is not known when or why Adomnán's name became connected with these monuments at Tara. The text *Dindgnai Temrach* where this is first made manifest dates to the Middle Irish period, that is, after AD 900. The real Adomnán himself was closely associated with a number of kings of Tara. His own family, Cenél Conaill, had contributed a number of incumbents to that office and his relation, Loingsech mac Óenguso, was king of Tara from *c.*695 to 703, overlapping with the last years of Adomnán's own lifetime. As we saw above, at an earlier date Adomnán was also associated with the king of Tara, Finnechta Fledach.[38]

Nollaig Ó Muraíle's list of Adomnán-related sites was published in 1997.[39] He noted fourteen such sites in Ireland but several of those either overlapped with or were otherwise connected with each other in some way. He didn't include all the sites listed by Reeves. In Raphoe he listed *Leaba Adhamhnáin*, 'Adamnán's bed', most likely some significant recumbent stone slab to which a story about the saint had become attached. The 'beds' of local saints are a commonly-found monument at early medieval ecclesiastical sites in Ireland. It appears that Adamnán's Bed had ceased to be pointed out by 1857 when Reeves published his monumental *Life of St Columba*. Ó Muraíle also noted that according to AFM in 1203 (1204 in AU) Derry was burned from St Martin's Graveyard to

35 C. Newman, *Tara: an archaeological survey*, pp 98, 101.
36 So spelt in E. Bhreathnach, 'The topography of Tara', pp 71–2.
37 This is shown on fig. 36 (p. 70) in E. Bhreathnach, 'The topography of Tara', but not otherwise mentioned in that article. It may be that it is to be equated with the *Suidhe Adhamhnáin* mentioned above which is not shown on Petrie's plan.
38 It might be noted here that to the east of the Hill of Tara is located the Hill of Skreen, originally *Scrín Choluim Chille*. However, that dedication seems to date from the mid-to-late tenth century and to have been associated with the Norse king of Dublin, Amlaíb Cúarán. See E. Bhreathnach, 'Columban churches in Brega and Leinster', also Lacey *Saint Columba*, pp 181–2.
39 'The Columban onomastic legacy', pp 214–18.

Tioprait Adhamhnáin, 'Adamnán's Well'. The well was located beside two others, dedicated respectively to St Martin of Tours and St Colum Cille, in the street (now just a pedestrianized 'court') known as St Columb's Wells in the Bogside.[40]

Ó Muraíle's 1997 survey also included twenty-one sites in Scotland that either contained some remnant of the name Adomnán or Adamnán, or else had a dedication to him as a saint. Ó Muraíle noted that: 'The Scottish pattern [of distribution] is particularly noteworthy, the names being largely concentrated in the Grampian region, the ancient Druim Alban'.[41] Ó Muraíle's list had built on the work of the great Scottish place-names expert W.J. Watson and other earlier researchers such as Thomas Innes and William Reeves. In 1857, Reeves had published a list of eight sites in Scotland at which Adomnán's memory was honoured – sometimes in what looks to us as very garbled forms of his name that are not easily identifiable now if we did not know their origins from other sources:

> [Inis] Abhuinn, Adaman, Adamani, Adamannan, Adamannus, Adampnani, Ainan, Arnold, [Inis] Avonia, Awyn, Eunan, Eunendi, Fidamnan, [Kill]ewnane, [Kily]ownane, [T]Eunan, [T]eunan, [Th]eunan, [Th]ewnan, and [Th]ewnanus.[42]

In 1999, Simon Taylor published a survey of references to abbots of Iona in Scottish place-names.[43] That study included a specially detailed appendix concerning Adomnán-related place-names, noting similarly to Ó Muraíle (above) that 'their distribution shows a distinctly eastern Scottish bias.' The significance of this is that the bulk of those places were located in what would have been Pictish territories at the time, no doubt reflecting Adomnán's own direct engagement with those people. To those with specific Adomnán associations that had been listed by previous researchers, Taylor added places connected with Coeddi and other clerics probably associated with Iona at the time of the ninth abbacy. Coeddi who was a contemporary of Adomnán was the bishop of Iona and one of the 'guarantors' of the 697 *Cáin Adomnáin*. He died in 712.

Taylor's study is too detailed to be summarized here but below is added a list of possible variations on Adomnán's name as cited by him:

> Adampnanus, Áibind, Anniani, [Ard]enan, [Ard]eonaig, [Ard]ewnan, [Ard]oueny, Edheunanus, Eódhnain, Eonan, [Erd]onny, Eunandis, [Kill]ewnan, [Kille]onan, [Killi]onan, [Kilmav]eonaig, [Kilmaw]ewinok,

---

40 B. Lacey, *Medieval and monastic Derry*, pp 90–1.
41 'The Columban onomastic legacy', p. 218.
42 Brackets added here and below to separate the personal element from the other aspects of the place-names.
43 S. Taylor, 'Seventh-century Iona abbots in Scottish place-names', especially pp 57–60, 62–70 and map, fig. 2, p. 39.

[Kilm]eunoc, [Kill]unan, [Lag]eonan, Odamnanus, Owen, Oyne, [Roward]ennan.

An old church at Lonan on the east coast of the Isle of Man, with ancient connections to Cumbria on mainland Britain, is also said to be dedicated to St Adamhnán.

As well as in place-names, Adomnán was also commemorated in personal names in Ireland and Scotland: both as 'Christian' (first) names and surnames. As first noted in 1857 by William Reeves, Gilla ['servant of'] Adomnáin Ua Coirthén is mentioned in the charters in the Book of Kells.[44] He was comarba of Colum Cille and abbot of Kells for some time from about 1117, but we don't know when he died or left that office. Reeves had noted that Somhairle (or Somerled) Mac Donald, the lord of Argyll who died in 1164, was the son of Gilla Adhamhnáin but Ó Muraíle took the latter to have been a surname. The name allegedly became a favourite in the Mac Donald family and among their offspring, the Mac Neills of Barra. For instance, for 1495 Reeves cites Gilleownan Makneill, grandson of another Gilleownan, and G.F. Black provided many instances of the name between the early thirteenth and late seventeenth centuries.[45] Nollaig Ó Muraíle also noted the death of the appropriately named Giolla Adhamhnáin Ó Firghil, comarba of Adamnán,[46] as recorded in AFM for 1328. The same name, 'and quite possibly the very same individual', occurs in Dubhaltach Mac Fhirbhisigh's genealogies (152.3) as do the names 'Giolla Adhamhnáin mac Soloimh, the great-great-grandfather of Domhnall eponymous ancestor of [the Scottish] Clann Domhnaill [341.1] ... [and] Giolla Adhamhnáin mac Alusdrain Óig, a great grandson of that same Domhnall [345.11].' Adomnán also became the root of several surnames: Reeves cites the Mac Lennans (*Mac Gilla-Adhamhnáin*) of Glensheil in Rosshire, who derived their surname from Gilla-agamman, son of Cormac, son of Oirbertach. Ó Muraíle references Woulfe as claiming that MacAlonan, MacLennon, MacLennan and M'Eleownan(e), all Co. Down surnames, derive ultimately from Adomnán.[47]

44 Spelt Gilla Adomnáin in M. Herbert, *Iona, Kells and Derry*, pp 98 and 101, but as Giolla Adhamhnain in W. Reeves, *The Life of St Columba*, pp lxvii and 404.

45 G. Black, *The surnames of Scotland*, p. 305, quoted in N. Ó Muraíle, 'The Columban onomastic legacy', p. 215.

46 The Ó Firghils (anglicized as O'Friel) claimed to descend directly from Columba's brother Iogen (Éogan?). For an account of their genealogies back to the eponymous Firgheal in the mid-twelfth century see T. Ó Canann, 'Review article', p. 131. The family of that surname still maintain an important position in the Columban traditions of the Gartan area of Donegal, being the only people allowed to retrieve the celebrated Gartan clay.

47 *Sloinnte Gaedheal is Gall*, pp 366–7. Ó Muraíle also noted that Mac Lysaght (*The surnames of Ireland*, p. 5) 'locates the surname Mac Alonan [Mac Giolla Adhamhnáin] in Cos Antrim and Derry.'

CHAPTER TWELVE

Adomnán and Adhamhnán: since the Middle Ages

As we have seen, sporadic references to the name of and devotion to Adamnán survive from throughout the later Middle Ages. 'His' church at Raphoe remained the seat of the bishopric of the diocese of the Cenél Conaill throughout that period and gave its name to both the Catholic and Protestant dioceses into modern times. Although they do not survive themselves, no doubt there were relics of some sort connected with him and manuscript texts about him preserved by the clergy at the cathedral there.

The great cathedral at Durham in England also helped to preserve Adomnán's memory, albeit indirectly by transmitting copies of the so-called B manuscript tradition of the *Vita Columbae*.[1] Durham was the institutional heir of an ecclesiastical tradition that stretched back to the foundation of the Columban monastery on the island of Lindisfarne. The Durham library preserved a number of manuscripts that reflected that Columban pedigree. Three manuscripts from that B tradition, dating from the late twelfth to the late fifteenth century, survive, and are now all preserved in the British Museum. The B manuscripts have slight differences among themselves but demonstrate greater differences with the A manuscript (Dorbbénne's copy in Schaffhausen). The oldest of the three Durham copies, B1,[2] dates to the late twelfth century. We know that the Durham cathedral library had an older copy that was used in the 1150s or 1160s in the composition of a Life of Saint Oswald, the seventh-century king of Northumbria. Adomnán had referred to the king in the first chapter of the *Vita Columbae*, telling how Oswald had won a victory over the British ('Welsh') king, Cadwallon, in the battle of Heavenfield near Hexham in Northumberland with the aid of a vision of Saint Columba. The copy used for the Life of Oswald does not survive but it had probably been the exemplar for B1 which was certainly made in Durham before the end of that century. Later B1 was housed in the library of the Augustinian canons in Newcastle-upon-Tyne. B2[3] seems to be of roughly the same date as B1 or maybe a little later but, significantly, it has some slight differences when compared to the latter. B2 was badly damaged in a fire in

---

1 This section is indebted to accounts by Anderson & Anderson (eds), *Adomnan's Life of Columba*, pp 4–11 and R. Sharpe, *Adomnán of Iona*, pp 236–7.
2 British Library, MS Additional 35110.
3 British Library, MS Cotton Tiberius D. iii.

1731 and parts of all its pages are either missing or illegible. B3[4] dates to the late fifteenth or early sixteenth century and is more closely related to B1 than is B2; in fact, Richard Sharpe suggested that B3 may have been copied from B1. B3 was made in an Augustinian house, but around 1600 it belonged to a Co. Durham nobleman, Lord John Lumley. Shortly afterwards the lord's books, including B3, were purchased by King James (I of England and Ireland, VI of Scotland) and passed into the royal collections at St James's Palace in London.

Back in Ireland in the 1220s a monk, probably working in Ferns (Co. Wexford), assembled a collection of saints' Lives that included a shortened version of Adomnán's *Vita Columbae*. The collection is preserved in an early fifteenth-century manuscript in Marsh's Library in Dublin.[5] That abbreviated text, or a copy very close to it, was used in the next major literary project dealing with the hagiography of St Columba, the extraordinary *Betha Colaim Chille* by Manus Ó Domnaill finished in the year 1532.[6] Adamnán appears quite frequently in Ó Domnaill's text as a source for stories about Columba. But other than suggesting at one point that the latter had miraculously predicted his birth, there is no further information about Adomnán/Adamnán himself. Perhaps peculiarly, Ó Domnaill did not have access to a full version of Adomnán's *Vita Columbae*. Indeed, Richard Sharpe stated ironically that: 'Although copies of this were known in England [the B manuscripts, and of course manuscripts of the A tradition on the Continent], there is no evidence that any copy was available in Ireland in the sixteenth century.'[7]

By the end of the sixteenth and the beginning of the seventeenth century things had all changed utterly. The eastern part of Donegal, where all the monuments associated with both Columba and Adomnán were located, was confiscated and distributed among new colonial settlers who would have had no knowledge of and presumably very little respect for, or interest in, the ancient sites and the traditions that made them meaningful to the native population. This was all the more catastrophic as it was in precisely that agriculturally rich part of the county that most of the major archaeological sites had been located. Most of the medieval church sites including the cathedral at Raphoe did survive as centres of Protestant worship but the newly introduced religion did not have much time for the 'superstitions' associated with the ancient Irish saints. Donegal Catholicism, indeed Irish culture in general, was in disarray as a result of the loss of the Gaelic aristocracy in the 'Flight of the Earls' (1607) and the seismic social shift created by the Plantations in Ulster.

4 British Library, MS Royal 8 D. ix.
5 R. Sharpe, 'Maghnus Ó Domhnaill's source', p. 604.
6 O'Kelleher & Schoepperle, *Betha Colaim Chille*; B. Lacey, *The Life of Colum Cille by Manus O'Donnell*.
7 R. Sharpe, 'Maghnus Ó Domhnaill's source', p. 604.

But a fight-back of sorts was being planned by Irish, especially Catholic clerical, exiles on the Continent. The intellectual headquarters of this response was at St Anthony's Irish Franciscan College in Leuven, in the then Spanish Netherlands (now Belgium), which had been founded in 1607. One of the main champions of that fight-back was Brother Mícheál Ó Cléirigh ('an bráthar bocht'). Mícheál had been born at Kilbarron in south Donegal about 1590 and then given the name Tadhg (sometimes called Tadhg an tSléibhe); Mícheál was his adopted religious name. His family, the Uí Chléirigh, had been the official historians for the Uí Domnaill perhaps since the mid-fourteenth century.[8] Following the collapse of Gaelic rule in Donegal, Tadhg seems to have gone to the Continent to become a soldier. But about 1623 he entered St Anthony's where he took Mícheál as his 'name in religion'. Coming from a family of Gaelic scholars and being a 'brother' rather than a priest (which would have made things more dangerous for him) the Guardian of the college, another Donegal man, Fr Hugh Ward, sent Mícheál back to Ireland in 1626 to collect documentary materials for the study of Irish secular and ecclesiastical history.[9] As we saw above several of the important texts relating to Adomnán, or more correctly to Adamnán, owe their survival for us to Ó Cléirigh's extraordinary travels around Ireland seeking out and copying older manuscripts. He copied the *Cáin Adamnáin* – one of only two surviving copies – at the Franciscan Convent at Bundrowse in Donegal on 31 March 1627, the *Fís Adamnáin* also at Bundrowse in May 1628, and the *Betha Adamnáin* sometime in 1628 or 1629. Ó Cléirigh was, of course, also the principal compiler of the Annals of the Kingdom of Ireland, better known as the Annals of the Four Masters, which contains the following evidently non-contemporary, retrospective obituary for Adomnán at the incorrect year of 703:

> Adamnán, son of Ronan, abbot of Ia Coluim Cille, died on 23 of September [704] after having been twenty-six [twenty-five?] years in the abbacy, and after the seventy-seventh [?] year of his age. Adamnán was a good man, according to the testimony of St Bede [*naoimh Béda*], for he was tearful, penitent, given to prayer, diligent, ascetic[10] and temperate; for he never used to eat excepting on Sunday and Thursday only; he made a slave [*mogh*] of himself to these virtues; and moreover, he was a wise man and learned in the clear understanding of the holy Scriptures of God.

8   T. Ó Canann, 'Máel Coba', p. 62, n. 3, provides a brief, critical account with references to the story of Matha Ó Scingín – then Uí Domnaill historian but without a male heir – marrying his daughter to Cormac mac Diarmada Ó Cléirigh and thus introducing the latter family to Donegal.

9   Mícheál Ó Cléirigh's story is remarkable in its own right. See, for instance, E. Bhreathnach & B. Cunningham, *Writing Irish history: the Four Masters and their world*.

10 These last four compliments form a beautiful alliterative run in Irish: *ba haithrighech, ba hurnuighthech, ba hinnneithmhech, ba haointeach*.

Mícheál Ó Cléirigh was also the compiler of the Martyrology of Donegal. Under 23 September, his feastday, the Martyrology has a fairly long entry on Adomnán. It opens with details of his family's background and tells us that he spent over twenty years in the abbacy of Iona. It then repeats a story told in earlier texts (see chapter 9) about three days and nights that Adomnán spent meditating and praying in the church. When the elders went to check on him, they found him with a radiant infant at his bosom.

> They were certain that it was Jesus who was in the shape of an infant, delighting Adomnán in this manner, and also that he was his satisfaction and gratification [the alternative to food and sustenance] during these three days and three nights.
>
> He [Adomnán] was a vessel of wisdom, and a man full of the grace of God, and of the knowledge of the holy Scriptures, and of every other wisdom; a burning lamp which illuminated and enlightened the west of Europe with the light of virtues and good morals, laws, and rules, wisdom and knowledge, humility and self-abasement ...
>
> His body was interred with great honour and respect at Iona, and ... [said, probably incorrectly, to have been] removed to Ireland after some time.
>
> It was to Adomnán were revealed the glory of the kingdom of heaven and the pains of hell, as contained in the Vision of Adomnán, which was copied from the Lebor na hUidre. And thenceforward it was the glory of heaven and the pains of hell he used to preach. The Life of Ciarán of Clonmacnoise states, chapter 47, that the [monastic] order of Adomnán was one of the eight orders that were in Ireland.
>
> A very ancient old vellum book ... states that Adomnán was, in his habits and life, like unto Silvester the Pope.

The Martyrology entry doesn't tell us anything new or even anything very interesting about Adomnán, made up as it is of extracts from earlier texts and stock hagiographical phrases. But it does tell us how the great seventh-century Donegal intellectual and scholar, Adomnán, was perceived by one of the greatest intellectual and scholarly Irishmen, also from Donegal, about a thousand years later.

William Reeves noted that the text of an abbreviated version of Adomnán's *Vita Columbae* from a manuscript in Windberg in Bavaria had been published first in 1604 and reprinted in 1624, and 1725.[11] But a few years before Mícheál Ó Cléirigh had entered St Anthony's College in Leuven, another Irish Catholic

11   W. Reeves, *The Life of St Columba*, pp viii–x.

cleric on the Continent had made an enormously important discovery relating to Adomnán, the full copy of the *Vita Columbae* made by Dorbbéne.[12] The cleric in question, Stephen White, a Jesuit, was born in Clonmel (Co. Tipperary) in 1574 and had become Professor of Theology at the Catholic University of Dillingen in Bavaria. Jean-Michel Picard described White as:

> one of the brightest and most learned men of his generation [who] played an important role in the creation of a modern Irish identity through his work on documents and sources attesting the achievements of the Irish in Europe throughout the Middle Ages.[13]

White had a great interest in the history of the early Irish church and its continental connections. He took every opportunity to search accessible libraries for manuscripts that could throw light on that history. One of those libraries was on Reichenau, an island in Lake Constance about 200km south-west of Dillingen. Its ancient monastery had many previous connections with Ireland. It was there that Stephen White found Dorbbéne's manuscript of Adomnán's *Vita Columbae*, the codex that we now know as Generalia I, preserved in the stadtbibliotek of Schaffhausen in Switzerland. White was allowed to bring the manuscript back to Dillingen with him where he made a copy of it dated 31 May 1621. Unfortunately, that copy is itself now missing.

White disseminated his knowledge of the existence of the Dorbénne manuscript to other scholars who had an interest in the early medieval period of Irish church history. He sent a copy to St Anthony's in Leuven from which John Colgan, another Donegal man, published the first printed copy of the text in 1647, in his book *Trias Thaumaturga*. That book dealt with the three patron saints of Ireland: Brigid, Columba and Patrick. White also sent a copy to Heribert Rosweyde in Antwerp before his death in 1629. Rosweyde, another Jesuit, was the leading scholar behind a huge Catholic counter-reformation enterprise designed to gather, critically analyse and publish the Lives of all the saints. Rosweyde's work would later grow into the famous Bollandist project, which published Adomnán's *Vita Columbae* in 1698. Although Irish Catholicism was under severe attack from the British state and the Protestant church at the time, we know that those interested in early church history across the religious divide continued to communicate and even co-operate with each other on research matters. Stephen White sent a copy of his transcript of the Schaffhausen manuscript to

---

12 Outlines of the story of the discovery and the later history of the manuscript can be found in R. Sharpe, *Adomnán of Iona*, pp 235–6; J.M. Picard, 'Schaffhausen, Stadtbibliotek, Generalia I', pp 56–62, which gives greater detail; and W. Reeves, *The Life of St Columba*, pp xxiii–xxiv. The outline here is a summary of those three accounts.

13 J.M. Picard, 'Schaffhausen, Stadtbibliotek, Generalia I', p. 60. For a brief account of White's life see R. Sharpe, *Medieval Irish saints' Lives*, pp 44–6.

James Ussher sometime between 1632 and 1639. Ussher, the Church of Ireland archbishop of Armagh, was the leading Protestant scholar on the early church. He was in the process of preparing his *Britannicarum ecclesiarum antiquitates* (published in 1639) when he received White's transcript. Unfortunately, it was too late for Ussher to include fully much of the *Vita* material in his main text, but some of it did make its way into the *addenda*.

White returned the original Dorbbéne manuscript to the monastery at Reichenau but sometime in the following century it was transferred to Schaffhausen. When and under what circumstances it came there is not known but its identity seems to have become obscured again. Jean-Michel Picard points out that it could have been in Schaffhausen as early as 1724 but was most definitely there by 1772. But before he died, in 1795, a Swiss Benedictine historian, Moritz van der Meer, made a study of the manuscript. Van der Meer had an interest in early Irish church history and wrote a Life of St Fintan, the patron of the separate monastery of Rheinau nearby. It was van der Meer who, among other points of interest about the manuscript, determined that it was a Life of St Columba, not his near Irish and perhaps (on the Continent) more famous name-sake St Columbanus, as had been supposed by some.

After van der Meer the manuscript, as it were, disappeared or at least receded from view again until 1845 when it was rediscovered by Dr Ferdinand Keller, a Swiss archaeologist. Recognizing its importance, Keller wrote about it to J.H. Todd in Dublin, the scholar who had been the founder of the Irish Archaeological Society in 1840. It would be the latter society (by then the words 'and Celtic' had been inserted in its title) that seventeen years later would publish William Reeves's magnificent, annotated edition of the text. Keller had also included in his letter to Todd facsimiles of a few pages of the original. Some of Keller's facsimiles of the decorated capitals in the manuscript would be used to illustrate Reeves's edition. Todd, a Church of Ireland clergyman, drew Keller's letter to the attention of Dr Reeves, who was also a leading Church of Ireland scholar (and later bishop), and the latter began a correspondence with the Swiss antiquarian. In his introductory material to the 1857 edition Reeves quoted a letter he received from Keller in January 1851 outlining the condition in which the latter had found the manuscript.

> The present proprieter of the MS. of S. Columba is the Town-library (public library) of Schaffhausen. Here I found this codex in 1845 at the bottom of a high book-chest, where it lay pêle-mêle with some other MSS. and old books totally neglected, bearing neither title nor number.[14]

14   *The Life of St Columba*, pp xxiii–xxiv. It must be said that the manuscript is now treated with the utmost care and respect by its curators in Schaffhausen.

Jean-Michel Picard, commenting on the state of the manuscript then, wrote: 'it is frightening to think that such a treasure was nearly lost.'[15]

Keller made a copy of the text available to Dr Reeves from which the latter published his encyclopedic edition in 1857. Apart from faithfully respecting Dorbbéne's manuscript and Adomnán's text, Reeves's book was a major step in the evolution of the writing of early Irish history.[16] It has been a personal 'misfortune' of mine from time to time to think that I had discovered some new thought about the history of Columba or the Columban story only to find that Reeves had not only discovered it already but published it 150 years ago. His book is over 550 pages of small type with extensive commentary and notes, well exceeding the length of Adomnán's original. From a modern point of view the only negative thing that might be said about Reeves's edition was that it did not include a translation of Adomnán's Latin into English. Notwithstanding that, it remains the essential jumping off point for any study of this subject.

Although various editions and reprints based on Reeves's 1857 book followed, it was not until a century later that another major step forward took place with the publication in 1961 of the annotated edition and translation of Dorbénne's text by Dr Alan Anderson and his wife Marjorie.[17] This was followed in 1995 by Richard Sharpe's translation with voluminous notes and explications.[18] Sharpe's text has been characterized by Professor Thomas Charles-Edwards as 'the best translation'.[19] Both of those books brought about a much wider appreciation of Adomnán's original text and facilitated the growth of detailed academic studies and research on his life and work, quite literally all over the world. Among the other leading scholars who pioneered modern studies about Adomnán himself, the texts he created, and the dissemination, use and exploitation of those texts in later centuries, are Máirín Ní Dhonnchadha, Máire Herbert, Jean-Michel Picard and Pádraig Ó Riain. Just some of their many contributions have been quoted and referred to above and are listed in the bibliography below.

The year 1997, understood then as the 1400th anniversary of the death of Columba and the actual 1300th anniversary of the Synod of Birr and the promulgation of the *Lex Innocentium*, saw a series of lectures, international conferences and publications on various aspects of the subject. That was followed in 2004 by the 1300th anniversary of the death of Adomnán with a similar array

15 'Schaffhausen, Stadtbibliotek, Generalia 1', p. 56.
16 For a brief but detailed outline of Reeves's achievements see R. Sharpe, *Medieval Irish saints Lives*, p. 75 and the references cited there. Sharpe says of Reeves': 'a new era in the study of Irish saints' Lives begins with the work of the Revd William Reeves (1813–91)'.
17 *Adomnan's Life of Columba* (with a revised edition in 1991). As Richard Sharpe pointed out, the Andersons actually completed work on the book in 1957 but it took another four years before it was published (*Medieval Irish saints' Lives*, p. 88, n. 31).
18 *Adomnán of Iona*.
19 T. Charles-Edwards, 'The structure and purpose of Adomnán's *Vita Columbae*', p. 205, n. 1.

of academic studies and memorial events. Perhaps the most outstanding of those events was the conference organized on Iona by the Centre for the Study of Religion in Celtic Societies of the University of Wales, Lampeter, in association with Historic Scotland. A selection of the papers presented at that conference together with some additions became the basis for the book *Adomnán of Iona: theologian, lawmaker, peacemaker* published in 2010, which has been used and quoted from extensively in the preparation of this study.

2014 saw another major step in the modern recognition and appreciation of Adomnán's work with the publication by the *Armarium Codicum Hibernensium* (ArCH) Project at the School of History, University College Cork, and Cork University Press, of a magnificent facsimile of the Schaffhausen manuscript of the *Vita Columbae*.[20] That publication comprised two volumes: vol. I is a perfect photographic reproduction of the complete manuscript at a 1:1 scale; vol. II contains five analytical essays by leading experts on the manuscript and its contexts. This beautiful publication provides most of us with the first opportunity to encounter the full manuscript itself, if only in facsimile. It allows us to see how the book was made and decorated. Like an icon, it was deemed a sacred object and may have been treated as a relic. We can see in the facsimile what Adomnán and Dorbbéne intended us to see, but the accompanying analyses in vol. II allow us to discern some things that were not so intended. Anthony Harvey's technical but fascinating chapter on the book's orthographic features highlights several puzzles; as just one example, why Adomnán (or Dorbbéne) left a gap in the middle of the name *Fech reg.* This is almost *Name of the Rose* territory!

Just as the first draft of this present book was being finished in June 2020, James Houlihan published his excellent *Adomnán's* Lex Innocentium *and the laws of war*. Apart from anything else that publication necessitated the rewriting of substantial parts of chapters 4 and 8 of this work. For example, Houlihan's studies had clarified much more than any previous writers the absolute distinction between the original documentation of the *Lex Innocentium* (the text of the Law itself and the list of its so-called 'guarantors') of 697 from the later added material in the recension that has come down to us: the Raphoe *Cáin Adamnáin* of *c*.1000. Houlihan's book also, for the first time, demonstrates the innovatory genius of Adomnan's Law when compared against contemporary native Irish law in the first place, and its importance in an international context when compared against its analogues across time and geography. The book contains not only a major advance in scholarship about Adomnán but, also, a timely tribute. As discussed above also, the very recent publication of an important article[21] based on Charles Thomas's excavations on

---

20   D. Bracken & E. Graff, *The Schaffhausen Adomnán*.
21   Campbell & Maldonado, 'A new Jerusalem'.

Iona between 1956 and 1963 allows another aspect of Adomnán's imaginative genius to be highlighted and appreciated.

During his lifetime Adomnán was many things but, primarily and fundamentally, he was a Christian cleric and, evidently, a very holy man. To many of his contemporaries and those who came after him, no matter how precisely they understood or used the term, he was also a 'saint'. From soon after his death he began to be publicly acknowledged and honoured as such. Any overall assessment of Adomnán's career and achievements, no matter whether prepared by a 'believing' Christian or not, would be obliged necessarily to consider the spiritual and theological aspects of his life, thought and legacy, in so far as we can know those things. This author is certainly not equipped in any way to do that but, fortunately, several others have approached his work and writings from that perspective. As far as we know Adomnán did not write anything systematically outlining his own beliefs relating to these matters, although there would be no surprise if he had done so. But, as we saw above, his book about the Holy Land, *De Locis Sanctis*, is not just a travel book in the modern sense but a work of exegesis to help guide those studying the messages of the Old and New Testaments. In addition, theological issues come up frequently and naturally in his book, the *Vita Columbae*. But in the latter it is difficult, if not impossible, to separate from the words he wrote there what Adomnán may have believed and argued himself as distinct from the views he puts into the quoted observations of his subject, Columba. We may be forgiven for thinking, however, that the book is really a gentle polemic dealing with Adomnán's own opinions on these matters, semi-hidden within the folds of an account of his patron's life. Certainly, many modern researchers have understood the book in that way.

Although there may well be older examples, studies specifically dealing with these aspects of Adomnán's thoughts seem to have begun to appear in the main in the 1990s. As stated already, this author is certainly not equipped to either comment on or adjudicate on what others have written about these matters. But in concluding this work, which has attempted to provide an overal picture of (i) Adomnán's extraordinary life in so far as we can know it, (ii) his literary works that transmit his ideas and values to people of later ages, and (iii) the way his memory was invoked and indeed exploited by some of the people of those later ages, it seems appropriate at very least to draw attention to some modern studies by individuals qualified to write about his exegetical and theological beliefs.

The following is a basic personal list with no pretensions to completeness or accuracy. It is set out in chronological order of date of publication. Fuller bibliographical details will be found in the main bibliography and, of course, the works cited here all contain references to other relevant studies and publications.

* * *

Bullough, D.A., 'Columba, Adomnán, and the achievement of Iona' (1964 and
    1965).
O'Reilly, J., 'Reading the Scriptures in the Life of Columba' (1997).
O'Reilly, J., 'The wisdom of the scribe and the fear of the Lord in the Life of
    Columba' (1999).
O'Loughlin, T., 'Res, tempus, locus, persona: Adomnán's exegetical method'
    (1999).
O'Loughlin, T., 'Adomnán: a man of many parts' (2001).
O'Loughlin, T., 'The tombs of the saints: their significance for Adomnán'
    (2001).
O'Loughlin, T., Adomnán and the holy places: the perceptions of an insular monk
    on the location of the biblical drama (2007).
Jenkins, D., Holy, holier, holiest: the layout of the Temple of Jerusalem ... (2010).
O'Loughlin, T., 'The De Locis Sanctis as a liturgical text' (2010).
O'Reilly, J., 'Adomnán and the art of teaching spiritual sons' (2010).
O'Sullivan, T., 'The anti-Pelagian motif of the "naturally good" pagan in
    Adomnán's Vita Columbae' (2010).
Ritari, K., 'Heavenly apparitions and heavenly life in Adomnán's Vita Columbae'
    (2010).
Sharman, S., 'Visions of divine light in the writings of Adomnán and Bede'
    (2010).
Enright, M.J., Prophecy and kingship in Adomnán's 'Life of Saint Columba' (2013).
Houlihan, J., Adomnán's Lex Innocentium and the laws of war (2020).

* * *

Adomnán was a remarkable man in many ways. It is absolutely fitting that we
should remember his life, the things he achieved and the values he bequeathed
to his contemporaries and to those, later, that came and will come to learn more
about him.

Bibliography

Aist, R., 'Adomnán, Arculf and the source material of De Locis Sanctis' in Wooding, Aist, Clancy & O'Loughlin (eds), *Adomnán of Iona: theologian, lawmaker, peacemaker* (Dublin, 2010), pp 162–80.

Anderson, A.O. & Anderson, M.O. (eds and trans.), *Adomnán's Life of Columba* (London, 1961; revised 1991).

Bede, *A history of the English church and people*, translated by Leo Sherley-Price, revised by R.E. Latham (London, 1972).

Bernard, J. & Atkinson, R. (eds & trans.), *The Irish Liber hymnorum*, 2 vols (London, 1898).

Bhreathnach, E., 'The topography of Tara: the documentary evidence', *Discovery Programme Reports*, 2 (1993), 68–76.

Bhreathnach, E., 'Columban churches in Brega and Leinster: relations with the Norse and the Anglo-Normans', *JRSAI*, 129 (1999), 5–18.

Bhreathnach, E., 'The political context of *Baile Chuinn Chétchathaig*' in E. Bhreathnach (ed.), *The kingship and landscape of Tara* (Dublin, 2005), pp 49–68.

Bhreathnach, E. (ed.), *The kingship and landscape of Tara* (Dublin, 2005).

Bhreathnach, E., *Ireland in the medieval world, AD 400–1000: landscape, kingship and religion* (Dublin, 2014).

Bhreathnach, E. & Cunningham, B., *Writing Irish history: the Four Masters and their world* (Dublin, 2007).

Bieler, L. (ed. & trans.), *The Irish penitentials* (Dublin, 1975).

Bieler, L. (ed. & trans.) with a contribution by Fergus Kelly, *The Patrician texts in the Book of Armagh* (Dublin, 1979).

Binchy, D.A. (ed.), *Crith Gablach* (Dublin, 1970).

Binchy, D.A. (ed.), *Corpus iuris Hibernici*, 6 vols (Dublin, 1978).

Bisagni, J. (ed. and trans.), *Amrae Coluimb Chille: a critical edition* (Dublin, 2019).

Bjork, R.E. (ed.), *Catastrophes and the apocalyptic in the Middle Ages and the Renaissance* (Turnhout, 2019).

Black, G., *The surnames of Scotland: their origin, meaning and history* (New York, 1946).

Blackwell, A. (ed.), *Scotland in early medieval Europe* (Leiden, 2019).

Borsje, J., 'The monster in the River Ness in *Vita Sancti Columbae*: a study of a miracle', *Peritia*, 8 (1994), 27–34.

Boswell, C.S., *An Irish precursor of Dante: a study on the vision of Heaven and Hell ascribed to the eighth-century Irish Saint Adamnán with translation of the Irish text* (London, 1908).

Bourke, C. (ed.), *From the Isles of the North: early medieval art in Ireland and Britain* (Belfast, 1995).

Bourke, C. (ed.), *Studies in the cult of Saint Columba* (Dublin, 1997).

Bracken, D. & Graff, E. (eds), *The Schaffhausen Adomnán: Schaffhausen, Stadtbibliotek, MS Generalia 1, Part II: Commentary* (Cork, 2014).

Breathnach, C., 'Review of Herbert and Ó Riain, *Betha Adamnáin*', *Éigse*, 26 (1992), 77–87.

Broun, D. & Clancy, T.O. (eds), *Spes Scotorum: Hope of Scots* (Edinburgh, 1999).

Bryson, J., *The streets of Derry, 1625–2001* (Derry, 2001).

Bullough, D.A., 'Columba, Adomnán, and the achievement of Iona', *Scottish Historical Review*, 43 (1964), 111–30 and *Scottish Historical Review*, 44 (1965), 17–33.

Byrne, F.J., *Irish kings and high kings* (London, 1973; repr. with additional notes Dublin, 2001).

Byrne, M.E., 'Féilire Adamnáin', *Ériu*, 1 (1904), 225–8.

Campbell, E., 'The archaeology of writing in the time of Adomnán' in Wooding, Aist, Clancy & O'Loughlin (eds), *Adomnán of Iona: theologian, lawmaker, peacemaker* (Dublin, 2010), pp 139–44.

Campbell, E., 'Peripheral vision: Scotland in early medieval Europe' in A. Blackwell (ed.), *Scotland in early medieval Europe* (Leiden, 2019), pp 17–33.

Campell, E. & Maldonado, A., 'A new Jerusalem "at the ends of the earth": interpreting Charles Thomas's excavations at Iona Abbey 1956–63', *The Antiquaries Journal*, 100 (2020), 33–85.

Carey, J., '*Fís Adomnáin*: The Vision of Adomnán' in J. Carey (ed. and trans.), *King of mysteries: early Irish religious writings* (Dublin, 2000), pp 261–74.

Carey, J. (ed. and trans.), *King of mysteries: early Irish religious writings* (Dublin, 2000).

Carey, J., Herbert, M., & Ó Riain, P. (eds), *Studies in Irish hagiography: saints and scholars* (Dublin, 2001).

Carey, J., Nic Cárthaigh, E. & Ó Dochartaigh, C. (eds), *The end and beyond: medieval Irish eschatology* (Aberystwyth, 2014).

Charles-Edwards, T., *Early Christian Ireland* (Cambridge, 2000).

Charles-Edwards, T., 'The structure and purpose of Adomnán's *Vita Columbae*' in Wooding, Aist, Clancy & O'Loughlin (eds), *Adomnán of Iona: theologian, lawmaker, peacemaker* (Dublin, 2010), pp 205–18.

Clancy, T., 'Diarmait *sapientisssimus*: the career of Diarmait dalta Daigre, abbot of Iona, 814–839', *Peritia*, 17–18 (2003–4), 215–32.

Clancy, T., 'Adomnán in medieval Gaelic literary tradition' in Wooding, Aist, Clancy & O'Loughlin (eds), *Adomnán of Iona: theologian, lawmaker, peacemaker* (Dublin, 2010), pp 112–22.

Clancy, T. & Márkus, G. (eds), *Iona: the earliest poetry of a Celtic monastery* (Edinburgh, 1995).

Condit, T. & Corlett, C. (eds), *Above and beyond: essays in memory of Leo Swan* (Dublin, 2005).

Day, A. & McWilliams, P. (eds), *Ordnance Survey memoirs of Ireland: parishes of County Donegal II, 1835–6, Mid, West and South Donegal*, vol. 39 (Belfast, 1997).

de Brún, P., Ó Coileáin, S. & Ó Riain, P. (eds), *Folia Gadelica* (Cork, 1983).

DIL Dictionary of the Irish language (compact edition) (Dublin, 1983, repr. 1998).

Dillon, C. & Jefferies, H.A. (eds), *Tyrone: history and society* (Dublin, 2000).

Dinneen, P., (comp. & ed.), *Foclóir Gaeidhilge agus Béarla* (Dublin 1927, repr. 1979).

Dobbs, M., 'A poem ascribed to Flann mac Lonáin', *Ériu*, 17 (1955), 16–34.

Doherty, W.J., *The abbey of Fahan in Inishowen, County Donegal: a paper read at a meeting of the Royal Irish Academy, February 28th 1881* (Dublin, 1881).

Enright, M., 'Royal succession and abbatial prerogative in Adomnán's *Vita Columbae*', *Peritia*, 4 (1985) 83–103.

Enright, M., *Prophecy and kingship in Adomnán's 'Life of Saint Columba'* (Dublin, 2013).

Etchingham, C., *Church organization in Ireland, AD 650–1000* (Maynooth, 1999).

Fisher, I., *Early medieval sculpture in the West Highlands and Islands* (Edinburgh, 2001).

Flechner, R., *A study, edition and translation of the* Hibernensis, *with commentary* (Dublin, forthcoming).

Fraser, J., *From Caledonia to Pictland: Scotland to 795* (Edinburgh, 2009).

Fraser, J., 'Adomnán and the morality of war' in Wooding, Aist, Clancy & O'Loughlin (eds), *Adomnán of Iona* (Dublin, 2010), pp 95–111.

Gérardy, G., *Henri Pirenne, 1862–1935* (Bruxelles, 1962).

Gillespie, R., Ryan, S. & Scott, B. (eds), *Making the Book of Fenagh: context and text* (Cumann Seanchais Bhreifne, 2016).

Graff, E., 'Report on codex: Schaffhausen, Stadtbibliotek, Generalia 1' in Bracken & Graff (eds), *The Schaffhausen Adomnán: Schaffhausen, Stadtbibliotek, MS Generalia 1, Part II: Commentary* (Cork, 2014), pp 17–55.

Gwynn, A. & Hadcock, R.N., *Medieval religious houses Ireland* (Dublin, 1970, repr. 1988).

Gwynn, E. (ed. & trans.), *The Metrical Dindshenchas*, Royal Irish Academy Todd Lecture Series, vol. xi, part iv (Dublin, 1924).

Gwynn, L., 'The reliquary of Adamnan', *Archivium Hibernicum*, 4 (1915), 199–214.

Harbison, P., 'The biblical iconography of the Irish Romanesque architectural sculpture' in C. Bourke (ed.), *From the Isles of the North* (Belfast, 1995), pp 271–80.

Harvey, A., 'Some orthographic features of the Schaffhausen manuscript' in Bracken & Graff (eds), *The Schaffhausen Adomnán: Schaffhausen, Stadtbibliotek, MS Generalia 1, Part II: Commentary* (Cork, 2014), pp 90–104.

Hennessy, W.M. (ed. and trans.), *Chronicum Scotorum* (London, 1866; repr. Wiesbaden, 1964).

Hennessy, W.M. & Kelly, D.H. (eds and trans.), *The Book of Fenagh* (Dublin, 1875).

Henry, P., *Saoithiúlacht na Sean-Ghaeilge* (Baile Átha Cliath, 1976).

Herbert, M., *Iona, Kells and Derry: the history and hagiography of the monastic* familia *of Columba* (Oxford, 1988; repr. Dublin 2021).

Herbert, M. & Ó Riain, P. (eds), *Betha Adamnáin: The Irish Life of Adamnán*, Irish Texts Society, vol. 54 (London, 1988).

Herity, M. (ed.), *Ordnance Survey letters, Donegal* (Dublin, 2000).

Hogan, E., *Onomasticon Goedelicum: locorum et tribuum Hiberniae et Scotiae – An index, with identifications to the Gaelic names of places and tribes* (Dublin, 1910; repr. Dublin, 1993).

Houlihan, J., *Adomnán's* Lex Innocentium *and the laws of war* (Dublin, 2020).

Hughes, K., *Early Christian Ireland: introduction to the sources* (London, 1972).

Ireland, C., 'Aldfrith of Northumbria and his Irish genealogies', *Celtica,* 22 (1991), 64–78.

Ireland, C., 'Aldfrith of Northumbria and the learning of a *sapiens*' in K. Klar, E. Sweetser and C. Thomas (eds), *A Celtic florilegium: studies in memory of Brendan O Hehir* (Lawrence, MA, 1996), pp 63–77.

Ireland, C. (ed. & trans.), *Old Irish wisdom attributed to Aldfrith of Northumbria: an edition of* Bríathra Flainn Fína maic Ossu (Tempe, AZ, 1999).

Ireland, C., 'Where was king Aldfrith of Northumbria educated? An exploration of seventh-century insular learning', *Traditio,* 70 (2015), 29–74.

Ireland, C., 'What constitutes the learning of a sapiens? The case of Cenn Fáelad', *Peritia,* 27 (2016), 63–78.

Ireland, C., 'Lutting of Lindisfarne and the earliest recorded use of Dionysiac *annus Domini* chronology in Northumbria', *Peritia* (forthcoming).

James, E., 'Bede and the tonsure question', *Peritia,* 3 (1984), 85–98.

Jenkins, D., *Holy, holier, holiest: the layout of the Temple of Jerusalem as a paradigm for the topography of religious settlement within the early medieval Irish church* (Turnhout, 2010).

Johnston, E., *Literacy and identity in early medieval Ireland* (Woodbridge, 2013).

Kelleher, John V., *Too small for stove wood, too big for kindling* (Dublin, 1979).

Kelly, F., *A guide to early Irish law* (Dublin, 1988).

Kenney, J.F., *The sources for the early history of Ireland – ecclesiastical: an introduction and guide* (New York, 1929; repr. Dublin 1979).

Lac[e]y, B., 'The Ui Meic Cairthinn of Lough Foyle', *Derriana* (1979), 3–24.

Lac[e]y, B. [et al.], *Archaeological survey of County Donegal* (Lifford, 1983).

Lacey, B., *The Life of Colum Cille by Manus O'Donnell* (Dublin, 1998).

Lacey, B., 'County Derry in the early historic period' in G. O'Brien (ed.), *Derry and Londonderry: history and society* (1999), pp 115–48.

Lacey, B., 'The Grianán of Aíleach – a note on its identification', *JRSAI,* 131 (2001), 145–9.

Lacey, B., 'Tírechán's Sírdruimm, Adomnán's Dorsum Tómme', *JRSAI,* 132 (2002), 148–50.

Lacey, B., 'The church of Ráith Maige Oenaig and the Donegal Cenél nÉnnai' in Condit & Corlett (eds), *Above and beyond: essays in memory of Leo Swan* (Dublin, 2005), pp 214–18.

Lacey, B., *Cenél Conaill and the Donegal kingdoms: AD 500–800* (Dublin, 2006).

Lacey, B., 'The "Bend of the Finn": an archaeological landscape in east Donegal' in C. Manning (ed.), *From ringforts to fortified houses* (2007), pp 107–17.

Lacey, B., 'Fahan, Tory, Cenél nEogain and the Picts', *Peritia,* 20 (2008), 331–45.

Lacey, B., 'Adomnán and Donegal' in Wooding, Aist, Clancy & O'Loughlin (eds) *Adomnán of Iona* (Dublin, 2010), pp 20–35.

Lacey, B., *Lug's forgotten Donegal kingdom: the archaeology, history and folklore of the Síl Lugdach of Cloghaneely* (Dublin, 2012).

Lacey, B., *Medieval and monastic Derry: sixth century to 1600* (Dublin, 2013).

Lacey, B., *Saint Columba: his life and legacy* (Dublin, 2013).

Lacey, B., 'The ringed cross at Ray, Co. Donegal; context and date', *Journal of Irish Archaeology*, 25 (2016), 49–65.

Lacey, B., 'The origins of the Uí Dochartaigh of Inishowen', *Donegal Annual*, 72 (2020), 59–64.

Lacey, B., 'Cúl Dreimne, Drumcliff and other Sligo associations with Colum Cille', *Sligo Field Club Journal*, 6 (2020), 47–58.

Mac Airt, S. & Mac Niocaill G. (eds), *Annals of Ulster* (Dublin, 1983).

Mac Giolla Easpaig, D., 'Places and early settlement in County Donegal' in Nolan, W., Ronayne, L. & Dunlevy, M. (eds), *Donegal: history and society* (Dublin, 1995), pp 149–82.

Mac Niocaill, G., *Ireland before the Vikings* (Dublin, 1972).

Mac Shamhráin, A., '*Nebulae discutiuntur*? The emergence of Clann Cholmáin, sixth-eighth centuries' in Smyth (ed.), *Seanchas: studies in early and medieval Irish archaeology, history and literature in honour of Francis J. Byrne* (Dublin, 2000), pp 83–97.

Mac Shamhráin, A., 'The making of Tír nEogain: Cenél nEogain and the Airgialla from the sixth to the eleventh centuries' in Dillon & Jefferies (eds), *Tyrone: history and society* (Dublin, 2000), pp 55–84.

Macalister, R.A.S., 'The inscription on the slab at Fahan Mura, Co. Donegal', *JRSAI*, 59 (1929), 89–98.

Macalister, R.A.S., *Book of Fenagh: supplementary volume* (Dublin, 1939).

Macalister, R.A.S., *Corpus inscriptionum insularum celticarum* (Dublin, 1949).

MacDonald, A., 'Adomnán's monastery; and aspects of the monastic landscape in Adomnán's Life of Columba' in Carey, Herbert & Ó Riain (eds), *Studies in Irish hagiography: saints and scholars* (Dublin, 2001), pp 15–30.

MacLysaght, E., *The surnames of Ireland*, 5th ed. (Dublin, 1980).

Macquarrie, A. (ed.), *Legends of the Scottish saints: readings, hymns and prayers for the commemorations of Scottish saints in the Aberdeen Breviary* (Dublin, 2012).

Mac Suibhne, B. & Dickson, D. (eds), *The outer edge of Ulster: a memoir of social life in nineteenth-century Donegal* (Dublin, 2000).

Manning, C. (ed.), *From ringforts to fortified houses: studies on castles and other monuments in honour of David Sweetman* (Dublin, 2007).

Márkus, G. (trans.), *Adomnán's 'Law of the Innocents'* (Glasgow, 1997).

Márkus, G. '*Adiutor Laborantium* – a poem by Adomnán?' in Wooding, Aist, Clancy & O'Loughlin (eds), *Adomnán of Iona: theologian, lawmaker, peacemaker* (Dublin, 2010), pp 145–61.

Marsden, J., *The illustrated Columcille* (London, 1991).

Mc Carthy, D., 'The original compilation of the Annals of Ulster', *Studia Celtica*, 38 (2004), 69–95.

Mc Carthy, D., *The Irish Annals: their genesis, evolution and history* (Dublin, 2008).

Mc Carthy, D., 'The illustration and text on the Book of Kells, folio 114RV', *Studies in Iconography*, 35 (2014), 1–38.

Mc Carthy, D., 'Representations of tonsure in the Book of Kells', *Studia Celtica*, 51 (2017), 89–103.

McCormick, F., 'Excavations at Iona, 1988', *Ulster Journal of Archaeology*, 56 (1993), 78–107.

McCracken, E., 'The woodlands of Donegal', *Donegal Annual* (1958), 62–4.

Meehan, B., *The Book of Durrow: a medieval masterpiece at Trinity College Dublin* (Dublin, 1996).

Meehan, D. (ed.), *Adamnan's De Locis Sanctis* (Dublin, 1958, repr. 1983).

Meyer, K. (ed. and trans.) *Cáin Adamnáin: an Old Irish treatise on the Law of Adamnán* (Oxford, 1905).

Meyer, K., 'The Laud genealogies and tribal histories', *Zeitschrift für celtische Philologie*, 8 (1912), 291–338.

Meyer, K., *Sanas Cormaic (Cormac's Glossary) compiled by Cormac Úa Cuilennáin, king-bishop of Cashel in the tenth century ...* (Dublin, 1913).

Moisl, H., 'The Bernician royal dynasty and the Irish in the seventh century', *Peritia*, 2 (1982), 99–126.

Newman, C., *Tara: an archaeological survey* (Dublin, 1997).

Ní Dhonnchadha, M., 'The guarantor-list of *Cáin Adomnáin*, 697', *Peritia*, 1 (1982), 178–215.

Ní Dhonnchadha, M. (trans.), 'Birr and the Law of the Innocents', in O'Loughlin (ed.), *Adomnán at Birr, AD 697* (Dublin, 2001), pp 13–32.

Ní Dhonnchadha, M., 'The Law of Adomnán: a translation' in O'Loughlin (ed.), *Adomnán at Birr, AD 697* (Dublin, 2001), pp 53–68.

Nolan, W., Ronayne, L. & Dunlevy, M. (eds), *Donegal: history and society* (Dublin, 1995).

Nugent, L., *Journeys of faith: stories of pilgrimage from medieval Ireland* (Dublin, 2020).

Ó Briain, M., 'Review of Herbert and Ó Riain, *Betha Adamnáin*', *Studia Hibernica*, 27 (1993), 155–8.

O'Brien, G. (ed.), *Derry and Londonderry: history and society* (Dublin, 1999).

O'Brien, M.A. (ed.), *Corpus genealogiarum Hiberniae*, vol. 1 (Dublin, 1962).

Ó Canann, T., 'Trí Saorthuatha Mhuintire Chanannáin: a forgotten medieval placename', *Donegal Annual*, 38 (1986), 19–46.

Ó Canann, T., 'Ua Canannáin genealogies in the Irish manuscript tradition', *Studia Hibernica*, 30 (1998–99), 167–229.

Ó Canann, T., 'Review article: Leabhar Mór na nGenealach – The Great Book of Irish Genealogies', *JRSAI*, 132 (2002), 127–37.

Ó Canann, T., 'Máel Coba Ua Gallchubhair and his early family background', *JRSAI*, 134 (2004), 33–79.

Ó Canann, T., 'Clann Fhiangusa and the pedigree of Flann mac Maíle Dúin', *Donegal Annual*, 56 (2004), 20–6.

Ó Canann, T., 'Notes on medieval Donegal II', *Donegal Annual*, 67 (2015), 67–86.

Ó Carragáin, T., 'The architectural setting of the cult of relics in early medieval Ireland', *JRSAI*, 133 (2003), 130–76.

Ó Cróinín, D., *Early medieval Ireland* (London, 1995).

O'Donovan, J. (ed.), *Annals of the kingdom of Ireland by the Four Masters*, 7 vols, 2nd ed., (Dublin, 1851–6; repr. 1990).

Ó Duígeannáin, M., 'Notes on the history of the kingdom of Bréifne', *JRSAI*, 65, (1935), 113–40.

O'Grady, S.H., *Silva Gadelica*, 2 vols (London, 1892).

O'Kelleher, A. & Schoepperle, G. (eds & trans.), *Betha Colaim Chille: Life of Columcille* (Urbana, IL, 1918).

O'Loughlin, T., 'The library of Iona in the late seventh century: the evidence from Adomnán's *De Locis Sanctis*', *Ériu*, 45 (1994), 33–52.

O'Loughlin, T., 'Adomnán the illustrious', *Innes Review*, 46 (1995), 1–14.

O'Loughlin, T., '*Res, tempus, locus, persona*: Adomnán's exegetical method' in Broun & Clancy (eds), *Spes Scotorum* (Edinburgh, 1999), pp 139–58.

O'Loughlin, T., 'Palestine in the aftermath of the Arab conquest: the earliest Latin account' in R.N. Swanson (ed.), *Studies in church history*, 38 (2000), 78–89.

O'Loughlin, T. (ed.), *Adomnán at Birr, AD 697: essays in commemoration of the Law of the Innocents* (Dublin, 2001).

O'Loughlin, T., 'Adomnán: a man of many parts' in O'Loughlin (ed.), *Adomnán at Birr, AD 697* (Dublin, 2001), pp 41–51.

O'Loughlin, T., 'The tombs of the saints: their significance for Adomnán' in Carey, Herbert, & Ó Riain (eds), *Studies in Irish hagiography: saints and scholars* (Dublin, 2001).

O'Loughlin, T., *Adomnán and the holy places: the perceptions of an insular monk on the location of the biblical drama* (London, 2007).

O'Loughlin, T., 'The *De Locis Sanctis* as a liturgical text' in Wooding, Aist, Clancy & O'Loughlin (eds), *Adomnán of Iona: theologian, lawmaker, peacemaker* (Dublin, 2010), pp 181–92.

O'Loughlin, T., 'The diffusion of Adomnán's *De Locis Sanctis* in the medieval period', *Ériu*, 51 (2000), 93–106.

Ó Muraíle, N., 'The Columban onomastic legacy' in C. Bourke (ed.), *Studies in the cult of Saint Columba* (Dublin, 1997), pp 193–228.

Ó Muraíle, N. (ed. & trans.), *Leabhar Mór na nGenealach, The Great Book of Irish Genealogies, compiled 1645–66 by Dubhaltach Mac Fhirbhisigh*, 5 vols (Dublin, 2003).

O'Neill, P., 'A Middle Irish poem on the maledictory Psalms', *Journal of Celtic Studies*, 3:1 (1981), 40–50.

Ó Néill, P. & Dumville, D. (eds and trans.), *Cáin Adomnáin and Canones Adomnani* (Cambridge, 2003).

O'Reilly, J., 'Reading the Scriptures in the Life of Columba' in C. Bourke (ed.), *Studies in the cult of Saint Columba* (Dublin, 1997), pp 80–106.

O'Reilly, J., 'The wisdom of the scribe and the fear of the Lord in the Life of Columba' in Broun & Clancy (eds), *Spes Scotorum* (Edinburgh, 1999), pp 159–211.

O'Reilly, J., 'Adomnán and the art of teaching spiritual sons' in Wooding, Aist, Clancy & O'Loughlin (eds), *Adomnán of Iona: theologian, lawmaker, peacemaker* (Dublin, 2010), pp 69–94.

Ó Riain, P., 'Cainnech *alias* Colum Cille, patron of Ossory' in de Brún, Ó Coleáin & Ó Riain (eds), *Folia Gadelica* (Cork, 1983), pp 20–35.

Ó Riain, P., 'A misunderstood annal: a hitherto unnoticed *cáin*', *Celtica*, 21 (1990), 561–6.

Ó Riain, P. (ed.), *Corpus genealogiarum sanctorum Hiberniae* (Dublin, 1985).

Ó Riain, P., *Feastdays of the saints: a history of Irish martyrologies* (Bruxelles, 2006).

Ó Riain, P., *A dictionary of Irish saints* (Dublin, 2011).

O'Sullivan, J., 'Iona: archaeological investigations, 1875–1996' in Broun & Clancy (eds), *Spes Scotorum: Hope of Scots* (Edinburgh, 1999), pp 215–43.

O'Sullivan, J. & Ó Carragáin, T., *Inishmurray: Monks and pilgrims in an Atlantic landscape* (Cork, 2008).

O'Sullivan, T., 'The anti-Pelagian motif of the "naturally good" pagan in Adomnán's *Vita Columbae*' in Wooding, Aist, Clancy & O'Loughlin (eds), *Adomnán of Iona: theologian, lawmaker, peacemaker* (Dublin, 2010), pp 253–73.

Picard, J.M., 'The purpose of Adomnán's *Vita Columbae*', *Peritia*, 1 (1982), 160–77.

Picard, J.M., 'Bede, Adomnán and the writing of history', *Peritia*, 3 (1984), 50–70.

Picard, J.M., 'Adomnán and the writing of the "Life of Columba"', *Donegal Annual*, 37 (1985), 3–18.

Picard, J.M., 'Adomnán's *Vita Columbae* and the cult of Colum Cille in continental Europe', *Proceedings of the Royal Irish Academy*, 98 (1998), 1–23.

Picard, J.M., 'Schaffhausen, Stadtbibliotek, Generalia 1: the history of the manuscript' in Bracken & Graff (eds), *The Schaffhausen Adomnán: Schaffhausen, Stadtbibliotek, MS Generalia 1, Part II: Commentary* (Cork, 2014), pp 56–69.

Plummer, C. (ed. & trans.) *Lives of Irish saints*, 2 vols (Oxford, 1922; repr. 1997).

Radner, J.N. (ed. and trans.), *Fragmentary Annals of Ireland* (Dublin, 1978).

Reeves, W., *Acts of Archbishop Colton in his metropolitan visitation of the diocese of Derry* (Dublin, 1850).

Reeves, W., 'St Mura', *Ulster Journal of Archaeology*, 1 (1853), 271–3.

Reeves, W. (ed.), *The Life of St Columba, founder of Hy; written by Adomnan, ninth abbot of that monastery* (Dublin, 1857; 2nd ed., Edinburgh, 1874).

Ritari, K., 'Heavenly apparitions and heavenly life in Adomnán's *Vita Columbae*' in Wooding, Aist, Clancy & O'Loughlin (eds), *Adomnán of Iona: theologian, lawmaker, peacemaker* (Dublin, 2010), pp 274–88.

Sharman, S., 'Visions of divine light in the writings of Adomnán and Bede' in Wooding, Aist, Clancy & O'Loughlin (eds), *Adomnán of Iona: theologian, lawmaker, peacemaker* (Dublin, 2010), pp 289–302.

Sharpe, R. (trans.), *Adomnán of Iona: Life of St Columba* (London, 1995).

Sharpe, R., 'Maghnus Ó Domhnaill's source for Adomnán's *Vita S. Columbae* and other vitae', *Celtica*, 21 (1990), 604–7.

Sharpe, R., *Medieval Irish saints' Lives* (Oxford, 1991).

Sherley-Price, L. (trans.), revised by R.E. Latham, *Bede: A history of the English church and people* (London, 1972).

Silke, J., *Two abbots* (Letterkenny, 1997).

Smyth, A., *Celtic Leinster: towards an histoical geography of early Irish civilization, AD 500–1000* (Dublin, 1982).

Smyth, A. (ed.), *Seanchas: studies in early and medieval Irish archaeology, history and literature in honour of Francis J. Byrne* (Dublin, 2000).

Smyth, A., *Warlords and holy men: Scotland AD 80–1000* (Edinburgh, 2003).

Spears, A., '"An Scuab as Fánaid" and the XIth century pandemonium', *Donegal Annual*, 35 (1983), 5–20.

Spears, A., 'Vestiges of ancient Raphoe from an aerial photograph', *Donegal Annual*, 39 (1987), 16–23.

Stancliffe, C., '"Charity with peace": Adomnán and the Easter question' in Wooding, Aist, Clancy & O'Loughlin (eds), *Adomnán of Iona: theologian, lawmaker, peacemaker* (Dublin, 2010), pp 51–68.

Stansbury, M., 'The Schaffhausen manuscript and the composition of the Life of Columba' in Bracken & Graff (eds), *The Schaffhausen Adomnán: Schaffhausen, Stadtbibliotek, MS Generalia 1, Part II: Commentary* (Cork, 2014), pp 70–89.

Stokes, W. (ed. and trans.), *The Tripartite Life of Patrick with other documents related to the saint*, 2 vols (London, 1887).

Stokes, W. (ed.), 'The Annals of Tigernach', *Revue Celtique*, 16–18 (1895–7).

Stokes, W. (ed. and trans.), *The Martyrology of Oengus the Culdee* (London, 1905).

Swanson, R.N. (ed.), *Studies in church history*, 38 (Woodbridge, 2000).

Taylor, S., 'Seventh-century Iona abbots in Scottish place-names' in Broun & Clancy (eds), *Spes Scotorum: Hope of Scots* (Edinburgh, 1999), pp 35–70.

Volmering, N., 'The rhetoric of catastrophe in eleventh-century medieval Ireland: the case of the Second Vision of Adomnán' in R.E. Bjork (ed.), *Catastrophes and the apocalyptic in the Middle Ages and the Renaissance* (Leiden, 2019), pp 1–14.

Volmering, N. (ed.), 'The Second Vision of Adamnán' in J. Carey, E. Nic Cárthaigh & C. Ó Dochartaigh (eds), *The end and beyond: medieval Irish eschatology* (Aberystwyth, 2014), pp 647–81.

Walsh, P., 'The monastic settlement on Rathlin O'Byrne Island, County Donegal', *JRSAI*, 113 (1983), 53–66.

Wooding, J.M., Aist, R., Clancy, T.O. & O'Loughlin, T. (eds), *Adomnán of Iona: theologian, lawmaker, peacemaker* (Dublin, 2010).

Woods, D., 'Arculf's luggage: the sources for Adomnán's *De Locis Sanctis*', *Ériu*, 52 (2002), 25–52.

Woods, D., 'On the circumstances of Adomnán's composition of the *De Locis Sanctis*' in Wooding, Aist, Clancy & O'Loughlin (eds), *Adomnán of Iona: theologian, lawmaker, peacemaker* (Dublin, 2010), pp 193–204.

Woulfe, P., *Sloinnte Gaedheal is Gall* (Dublin, 1923).

Yorke, B., 'Adomnán at the court of King Aldfrith' in Wooding, Aist, Clancy & O'Loughlin (eds), *Adomnán of Iona: theologian, lawmaker, peacemaker* (Dublin, 2010), pp 36–50.

Index